ACCESS CHINESE

汉语入门

Student Book | 学生用书 1

主编：刘　骏 Jun Liu

编者：康　燕 Kang Yan　魏慧萍 Wei Huiping　种一凡 Chong Yifan

FOREIGN LANGUAGE TEACHING AND RESEARCH PRESS　BEIJING

McGraw-Hill Higher Education

ACCESS CHINESE STUDENT BOOK 1, FIRST EDITION

Co-Published by McGraw-Hill, an imprint of The McGraw-Hill Companies, Inc., 1221 Avenue of the Americas, New York, NY 10020 and Foreign Language Teaching and Research Press, No. 19 Xisanhuan Beilu, Beijing, China, 100089. Copyright © 2013 McGraw-Hill Companies, Inc. and Foreign Language Teaching and Research Press. Printed in China.

ISBN: 978-0-07-337188-7
MHID: 0-07-337188-2

McGraw-Hill:
Vice President, Products and Markets: Michael Ryan
Editorial Director: William R. Glass
Publisher: Katie Stevens
Senior Sponsoring Editor: Katherine K. Crouch
Senior Director of Development: Scott Tinetti
Development Editor: Jennifer Kirk
Editorial Coordinator: Erin Blaze
Executive Marketing Manager: Craig Gill
Faculty Development Manager: Jorge Arbujas

FLTRP:
Publisher: Cai Jianfeng
Editor in Chief: Xu Jianzhong
Project Planning: Man Xingyuan
Project Management: Ding Ning
Project Editor: Li Yang, Xie Danling
Editorial Supporting Team: Cai Ying, Liu Hongyan, Xu Yang, Yan Li, Yao Jun, Zhao Qing

Boston	Burr Ridge, IL	Dubuque, IA	Madison, WI	New York	San Francisco
St. Louis	Bangkok	Bogotá	Caracas	Kuala Lumpur	Lisbon
London	Madrid	Mexico City	Milan	Montreal	New Delhi
Santiago	Seoul	Singapore	Sydney	Taipei	Toronto

www.mhhe.com

www.fltrp.com
www.chineseplus.com

To the Instructor

As you well know, the Chinese language is often perceived as more difficult to learn than other foreign languages. Many find Chinese characters, in particular, to be intimidating because they look more like pictures than the writing systems to which most students are accustomed. Combine that with the use of tones and unfamiliar grammatical structures, and many students give up before even giving it a try. While some perceptions of Chinese language learning are true, most of them are overgeneralized, as evidenced by the many English speakers who have learned Chinese very well. What is their secret?

When I taught Chinese to college freshmen at the Ohio State University in the mid-90s, I had great fun interacting with my students. They showed genuine interest in communicating with one another while completing tasks such as meeting new friends, asking for directions, bargaining at the market, and ordering food in a Chinese restaurant. This level of enthusiasm toward learning about Chinese culture through the study of the Chinese language has inspired me to create a better way to teach Chinese to college students in the U.S.

Whether Chinese can be learned well or not depends on three crucial factors: the textbook program, the teaching methodology, and the instructor. An appropriate, high-quality textbook is the fundamental factor that will either help engage students or cause them to lose interest in the learning process.

I have had great opportunities to interact with learners of Chinese around the world, and to familiarize myself with Chinese curricula and Chinese textbooks available on the market while working in several capacities, including as Associate Provost for International Initiatives and Professor of Applied Linguistics at Georgia State University, former Director of the Confucius Institute at the University of Arizona, Vice President of International Society of Chinese Language Teaching (ISCLT), and Senior Advisor of the Office of Chinese Language Council International (Hanban). In my experience, many textbooks are designed specifically for international students studying Chinese in the Chinese context. Some materials are of superb quality, but are too difficult for beginners studying Chinese in a non-Chinese context. Some are very easy to use, but focus too much on grammar and pattern drills and too little on communication and culture.

An ideal textbook, in my mind, should be designed to harmonize the following key elements critical in learning Chinese as a foreign language:

- linking language with culture

- balancing forms with meaning

- developing literacy skills through both oral and written Chinese

Equally important is the fact that the textbook must be interesting, engaging, and entertaining for both students and instructors.

Access Chinese is designed to blend the above three elements while making learning fun. In *Access Chinese*, students will experience Chinese language and culture through a dual storyline about twins Bill and Jenny. During their freshman year, both siblings are learning Chinese — Bill in China, and Jenny in the U.S. These two contexts depict different but authentic learning environments where language and culture are intertwined, at the same time controlling the level of difficulty of grammar and vocabulary as well as providing sufficient communicative tasks and activities. In this way, *Access Chinese* presents students with contemporary Chinese language and life, provides a practical communicative context for learners, and controls the level of difficulty while still providing the linguistic information necessary to be successful Chinese language learners.

I would like to take this opportunity to thank my team for working tirelessly on this project over the past several years. First and foremost, I am thankful to the lead member of the team, Wei Huiping, whose expertise, experience and extraordinary work ethic have been instrumental to the quality of the series. I am equally grateful to Kang Yan and Chong Yifan for their trust and belief in me and their great effort and conscientious work on different portions of this project since its inception. I would also like to thank Senior Sponsoring Editor Katherine K. Crouch and Development Editor Jennifer Kirk from McGraw-Hill Higher Education for their vision and enthusiasm in supporting *Access Chinese* and for holding the highest standard throughout its development. Likewise, I am extremely grateful to Foreign Language Teaching and Research Press (FLTRP) supervisors and editors Man Xingyuan, Deng Xiaojing, Ding Ning, Li Yang, and Xie Danling, among others, for their great coordination and editorial work. I am also grateful to Peng Donglin, Zhou Wei, and Zhou Fei for their great support and assistance at the early stages of this project. Last but not least, I am indebted to Chyi Chung of Northwestern University as well as the rest of our enthusiastic reviewers for their thoughtful and detailed notes and suggestions, and for making numerous constructive comments in the process of textbook development based on their years of college-level Chinese teaching experience in Chinese in the U.S.

Susan Butler — Spokane Community College

Guozhong Cao — University of Washington

Der-lin Chao — New York University

Cecilia Chu — University of California, Berkeley

Liancheng Chief — University of California, Los Angeles

Wei Hong — Purdue University

Hong Jiang — Northwestern University

Steven Kincely — Ohio State University

Bruce Knickerbocker — Northwestern University

Cornelius Kubler — Williams College

Horng-Yi Lee — Whittier College

Yufen Lee Mehta — Cornell University

Winnie Leong — City College of San Francisco

Hong Li — Emory University

Hong Li — Ithaca College

Sue Li — San Francisco State University

Xiaoliang Li — Georgia Institute of Technology

Xiaosu Li — San Francisco State University

Haiyong Liu — Wayne State University

Jin Liu — California State University, Fullerton

Jing Luo — Bloomsburg University

Chris Magriney — University of Southern California

Charles Marshal McArthur — University of Houston

Lei Shen — Brigham Young University

Curtis Smith — Grand Valley State University

Weiqing Su George — Cornell University

Hongyin Tao — University of California, Los Angeles

Jenny Zhijie Wang — United States Naval Academy

Mingqian Wang — Tufts University

Youquin Wang — University of Chicago

Jing Wu — College of San Mateo

Tina Wu — Central Connecticut State University

Jinglin Xiong — Wake Forest University

Jun Yang — University of Chicago

Lijuan Ye — Georgia State University

Yueming Yu — Carnegie Mellon University

Lan Zhang — University of Memphis

Xia Zhang — Arizona State University

Yi Zhou — University of North Carolina at Chapel Hill

Without their support, encouragement, and constructive criticism, this textbook would not be what it is today.

It is my sincere hope that *Access Chinese* will provide you and your students with the tools you need in order to truly experience Chinese language and culture.

Good luck, and have fun!

Jun Liu
Lead Author

Framework

Access Chinese is designed for beginners of Chinese as a second or foreign language. While the primary audience is college-level beginning Chinese learners in North America, this program also targets high school students and adult learners in non-Chinese contexts. The goal of *Access Chinese* is to help learners gradually develop communicative competence through integrative training of language elements (pronunciation, vocabulary, and grammar) and linguistic skills (listening, speaking, reading, and writing) in a graded series.

Key Features

In *Access Chinese*, contextualized grammar, communicative practice, and engaging cultural information are all intertwined, creating a learning environment appropriate for successful language acquisition as well as an opportunity to explore cultural contexts.

The storyline throughout the *Access Chinese* serves to engage students and to link the content throughout the series. Each episode provides the context for practical functions designed specifically for communication. Cultural themes are imbedded in each episode, along with a *Culture Snapshot* section that further explains cultural elements and teaches communication strategies. The grammar explanations are brief and aimed toward production in both written and oral Chinese. Each of these sections is accompanied by a number of practice activities.

Chinese and Global Content

Access Chinese deals with contemporary topics that are of high interest and relevance to students and teachers around the world. The topics have been selected to reflect both global perspectives and local contexts in order to stimulate cross-cultural awareness and discussion. The storyline of *Access Chinese* weaves together the experiences of learning Chinese in China and America, covering basic topics such as greetings, food, and sports, as well as more in-depth topics like foreign study partners, movie stars and online interaction. Students will also learn intercultural communication through the story.

Scalable Vocabulary

In order to avoid overwhelming learners, the words and expressions in *Access Chinese* are divided in three groups as follows:

1. *Required Words and Expressions* are intended for oral and written comprehension and communication. These are typically words and expressions frequently used in oral and written communication.

2. *Expanded Words and Expressions* are meant for comprehension and oral communication. They are considered common words and expressions frequently used in oral communication.

3. *Suggested Words and Expressions* are meant for comprehension only.

Online Learning Center

The Online Learning Center (www.mhhe.com/accesschinese) provides students with additional activities created for use with *Access Chinese*. In addition, student and instructor resources will be posted on the Online Learning Center, including the Instructor's Manual and MP3 files for the student book and workbook audio programs.

Unit Structure

Unit Opener

The *Unit Opener* provides a summary of the information covered in the unit's two episodes. In addition, you will find a list of the communicative functions, grammar points, and cultural topics to be covered in the unit, in order to orient students in their learning process and give them a clear expectation of what is to come.

Episodes

The two *Episodes* in each unit follow the storylines surrounding a set of twins — Bill and Jenny — who are both learning Chinese. In Unit 1, Bill goes to China for a one-year Chinese language program, while his twin sister, Jenny, learns Chinese in the U.S. Given their distinctly different learning environments, Bill and Jenny experience different challenges in learning the language, but they both find the learning very rewarding.

These short episodes introduce new grammar in a communicative context, present functional expressions, and reflect authentic Chinese culture and social etiquette.

The color-coded *Required Words and Expressions* and *Expanded Words and Expressions* boxes, provide a guide to the vocabulary presented in context, with English definitions and additional explanation as needed.

Activities

Individual, pair, and group activities, as well as whole class and role-play activities are included throughout the program, providing ample opportunities for practice in the classroom.

Sentence Patterns and Communicative Practice

Sentence Patterns is the first of two grammar presentations in each unit. This section focuses on introducing sentence patterns commonly used in real communication. The presentation of the sentence patterns is typically followed by communicative activities that range from more controlled to more open-ended practice.

Expanded Functions

Each *Episode* is followed by one or two expansions on functional usage, such as *Saying Hello* or *Time*. A variety of real-life materials and activities enable students to put into practice what they have learned.

Culture Snapshot

Culture Snapshot highlights major cultural differences in communication, for example, the practices of gift giving or accepting a compliment. These cultural topics are meant to raise cultural awareness and encourage adaptation, and are related to the contents of *Episodes 1* and *2* of each unit.

Grammar Kit

The *Grammar Kit* presents the new grammar of each unit, including three or more highlighted grammar structures with English explanations and examples of sentence usage. Grammar is placed at the end of each unit as a point of reference and language-learning tool rather than a main focus of study. Rather, students should concentrate on learning by doing, which can be achieved with the help of the numerous opportunities provided in the episodes and activities throughout *Access Chinese*.

Pronunciation Tips

This section gives suggestions to deal with pronunciation difficulties common among non-native Chinese speakers.

Writing Chinese Characters

Writing Chinese Characters encourages students to improve their writing skills by providing guidance on stroke order, character practice, and the evolution of Chinese characters.

Integrative Practice

The unit-culminating *Integrative Practice* section provides four skills practice, including activities for listening, speaking, reading and writing, all aligned with the themes of the unit.

Word List

A *Word List* appears at the end of each unit, including all of the *Required Words and Expressions*, *Expanded Words and Expressions*, and *Suggested Words and Expressions* presented in the unit.

Along with the previously outlined sections of the text, the following smaller features are scattered throughout the units to further enrich students' experiences in learning the Chinese language:

- **Break Time** boxes introduce the basic strokes in Chinese character writing, outlining the steps necessary to write basic simplified Chinese characters, as well as pronunciation training like poems, tongue twisters and so on.

- **Culture Boxes** give students extra support regarding cultural elements that appear within activities.

- **Tips** and **Notes** give background information, helpful word analysis and some useful grammar details.

Supplements

Workbook

Each student book in *Access Chinese* has a companion workbook that aims at providing learners with sufficient practice activities and tasks to strengthen the learning of materials in the student book. Both language knowledge and communication abilities are taken into consideration in the design of workbook.

The main types of practice in the workbook include: pronunciation practice, writing characters, grammar and vocabulary practice, and communicative tasks, as well as interview and discovery tasks. Every unit ends with a self-assessment tool that is designed to boost students' self-confidence in learning Chinese.

Online Supplements

For the Instructor

The Instructor's Edition of the Online Learning Center includes materials for instructors such as methodological suggestions, additional grammar explanations, guidance on cultural information, suggested additional activities or tasks, audio scripts, and guidance on testing and continuous assessment.

For the Student

The Online Learning Center provides a variety of reading, writing, and spelling exercises to reinforce grammar and vocabulary taught in *Access Chinese*. In addition to these activities, the complete audio program to accompany the *Access Chinese* student book and workbook, can also be found on the Online Learning Center, and is easily downloadable for use on the student's computer or MP3 player.

Contents 目录

Title	Topic	Function	Grammar
Intro and Synopsis 剧情和人物介绍 Page 14			
Introduction to Pinyin 拼音介绍 Page 16			
Introduction to Chinese Characters 汉字介绍 Page 40			
Unit 1 Meeting Each Other 见面寒暄 Page 48	Greetings; Chinese names	1. To greet each other 2. To introduce yourself 3. To ask someone's name 4. To give a compliment 5. To ask for a phone number	1. Word order in Chinese sentences 2. To express judgement using the verb 是 3. To confirm information using Yes-no questions ending with 吗 4. To use the adverb 很 in sentences with an adjectival predicate
Theme 1 Getting to Know Each Other — **Unit 2** Gifts and Courtesy 礼尚往来 Page 70	To give and accept gifts; Talking about age	1. To name objects 2. To give and accept gifts 3. To introduce people to each other 4. To ask someone's age	1. To use the proximal demonstrative pronoun 这 2. To ask what-questions with the interrogative pronoun 什么 3. To use the adverbs of range 也 and 都
Unit 3 Feel at Home Wherever You Are 四海为家 Page 92	Time; Familiy members; Career	1. To ask about and tell time 2. To ask about and give information about nationality 3. To talk about family members 4. To ask about and give information about work	1. How to tell time 2. To ask which-questions with the interrogative pronoun 哪 3. To ask others to confirm information using 吗 or verb+不+verb questions
Review Unit 1 复习单元1 Page 114			

Culture	Vocabulary	Pronunciation	Characters
1. How Chinese people respond to compliments 2. How Chinese people greet each other 3. Chinese name order	Words and expressions for greeting each other, especially for the first meeting	1. Chinese tones 2. Neutral tone 3. The changes of the 3rd tone	**Strokes:** horizontal stroke, vertical stroke, downward-left stroke, downward-right stroke **Stroke Order:** horizontal before vertical, downward-left before downward-right
1. Chinese small-talk topics such as age, marriage and salary 2. How Chinese people give and accept gifts 3. How Chinese people express and reciprocate courtesy	Words and expressions for giving and accepting presents, chatting with each other in the Chinese way	1. Initials *z,c,s* and *zh,ch,sh* 2. Intonation of the interrogative sentences	**Strokes:** dot, upward stroke, bending stroke, hook **Stroke Order:** from top to bottom, from left to right
1. About culture integration 2. How Chinese people address others 3. About respecting seniority	Words and expressions for talking about time, family members and career	1. How to pronounce *r* 2. How to pronounce the titles of family members 3. Pauses in a sentence	**Strokes Review** **Stroke Order:** from outside to inside, from outside to inside then enclose, center before sides

	Title	Topic	Function	Grammar
Theme 2 Making Friends	**Unit 4** In and Out of Class 课内课外 **Page 120**	To make plans; Invitations	1. To make plans 2. To make, accept and decline invitations, to make excuses 3. To ask about and give information about time and location	1. To express the time of an event or action using time phrases as adverbial phrases 2. To give a suggestion or request using the sentence final modal particle 吧 3. To form wh-questions using question words 谁, 什么, 什么时候, 哪儿, 哪个
	Unit 5 Shopping and Bargaining 讨价还价 **Page 142**	Bargining; Making comparisons; Colors	1. To ask about and describe goods and colors 2. To ask about prices 3. To make comparisons 4. To bargain	1. To express quantity using measure words 2. To express comparison using the preposition 比 3. Different usages of 了
	Unit 6 Fine Food 天下美食 **Page 166**	Chinese dishes; Table manners	1. To talk and ask about experiences 2. To ask about and describe the taste of food 3. To ask about opinions and make choices 4. To make suggestions	1. To express things you have done using the particle 过 2. To ask others to make a choice using "是……还是……？" 3. To use 的 phrases to indicate people or things

Review Unit 2 复习单元2   **Page 190**

Review of *Access Chinese 1* 总复习   **Page 195**

Grammar Kits 语法要点   **Page 197**

Word List 总词表   **Page 198**

Abbreviations of Grammatical Terms 语法术语缩写表   **Page 210**

Culture	Vocabulary	Pronunciation	Characters
1. Chinese youth life 2. Chinese way of declining invitations 3. Attitudes toward cultural differences	Words and expressions for giving and accepting invitations, talking about activities after class	1. *j, q, x* and *zh, ch, sh* 2. Intonation of wh-questions in Chinese	**Stroke Order:** the stroke order of semi-enclosed structure
1. Bargaining 2. Colors in Chinese culture	Words and expressions for shopping, bargaining, talking about colors and price	1. Tone changes of *yī* — 2. The semi-3rd tone 3. Sentence stress	**Stroke Order:** the stroke order of dot
1. Famous Chinese dishes 2. Courtesies at dining tables	Words and expressions for talking about food, restaurants and table manners	1. *-n* and *-ng* 2. R-ending retroflexion 3. Intonation of the exclamatory sentence	**Stroke Order:** the stroke order of three-side enclosure characters

Bill is in China for a one-year Chinese learning program in Beijing while his younger sister, Jenny, is learning Chinese in California. Given their distinctly different learning environments, Bill and Jenny experience different challenges in learning the language, and they both make good friends, Li Li and Wang Damin. They really enjoy their company though from time to time they experience anxieties and conflicts in intercultural communication. Happiness and dreams are coupled with their confusions and adventures — all being unfolded in this textbook: *Access Chinese*.

In Access Chinese, you will meet:

Zhēnnī

珍妮

Jenny, a 20-year-old American student studying Chinese at a university in California. Bill's twin sister.

Bǐ'ěr

比尔

Bill, a 20-year-old American student studying Chinese as an exchange student in China. Jenny's twin brother.

Wáng Dàmín
王 大民
Wang Damin, a 21-year-old American student, and Jenny's classmate.

Lǐ Lì
李丽
Li Li, a 20-year-old Chinese student, and Bill's good friend and classmate in China.

Shāntián
山田
Yamada, a 21-year-old Japanese student and Bill's classmate, studying Chinese in China.

Pinyin Step 1

Listen to the recording silently. 🎧

Nǐmen hǎo! Wǒmen kāishǐ xuéxí Hànyǔ. Nǐ zhīdào Hànyǔ pīnyīn ma?

■ Chinese Syllables

The **Pinyin** writing system uses the 26 letters of the Latin alphabet to represent Chinese characters phonetically. The syllable is the basic unit in Pinyin. One syllable can correspond to several Chinese characters with the same pronunciation. For instance, *zhōng* is the Pinyin representation of the characters 中 (center), 忠 (loyalty), and 终 (end).

Each Chinese syllable consists of three elements:

Initial: Most syllables begin with a consonant called an initial. Zero initials are the exception to this rule, which you will learn about later in the *Introduction to Pinyin*. There are 21 initials in Mandarin Chinese.

Final: The final of a Chinese syllable consists of the vowels, and sometimes consonants, that follow the initial. Single vowels, compound vowels or vowels combined with nasal endings can all play the role of finals. There are 39[1] finals in Mandarin Chinese.

Tone: Each syllable has a tone — a rising or falling sound — shown in Pinyin using tone marks. The tone mark appears above the main vowel of the syllable. You will learn more about these tone marks later in the *Introduction to Pinyin*.

For example, in the syllable *měi*, the initial is *m*, the final is *ei*, and the tone is ˇ (3rd tone).

A. **Listen and follow along as your teacher reads the chart in order to find the three elements of each syllable.**

Zhōngguó   Měiguó   rén
中国   (China)   美国   (the U.S.)   人 (person)

Syllable	Initial	Final	Tone	Syllable	Initial	Final	Tone
zhōng	zh	ong	—	guó	g	uo	´
měi	m	ei	ˇ	rén	r	en	´

B. **Can you identify these countries? Listen as your teacher reads the Pinyin of each country's name, then guess the English name of each country according to the picture.**

Fǎguó   Rìběn   Āijí
法国   日本   埃及

---

[1] Including -i[ɿ], -i[ʅ], ê[ɛ], er[ɚ].

C. Now identify the initial, final and tone of each syllable.

Syllable	Initial	Final	Tone
fǎ			
guó			
rì			
běn			
āi			
jí			

■ Zero Initial Syllables

Some Chinese syllables have no initial consonant, such as *ā*, *āi*, *ī*, and *ū*. These are called zero initial syllables (língshēngmǔ 零声母). Because zero initials do not have an initial consonant to distinguish them from the previous syllable, indicators are added in Pinyin in order to avoid confusion.

1. In cases like these, where a syllable is followed by a zero initial syllable that begins with *a*, *o* or *e*, a separator " ' " is added to distinguish between the two syllables. For example, 西安 *Xī'ān* (a city in China) is made up of the syllable *xī* and the zero initial syllable *ān*, whereas 鲜 *xiān* (fresh) is a single syllable with the initial *x* and the final *iān*. Other examples include:

Tiān' ānmén   Xī' ōu   Bǐ' ěr
天安门   西欧   比尔

2. If a zero initial syllable begins with *i* and the *i* is not followed by any other vowels, add *y* before *i*. For example:

ī ⟶ yī 一 (one)   īn ⟶ yīn 音 (sound)   īng ⟶ yīng 鹰 (eagle)

If there are other vowels following *i*, change the *i* to *y*.

iá ⟶ yá 牙 (tooth)   iě ⟶ yě 也 (too)   iòng ⟶ yòng 用 (to use)

3. If a zero initial syllable begins with *u* and the *u* is not followed by any other vowels, add *w* before *u*. For example:

ǔ ⟶ wǔ 五 (five)

If there are other vowels following *u*, change the *u* to *w*.

uǒ ⟶ wǒ 我 (I, me)   uán ⟶ wán 玩 (to play)

4. If a zero initial syllable begins with *ǚ*, always add *y* before *ǚ*, then omit the two dots over the *ǚ*. For example:

ǚ ⟶ yǔ 雨 (rain)   ǘn ⟶ yún 云 (cloud)   ǚe ⟶ yuè 月 (moon, month)

Now you can do it! ☺

A. Listen and read, then find the zero initial syllables. 🎧

Yīngyǔ	Hànyǔ	Éyǔ	yǔyán	wàiyǔ
英语	汉语	俄语	语言	外语
English	Chinese	Russian	language	foreign language

B. Listen and repeat after your teacher.

Wǒ xué Hànyǔ.
我 学 汉语 。   I study Chinese.

C. Pair Work

With a partner, write down the elements of each syllable in the sentence above.

Syllable	Initial	Final	Tone
wǒ			
xué			
hàn			
yǔ			

■ Tones

Tones are very important in Chinese. When two syllables have the same initial and final, different tones help to indicate that the two syllables have different meanings. For example, *tiān* 天 means "sky", while *tián* 甜 means "sweet".

Mandarin Chinese has four tones that appear in Pinyin as tone marks above the main vowel of a Chinese syllable. The shape of the mark indicates the direction of the rise or fall of the tone.

	1st tone	2nd tone	3rd tone	4th tone
	—	╱	╲╱	╲
	high and level tone	rising tone	falling-rising tone	falling tone

A. Listen and read, then add the missing tone marks. 🎧

a a a a   e e e e
i i i i   u u u u

wo	ni	ta	ta
我	你	他	她
I, me	you	he, him	she, her

é
鹅 (goose)

è
饿 (hungry)

Wo e le.
我 饿 了。 I am hungry.

Ni e ma?
你 饿 吗？ Are you hungry?

B. Pair Work

Take turns choosing the words from *wǒ* 我, *nǐ* 你, *tā* 他, *tā* 她 and expressing the meaning of the word by making a gesture. Then the other points out the character and reads it aloud.

C. Listen and read, paying close attention to the tones.

Nǐ shì nǎ guó rén?
A: 你 是 哪 国 人？ Where are you from?

Wǒ shì Měiguórén.
B: 我 是 美国人 。 I come from the U.S.

D. Pair Work

Practice the dialogue above and try substituting *tā* 他, *tā* 她, *Zhōngguó* 中国, *Fǎguó* 法国, *Rìběn* 日本.

E. Listen and repeat each syllable aloud.

mā	má	mǎ	mà
妈 (mother)	麻 (flax)	马 (horse)	骂 (to abuse)
tāng	táng	tǎng	tàng
汤 (soup)	糖 (sugar)	躺 (to lie down)	烫 (scalding)

■ Neutral Tone

As you learned in the first section on Pinyin, every Chinese syllable has a tone. Sometimes the original tone of a syllable becomes softer and shorter when it follows another syllable. These so-called neutral tones have no tone mark. For example, the forms of address of many family members have a neutral tone like *māma* 妈妈 (mother).

Neutral tone is not considered a fifth tone, but rather a changed tone with a softer and shorter sound. This change indicates a difference in meaning or lexical category. For instance, *Sūnzǐ* 孙子 is the name of a famous ancient Chinese military strategist while *sūnzi* 孙子 means "grandson".

A. Listen and read.

bàba	māma	gēge	jiějie	wǒmen	péngyou
爸爸	妈妈	哥哥	姐姐	我们	朋友
father	mother	elder brother	elder sister	we, us	friend

B. Listen to the recording, then circle the syllable with the neutral tone.

laozi
老子 (a famous ancient Chinese philosopher) —— laozi
老子 (an informal title of father)

maimai
买卖 (business) —— maimai
买卖 (to buy and to sell)

■ Placement of Tone Marks

The tone mark appears above the main vowel of a syllable. The order of preference is:

$$a \rightarrow o \rightarrow e \rightarrow i \rightarrow u \rightarrow ü$$

When two vowels occur in one syllable, the earlier vowel in the above progression usually wears the tone mark as in *hǎo* 好 (good) and *guójiā* 国家 (country).

Note: When the tone mark falls on the letter *i*, the tone mark should replace the dot on the *i*. When the final of the syllable is *iu* or *ui*, the tone mark appears on the last vowel of the syllable. For example:

shì	liù	jiǔ	duì
是	六	九	对
to be	six	nine	right

A. Listen and read.

Tā shì Lǐ Lì ma?
(1) A: 她 是 李 丽 吗?　　　A: Is she Li Li?

Bù, tā shì Liú Lì.
B: 不,她 是 刘 丽。　　　B: No, she is Liu Li.

Nǐ huì shuō Hànyǔ ma?
(2) A: 你 会 说 汉语 吗?　　　A: Can you speak Chinese?

Shìde, wǒ huì shuō Hànyǔ.
B: 是的,我 会 说 汉语。　B: Yes, I can.

> **Tip**
>
> The first letter of the sentence, as well as proper nouns should be capitalized in Pinyin. For instance: *Wǒ shì Měiguórén.* (我是美国人。 I am American.)

B. Pair Work

Read the dialogues above and try to use your own information, paying close attention to the position of the tone marks.

Now you can do it! ☺

A. Combine the different elements to create Chinese syllables.

Initial	+	Final	+	Tone	→	Syllable
t	+	a	+	‾	→	tā
sh	+	i	+	ˋ	→	
	+	uai	+	ˋ	→	
g	+	uo	+	ˊ	→	
p	+	eng	+	ˊ	→	
	+	iou	+		→	you

B. Write down the Pinyin of the syllables you created in Activity A to make a sentence, then read it aloud, making sure to pronounce the tones correctly.

_____.

他 是 外 国 朋 友。   He is a foreign friend.

C. Listen and read, then try to record the missing tones.

Ni hao! Wo shi Bi' er.
你 好！ 我 是 比尔。   Hello! I am Bill.

Ni hao! Wo shi Li Li.
你 好！ 我 是 李丽。   Hello! I am Li Li.

D. Pair Work

With a partner, read the dialogue in Activity C, then try it again using your own name.

Reminder

1. Chinese syllables have three elements: initial, final and tone.
2. The syllables that have no consonant initials are called zero initial syllables.
3. The four tones of Mandarian Chinese are: ā á ǎ à.
4. Neutral tone is a changed tone with softer and shorter sound without tone marks.

Pinyin Step 2

■ **Single Finals:** *a o e i u ü*

A. Listen to the recording and add the appropriate tone mark to each single final.

a   ā   á   ǎ   à   i   i   i   i   i

o   o   o   o   o   u   u   u   u   u

e   e   e   e   e   ü   ü   ü   ü   ü

B. Read the tips and try to pronounce accurately with your teacher's help.

Pinyin	Pronunciation Tips
a	Open the mouth wide, and pronounce **a** as in **father**.
o	Open the mouth and round the lips into an "o" shape, pronouncing **o** as in **more**.
e	Keep the mouth open as in *o*, then let lips form a natural smile and pronounce **e** as in **bachelor**.
i	Open the mouth a little bit, put the top of the tongue behind the lower front teeth, and pronounce **ee** as in **bee**.
u	Round the lips as much as possible, then pronounce **u** as in **put**.
ü	Pronounce *i* firstly, then keep the sound and round the lips as much as possible.

Tip

   When pronouncing *ü*, keep the situation of *i*, then round the lips and pronounce it. Keep the shape of the mouth until you pronounce this single-final totally and clearly. You could find the similar sound in the German **grün** or the French **lune**.

yú
鱼 (fish)

yǔ
雨 (rain)

C. Pair Work

   With a partner, take turns pointing at single finals from the chart in Activity A while the other tries to pronounce it correctly. Make sure to use the correct tone!

D. Group Work

   In groups of three, one member makes the shape of a single final with his or her mouth without actually pronouncing it while the others guess the correct vowel.

E. Listen and read each series of single finals slowly. Then go back and read each series quickly.

a – i   a – o   i – a   i – e   ü – e   e – i   u – o   o – u   u – a   i – ü

■ Labial Initials : *b p m f*   Alveolar Initials: *d t n l*

While the labial and alveolar initials are mostly pronounced similarly to their English counterparts, the aspirated sounds *p* and *t* are generally pronounced more forcefully in Chinese, while *b* and *d* are softer sounds.

Practice saying these initials to yourself using the pattern *bo, po, mo, fo, de, te, ne, le.*

A. Listen to the recording and repeat each syllable. Then fill in the missing finals for the given initials. 🎧

b   p   m   f   d   t   n   l

B. Listen and read. 🎧

ba – pa   da – ta   bo – po   di – ti   bu – pu   du – tu

C. Listen and write down the missing initials. 🎧

__ā	__ā	__ō	__ō
八	趴	波	坡
eight	to lie prone	wave	slope
__à	__à	__ú	__ú
大	踏	读	图
big	to tread	to read	picture

Now you can do it! ☺

■ Initial-Final Combinations

	b	p	m	f	d	t	n	l
a	ba	pa	ma	fa	da	ta	na	la
o	bo	po	mo	fo	–	–	–	–
e	–	–	me	–	de	te	ne	le
i	bi	pi	mi	–	di	ti	ni	li
u	bu	pu	mu	fu	du	tu	nu	lu
ü	–	–	–	–	–	–	nü	lü

A. Pair Work

In pairs, take turns as one partner reads the syllable list horizontally and the other reads it vertically.

B. Listen to the recording and write down the missing parts of the syllables, then read them aloud. 🎧

t __	w __	n __	t __	__ù	__à
他	我	你	她	不	那
he, him	I, me	you	she, her	no	that

bàb __	m __ ma	__ìdi	gēg __
爸爸	妈妈	弟弟	哥哥
father	mother	younger brother	elder brother

C. Listen and read as Li Li talks to Bill about her family photograph. 🎧

Tā shì wǒ bàba.
Lǐ Lì: 他 是 我 爸爸。

Tā shì nǐ māma, duì ma?
Bǐ'ěr: 她 是 你 妈妈，对 吗？

Duì, tā shì wǒ māma.
Lǐ Lì: 对，她 是 我 妈妈。

Nà shì nǐ dìdi ma?
Bǐ'ěr: 那 是 你 弟弟 吗？

Bú shì, nà shì wǒ gēge.
Lǐ Lì: 不 是，那 是 我 哥哥。

> Li Li: He is my father.
> Bill: She is your mother, right?
> Li Li: Yes, she is my mother.
> Bill: Is that your younger brother?
> Li Li: No, that's my elder brother.

D. Pair Work

Now read the dialogue between Bill and Li Li with a partner.

E. Group Work

In groups of three, one person writes the single finals, one writes initials, and the other one writes four tones as well as the neutral tone on small cards. Then one person picks up an initial, a single final and a tone in turn, reads it aloud and writes it down. The person who comes up with the most correct initial-final combinations is the winner.

F. Read the following sentences as quickly as you can, and try to pronounce each syllable accurately.

Mùmu de bàba fānù le.
木木 的 爸爸 发怒 了。   Mumu's father got angry.

Nàna de māma pífū hǎo.
娜娜 的 妈妈 皮肤 好。   Nana's mother has good skin.

Nīni de bóbo bù pápō.
妮妮 的 伯伯 不 爬坡。   Nini's uncle doesn't climb the slope.

Bōbo de pópo mílù le.
波波 的 婆婆 迷路 了。   Bobo's grandmother lost her way.

Reminder
1. There are six Single Finals: *a o e i u ü*
2. The four Labial Initials are: *b p m f*
3. The four Alveolar Initials are: *d t n l*

Pinyin Step 3

■ Compound Finals: *ai   ei   ao   ou   ua   uo   uai   ui (uei)*

Any compound final that has more than one vowel is made up of a main vowel and a secondary vowel. If the compound final is made up of two vowels, the first or main vowel of each of these compound finals receives the most stress. For example, in the compound final *ai*, the main vowel is *a* and the secondary vowel is *i*.

In a compound final with three vowels, the middle vowel receives the most stress. For example, in the compound final *uai*, *a* is the main vowel. The final *ui* is a contraction for the three vowel compound final *uei*, so the main vowel is *e*, even though it doesn't appear in the written form of Pinyin.

A. Listen and read.

ai   ei   ao   ou   ua   uo   uai   ui (uei)

B. Listen and write down the tones.

ai	fei	bao	tou	hua	duo	wai	dui
爱	飞	包	头	画	多	外	对
love	fly	bag	head	drawing	many	outside	right

C. Read the following syllables.

ài   bái   měi   fēi   ào   táo

ōu   lóu   wá   wài   wēi   wěi

D. Listen and read.

àihào	méi	huà huà	hǎo	mèimei	lái
爱好	没	画 画	好	妹妹	来
to be fond of; hobby	have not	to draw	good; all right	younger sister	to come

E. Read the following dialogues in pairs.

(1)
A: Nǐ hǎo!
你 好！   A: Hello!

B: Nǐ hǎo!
你 好！   B: Hi!

(2)
A: Mèimei láile ma?
妹妹 来了 吗？   A: Has your younger sister arrived?

B: Méi lái.
没 来。   B: Not yet.

(3)
A: Nǐ de àihào shì shénme?
你 的 爱好 是 什么？ A: What's your hobby?

B: Wǒ àihào huà huà.
我 爱好 画 画。   B: I love drawing.

■ Dental Sibilant Initials: z c s

To pronounce z, c, and s, put the tip of the tongue behind the upper front teeth, then release the tongue slightly to let the air flow between the narrow space between the tongue and teeth.

- z is similar to the **ds** in **lads**.
- c is similar to the **ts** in **cats**.
- s is similar to the **s** in **Sam**.

■ Retroflex Initials: zh ch sh r

To pronounce the retroflex initials zh, ch, sh and r, begin with the formation you learned for z, c, s, then open the mouth a little bit and curl the tip of the tongue up and back toward your soft palate so that the sound is produced farther back in the mouth.

- zh is similar to the **j** in **journey**, but with the tongue curled farther back.
- ch is similar to the **ch** in **chain**, but with the tongue curled farther back.
- sh is similar to the **sh** in **shine**, but with the tongue curled farther back.
- r is similar to the **r** in **run**, but with the tongue curled farther back.

When z, c, s and zh, ch, sh, r are combined with the single final i, the i is not pronounced as the typical ee sound. When paired with these initials, the tongue is held in the same position throughout the syllable, relaxing slightly at the pronunciation of the vowel.

A. Listen and read.

zī	zǐ	zì		cī	cí	cǐ	cì		sī	sǐ	sì	
zhī	zhí	zhǐ	zhì	chī	chí	chǐ	chì	shī	shí	shǐ	shì	rì

B. Listen to the recording and repeat each syllable. Then add the correct tone below.

zi	ci	si	sui	zhe	chi	shi	shei / shui
字	词	四	岁	这	吃	十	谁
character	word	four	year (of age)	this	to eat	ten	who

C. Listen and read.

zǐ – zhǐ   cí – chí   sì – shì   zǎo – zhǎo   cǎo – chǎo   sǎo – shǎo

D. Listen and read.

(1)
Nǐ mèimei jǐ suì?
A: 你 妹妹 几 岁？　　A: How old is your younger sister?

Tā sì suì.
B: 她四岁。　　B: She is four years old.

Shí suì?
A: 十岁？　　A: Ten years old?

Bù, sì suì.
B: 不，四岁。　　B: No, four years old.

Zhè shì shéi de shū?

(2) A: 这 是 谁 的 书 ？ A: Whose book is it?

Shì wǒ de shū .

B: 是 我 的 书 。 B: It's my book.

E. Practice the dialogues in Activity D with a partner.

Now you can do it! ☺

■ Initial-Final Combinations

	z	c	s	zh	ch	sh	r
ai	zai	cai	sai	zhai	chai	shai	–
ei	zei	cei	–	zhei	–	shei	–
ao	zao	cao	sao	zhao	chao	shao	rao
ou	zou	cou	sou	zhou	chou	shou	rou
ua	–	–	–	zhua	chua	shua	–
uo	zuo	cuo	suo	zhuo	chuo	shuo	ruo
uai	–	–	–	zhuai	chuai	shuai	–
ui	zui	cui	sui	zhui	chui	shui	rui

A. Pair Work

With a partner, take turns as one writing a final (with tone mark) in the center circle below. The other should write down all the possible initial-final combinations that can be made according to the chart above, then read them aloud.

        ch   s

zh   ◯   z   Possible Syllables: _____

sh   c   r   _____

B. Listen as your teacher says the following statement, then fill in the initials.

__ì __ī __ī míng

自 知 之 明   know oneself well

C. Team Competition

In teams of three, one person writes the finals him or her knows, one writes initials, and the other ones write four tones as well as the neutral tone on small cards. Then one person picks up an initial, a final and a tone in turn, reads it aloud and writes it down. The team that comes up with the most syllables wins.

D. Read the following sentences as quickly as you can, trying to pronounce each syllable accurately.

Sì shì sì, shí shì shí.

四 是 四 ， 十 是 十 。   4=4   10=10

Shísì shì shísì, sìshí shì sìshí.

十四 是 十四 ， 四十 是 四十 。

Pinyin Step 4

■ Compound Finals: *ia ie iao iu (iou) üe*

Listen to the recording silently.

ia   ie   iao   iu (iou)   üe

In compound finals that begin with *i* and *ü*, the second vowel serves as the main vowel. For example, in the compound final *üe*, the main vowel is *e* and the secondary vowel is *ü*. Review *Pinyin Step 1* for help on the usage of *y* in these zero initial syllables.

As you learned in *Pinyin Step 3*, the middle vowel receives the most stress in a compound final with three vowels. For example, in the compound final *iao*, *a* is the main vowel. Like *ui*, the final *iu* is a contraction for the three vowel compound final *iou*, so the main vowel is *o*, even though it doesn't appear in the written form of *iu*.

A. Listen and read.

ia	ie	iao	iu (iou)	üe
ai — ia	ei — ie	ao — iao	ou — iu (iou)	ü — üe

B. Listen and read.

yá	yě	yào	yǒu	yuè
牙	也	要	有	月
tooth	too	to want	to have	moon

C. Team Competition

In groups of three or four, find all possible vowel combinations as quickly as you can using the *a, o, e, i, u, ü*. For example, *ai* and *ia*.

■ Lingual Initials: *j q x*

- *j* is similar to the **j** in **jeep**, but keep the upper teeth and lower teeth together and keep the tongue flat.

- *q* is similar to the **ch** in **cheap**, but keep the same state of pronunciation of *j*, then give a puff of breath. It's an aspirated sound.

- *x* is similar to the **sh** in **sheep**, but keep the tongue flat and leave a seam between the upper and lower teeth to let a soft breath get through.

■ Velar Initials: *g k h*

While the velar initials are mostly pronounced similarly to their English counterparts, the aspirated sounds *k* and *h* are generally pronounced more forcefully in Chinese.

- ■ *g* is similar to the **g** in **gum**.
- ■ *k* is similar to the **c** in **cat**.
- ■ *h* is similar to the **h** in **hat**, with slightly more apsiration.

A. Listen and read. 🎧

jī	jí	jǐ	jì
qī	qí	qǐ	qì
xī	xí	xǐ	xì

Qīyuè qī, shì Qīxī, Qīxī jiérì yǒu qíjì.
七月 七，是 七夕，七夕 节日 有 奇迹。

Some miracle happens on the seventh evening of the seventh month of the lunar calendar.

gē	gé	gě	gè
kē	ké	kě	kè
hē	hé		hè

Gēge kǒu kě zhǎo shuǐ hē.
哥哥 口 渴 找 水 喝。

The elder brother is thirsty, and he is looking for some water to drink.

B. Listen and read, then write down the missing tones. 🎧

qiguai   kan   ge   xiexie   keqi   zaijian

𝒩ow you can do it! ☺

■ Initial-Final Combinations

	j	q	x	g	k	h
a	–	–	–	ga	ka	ha
ao	–	–	–	gao	kao	hao
ou	–	–	–	gou	kou	hou
e	–	–	–	ge	ke	he
i	ji	qi	xi	–	–	–
ia	jia	qia	xia	–	–	–
u	–	–	–	gu	ku	hu
uai	–	–	–	guai	kuai	huai
ü	ju	qu	xu	–	–	–
üe	jue	que	xue	–	–	–

If you noticed something special about *ü*, you are a good observer. When *ü* appears after *j*, *q*, and *x*, drop the two dots. Even though it looks like *u*, it should still be pronounced *ü*. There is a saying in Chinese:

j q x, xiǎo táoqì, jiànle ü yǎn jiù náqù.

j q x，小 淘气，见了 ü 眼 就 拿去。

j q x are so naughty that they always take away the eyes of *ü*. (In Chinese, *ü* sounds like *yú* 鱼 <fish>.)

j + ü ⟶ ju	jùzi	句子	sentence
q + ü ⟶ qu	qù	去	to go
x + üe ⟶ xue	xué	学	to learn

A. Group work

In groups of three, decide what kind of finals go with *j*, *q*, *x*, and what kind of finals go with *g*, *k*, *h*, according to the chart of initial-final combinations. Then share your list with the other groups to make sure everyone knows all the rules.

B. Listen and read. 🎧

qíguài	shūbāo	kàn	gè	xièxie	kèqi	zàijiàn
奇怪	书包	看	个	谢谢	客气	再见
strange	bag	to look	(a measure word)	thanks	courteous	goodbye

Qíguài! Wǒ de shūbāo ne?
A: 奇怪！我 的 书包 呢？

Nǐ kàn, zhège shūbāo shì bu shì nǐ de?
B: 你 看 ， 这个 书包 是 不 是 你 的？

Shìde. Xièxie!
A: 是的 。 谢谢 ！

Bú kèqi. Zàijiàn!
B: 不 客气。 再见 ！

Zàijiàn!
A: 再见 ！

> A: It's so weird! Where is my bag?
> B: Look, is this your bag?
> A: Yes. Thank you!
> B: You are welcome. Goodbye!
> A: Bye!

C. Pair Work

Now practice reading the dialogue in Activity B with a partner.

Reminder

1. There are five Compound Finals beginning with *i*, *ü*: *ia   ie   iao   iu (iou)   üe*
2. The three Lingual Initials are: *j   q   x*
3. The three Velar Initials are: *g   k   h*

Pinyin Step 5

■ **Front Nasal Finals:** *an   en   ian   in   uan   un (uen)   üan   ün*

Listen to the recording silently. 🎧

an   en   ian   in   uan   un (uen)   üan   ün

The front nasal finals end with *–n*. As in English, the Chinese *–n* is pronounced with the tip of the tongue at the back of the front upper teeth. These syllables are all zero initial syllables. Pay attention to the usages of *y* and *w* mentioned in *Pinyin Step 1*.

Like the compound finals *iu* and *ui*, *un* is a contraction of *uen*. For example, *liù* 六 (six), *huí* 回 (to come back), *tūn* 吞 (to swallow).

A. Listen and read. 🎧

an	en	ian	in	uan	un (uen)	üan	ün
ān	ēn	yán	yīn	wàn	wèn	yuǎn	yún
安	恩	盐	音	万	问	远	云
safe	favor	salt	sound	ten thousand	to ask	far	cloud

B. Listen and read, paying close attention to the differences of the finals. 🎧

tán — tián   chén — yín   wǎn — yuǎn   wèn — yùn
lán — lián   rèn — xìn   zǎn — zuǎn   juàn — jùn

■ Back Nasal Finals: *ang eng ong iang ing iong uang ueng*

Listen to the recording silently. 🎧

ang eng ong iang ing iong uang ueng

The back nasal finals end with –*ng*. As in English, the Chinese –*ng* is pronounced with back of the tongue touching the soft palate, with a stronger nasal sound than –*n*.

A. Listen and read. 🎧

an — ang   en — eng   in — ing
ian — iang   ian — ing   uan — uang
un — ueng   ün — iong   un — ong

B. Listen and read, then complete the syllables with the correct finals. 🎧

d___rán	zhēnch___	x___niàn	xīngch___
当然	真诚	想念	星辰
of course	sincere	to miss, to think of	star

xīnq___	niánq___	y___jing	wēif___
心情	年轻	眼睛	微风
mood	young	eye	breeze

Now you can do it! ☺

A. Listen and read. 🎧

Ràokǒulìng
绕口令 (Tongue Twister)

Tiānshang xǔduō xīngxing, wènqǐ wǒ de xīnqíng.
天上 许多 星星 ，问起 我 的 心情 。

Wǒ xiǎng guò de qīngsōng.
我 想 过 得 轻松 。

Xīngxing zhǎzhe yǎnjing, sòng wǒ yí zhèn wēifēng.
星星 眨着 眼睛 ，送 我 一 阵 微风 。

Stars in the sky asked me about my feelings.
I just wanted to have a pleasant life in this world.
The stars winked and gave me a breeze.

B. Pair Work

With a partner, take turns as one person reads the syllable and the other writes it down.

zh + un (uen) + 3声 → _____   iou   + 4声 → _____

k + uang   + 1声 → _____   üan   + 3声 → _____

x + in   + 4声 → _____   ing   + 2声 → _____

j + ü   + 2声 → _____   un (uen) + 3声 → _____

q + ün   + 1声 → _____   iang   + 1声 → _____

Reminder

1. There are eight Front Nasal Finals ending with –*n*: *an en ian in uan un (uen) üan ün*
2. There are eight Back Nasal Finals ending with –*ng*: *ang eng ong iang ing iong uang ueng*

Pinyin Step 6

■ –*er* and R-ending Retroflexion

Listen to the recording silently.

ér huār niǎor huàr zhèr nàr nǎr tiānr cír diànyǐngr

When *er* appears as an independent syllable, as in *ér* 儿 (son), *ér* 而 (however), *ěr* 耳 (ear), and *èr* 二 (two), try to pronounce *e* while curling the tongue back to get *er*.

R-ending retroflexion or *érhuà* 儿化 happens when –*er* is added to the end of another final. This is an addition of a retroflexion to the original final of the syllable. This change is made in writing by adding *r* to the end of the syllable in Pinyin and by adding 儿 after the final character of the word. For instance, *huā* 花 (flower) becomes *huār* 花儿. R-ending retroflexion is commonly used, especially in the Beijing area.

A. Listen and read.

érzi	értóng	dì-èr tiān	érqiě	ěrduo	èr líng èr líng nián
儿子	儿童	第二 天	而且	耳朵	二 零 二 零 年
son	children	the second day	furthermore	ear	the year of 2020

B. Listen and read, paying close attention to the changes of the finals.

zhè zhèr	nà nàr	tóu tóur	chē chēr
这 → 这儿	那 → 那儿	头 → 头儿	车 →车儿
this → here	that → there	head → leader	car

If the final syllable ends with *a*, *o*, *e*, or *u*, add *r* directly to the end of the word. Changes are more complex when the word ends with other vowels or with a consonant.

C. Listen carefully and try to pronounce the finals with r-ending retroflexion correctly. 🎧

		Changes
yǒuqù 有趣 (interesting) →	yǒuqùr 有趣儿	[tɕʻy] → [tɕʻyɚr]
cí 词 (word) →	cír 词儿	[tsʻɿ] → [tsʻɚr]
diànyǐng 电影 (film) →	diànyǐngr 电影儿	[iŋ] → [iɚr]

Sometimes r-ending retroflexion changes the meaning of the word, for example, *zhè* 这 (this) → *zhèr* 这儿 (here) and *tóu* 头 (head) → *tóur* 头儿 (leader).

Now you can do it! ☺

Listen and read the words following the recording. Note the changes in meaning of some of the words. 🎧

xìn 信 →	xìnr 信儿	wán 玩 →	wánr 玩儿	nǎ 哪 →	nǎr 哪儿
letter	message	to play		which	where

fànguǎn 饭馆 →	fànguǎnr 饭馆儿	yīdiǎn 一点 →	yīdiǎnr 一点儿	huà 画 →	huàr 画儿
restaurant		a little		to draw; drawing	

■ Tone Change

Listen to the recording silently. 🎧

nǐ hǎo   měilì   yì nián   yìzhí   yìqǐ   yí gè
bù'ān   bùwén búwèn   bù zhǔn   hǎo bu hǎo

When syllables are combined to make words and sentences, there are often changes in tone to allow for more natural and fluent speech. Here are the special rules for tone changes.

■ Tone Change for the 3rd Tone

1. 3rd tone + 3rd tone → 2nd tone + 3rd tone

For example: *nǐ* 你 + *hǎo* 好 → *nǐ* (*ní*) *hǎo* 你好 (hello)

2. 3rd tone + other tones (except 3rd tone)   semi-3rd tone + other tones

For example: *měi* 美 + *guó* 国 → *Měi* (semi-3rd tone) *guó* 美国 (the U.S.)

Semi-3rd tone means that only the front half of the 3rd tone is pronounced. There is no separate tone mark for semi-3rd tone, so these changes usually go unnoticed in Pinyin.

A. Listen and read, paying close attention to the changes in tone. 🎧

mǎi	shǒu	biǎo		mǎi	shǒu(shóu)biǎo	
买	手	表	⟶	**买**	**手**表	to buy a watch

zhǎo	yǔ	sǎn		zhǎo	yǔ(yú)sǎn	
找	雨	伞	⟶	**找**	**雨**伞	to look for an umbrella

hěn	měi	hǎo		hěn	měi(méi)hǎo	
很	美	好	⟶	**很**	**美**好	wonderful

B. Read the dialogue following the recording.

Wǒmen qù mǎi dōngxi ba.
A: 我们 去 买 东西 吧。　　A: Let's go shopping.

Nǐ xiǎng mǎi shénme?
B: 你 想 买 什么 ？　　B: What do you want to buy?

Wǒ xiǎng mǎi shǒubiǎo.
A: 我 想 买 手表 。　　A: I want to buy a watch.

Hǎo de, wǒmen zǒu ba.
B: 好 的， 我们 走 吧。　　B: OK, let's go.

C. Pair Work

Now practice reading the dialogue in Activity B with a partner.

■ Tone Change for yī 一

1. yī 一 (1st tone) + 4th tone → yí 一 (2nd tone) + 4th tone

   For example: yī 一 + yàng 样 → yíyàng 一样 (same)

2. yī 一 (1st tone) + other tones (except 4th tone) → yì 一 (4th tone) + other tones

   For example:

   yī 一 + ⎧ tiān 天 → yì tiān 一天 (one day)
          ⎨ píng 瓶 → yì píng 一瓶 (a bottle of)
          ⎩ qǐ 起 → yìqǐ 一起 (together)

3. verb + yī 一 (1st tone) + verb → verb + yi 一 (neutral tone) + verb

   For example:

   shì 试 + yī 一 + shì 试 → shì yi shì 试一试 (to have a try)

   zǒu 走 + yī 一 + zǒu 走 → zǒu yi zǒu 走一走 (to have a walk)

Pair Work

With a partner, take turns choosing a syllable to follow yī 一 while the other reads it. Don't forget to follow the rules for tone changes!

yī		jiā	nián	zhǒng	zhí	duǒ	dìng	qiè	shēng
一	+	家	年	种	直	朵	定	切	生

■ Tone Change for *bù* 不

1. *bù* 不 (4th tone) + 4th tone → *bú* 不 (2nd tone) + 4th tone

   For example: *bù* 不 + *qù* 去 → *bú qù* 不去 (not to go)

2. *bù* 不 + other tones (except 4th tone) → no change

   For example: *bù* 不 + *zhīdào* 知道 → *bù zhīdào* 不知道 (don't know)

3. verb/adjective + *bù* 不 + verb/adjective → verb/adjective + *bu* 不 (neutral tone) + verb/adjective

   For example:

   chī 吃 + *bù* 不 + *chī* 吃 → *chī bu chī* 吃不吃 (Eat or not?)

   hǎo 好 + *bù* 不 + *hǎo* 好 → *hǎo bu hǎo* 好不好 (Is it all right?)

Team Work

In groups of three, one person chooses a word from the following list to read aloud, another adds 不 prior to it, and the third person reads it in the verb/adjective+*bù* 不+verb/adjective model. For example, Student A says 吃, Student B says 不吃, and Student C says 吃不吃.

chī 吃	shuō 说	dú 读	kàn 看	lái 来	xiǎng 想	lěng 冷	rè 热	wèn 问
to eat	to say	to read	to look	to come	to think	cold	hot	to ask

---

Reminder

1. Er can appear as an independent syllable (*èr* 二). It also can be added to the end of another final (*huār* 花儿).

2. The 3rd tone changes to be a 2nd tone (*nǐ<ní> hǎo* 你好) or half 3rd tone (*měilì* 美丽).

3. Yī 一 changes to *yí* (*yíyàng* 一样), *yì* (*yìqǐ* 一起) or *yi* (*shì yi shì* 试一试).

4. Bù 不 changes to *bú* (*bú qù* 不去) or *bu*(*hǎo bu hǎo* 好不好).

Team Game

In groups of six, five members stand in a circle, and each person has some finals written on cards. The sixth member stands in the center of the circle holding cards with initials on them. The person in the middle closes his or her eyes and spins in the circle and then stops and reads aloud an initial. The member who faces the person in the middle reads aloud a final to see if they match and can come up with a proper initial-final combination to form a syllable. If not, try again until you come up with a syllable. The team that comes up with the most syllables in five minutes wins the game.

Supplementary

■ Sentence Pause

Punctuation such as comma (,) and pause mark (、) help us know when to pause in the middle or at the end of a sentence. However, most pauses are not called out with punctuation, so it is important to know where natural pauses occur in order to speak more fluently. The pause appears with the integrated meaning of each part of the sentence.

A. Listen and read, paying close attention to the pauses in each sentence. 🎧

Tā shì wǒ de péngyou Lǐ Lì.
她 是 | 我 的　朋友　| 李 丽。　　She is my friend Li Li.

Wǒ mǎile yí gè shūbāo.
我 买了 | 一 个　书包 。　　I bought a bag.

B. Pair Work

With a partner, have one person read the following sentence while the other marks the pause, then exchange roles. Did you both come up with the same sentence?

nǐ xǐhuan wǒ yě xǐhuan tā zěnme bàn
你 喜欢　我 也　喜欢　她　怎么　办

■ Sentence Stress

Placing stress on a particular word or words helps to indicate the most important part of a sentence. The word that expresses the main idea of the sentence should be emphasized.

A. Listen and read, paying close attention to where the stress is placed. 🎧

Bǐ'ěr huì shuō Hànyǔ.
比尔 会 说 汉语 。　　It's Bill who can speak Chinese.

Bǐ'ěr huì shuō Hànyǔ.
比尔 会 说 汉语 。　　The language that Bill can speak is Chinese.

Bǐ'ěr huì shuō Hànyǔ.
比尔 会 说 汉语 。　　Bill can speak Chinese. (But he cannot write Chinese characters.)

Bǐ'ěr huì shuō Hànyǔ.
比尔 会 说 汉语 。　　Bill can speak Chinese. (Why did you say that he cannot?)

B. Pair Work

With a partner, take turns reading the sentences in Activity A, while the other explains the main meaning indicated by the sentence stress without looking at the book.

■ Sentence Intonation

Declarative sentences, interrogative sentences, exclamatory sentences and imperative sentences have different intonations.

A. Repeat the following sentences after your teacher, paying close attention to the intonation of each type of sentence.

Tā shì wàixīngrén.
他 是 外星人 。

He is an alien.

Tā shì wàixīngrén?
他 是 外星人 ？

Is he an alien?

Tā shì wàixīngrén!
他 是 外星人 ！

He is an alien!

Nǐ zhǎo wàixīngrén? Qù zhǎo tā ba!
你 找 外星人 ？ 去 找 他 吧！

Are you looking for the alien? Go find him!

Āiyā, wǒ zhēn méi kàn chūlái, tā shì wàixīngrén a!
哎呀，我 真 没 看 出来，他 是 外星人 啊！

Wow, I really didn't know that he was an alien!

B. Take turns reading the sentences from Activity A with a partner.

■ Reciting

Reciting poems is an important training for students of Chinese culture.

A. Listen to the recording and read after it silently.

Jìngyè sī
静夜 思
Lǐ Bái (Táng)
—— 李 白（唐）

Chuáng qián míngyuèguāng,
床 前 明月光 ，
Yí shì dì shàng shuāng.
疑 是 地 上 霜 。
Jǔ tóu wàng míngyuè,
举 头 望 明月 ，
Dī tóu sī gùxiāng.
低 头 思 故乡 。

A Tranquil Night
— Li Bai (Tang Dynasty)

Abed, I see a silver light,
I wonder if it's frost aground.
Looking up, I find the moon bright;
Bowing, in homesickness I'm drowned.

(Translated by Xu Yuanchong)

B. Repeat the verses of this famous poem after your teacher, then take turns reciting the poem with a partner.

The Initials, Finals and Tones of Pinyin

Initials

	Unaspirated[7]	Aspirated[8]	Nasal[9]	Fricative[10]	Voiced[11]
Labial[1]	b[p]	p[p']	m[m]	f [f]	
Alveolar[2]	d [t]	t[t']	n[n]		l[l]
Velar[3]	g[k]	k[k']		h[x]	
Lingual[4]	j[tɕ]	q[tɕ']		x[ɕ]	
Retroflex[5]	zh[tʂ]	ch[tʂ']		sh[ʂ]	r[ʐ]
Dental[6]	z [ts]	c [ts']		s[s]	

1. Labial: made using one or both lips.
2. Alveolar: made by putting the tip of the tongue behind the upper front teeth.
3. Velar: made with the root of the tongue near the soft palatal.
4. Lingual: made by putting the tongue near the hard palatal.
5. Retroflex: made with the tip of the tongue curled upwards and backwards.
6. Dental: made by putting the tip of the tongue against the upper front teeth.
7. Unaspirated: made with weak breath.
8. Aspirated: made with audible breath.
9. Nasal: made with nasal resonance.
10. Fricative: made by letting the breath through a narrow channel.
11. Voiced: made when the vocal cords vibrate.

Finals

Single Finals	a[A]　o[o]　e[ɤ]　i[i]　u[u]　ü[y] -i[ɿ]　、-i [ʅ][1]　ê[ɛ][2]　er [ɚ][3]
Compound Finals	ai[ai]　ei[ei]　ao[au]　ou[ou] ia[iA]　ie[iɛ]　iao[iau]　iu (iou)[iou] ua[uA]　uo[uo]　uai[uai]　ui (uei)[uei] üe[yɛ]
Nasal Finals	an[an]　en[ən]　ang[aŋ]　eng[əŋ]　ong[uŋ] ian[iæn]　in[in]　iang[iaŋ]　ing[iŋ]　iong[yŋ] uan[uan]　un (uen)[uən]　uang[uaŋ]　ueng[uəŋ] üan[yan]　ün[yn]

1. -i[ɿ],[ʅ] are recorded as i in Pinyin system. -i [ɿ] only appears in zi, ci, si while -i[ʅ] occurring in zhi, chi, shi.
2. ê[ɛ] only appears in āi, ǎi 欸.
3. er [ɚ] can be a single syllable by itself and can attach to another final and occurs as the last part of this final.

The finals begin with i are written as yi, ya, ye, yao, you, yan, yin, yang, ying, yong when there are no initials before i. The finals begin with u are written as wu, wa, wo, wai, wei, wan, wen, wang, weng when there are no initials before u. The finals begin with ü are written as yu, yue, yuan, yun when there are no initials before ü, and ü drops the two dots on the top of it in this situation.

Tones

Tone	Mark	Pronunciation	Example	
1st tone	—	high and level tone	mā 妈	mother
2nd tone	ˊ	rising tone	má 麻	flax
3rd tone	˅	falling-rising tone	mǎ 马	horse
4th tone	ˋ	falling tone	mà 骂	to abuse
neutral tone	no mark	short and soft	ma 吗	(a particle)

The Syllables of Mandarin Chinese

韵母 \ 声母	∅	b	p	m	f	d	t	n	l	z	c	s	zh	ch	sh	r	j	q	x	g	k	h
un	yun																jun	qun	xun			
üan	yuan																juan	quan	xuan			
üe	yue							nüe	lüe								jue	que	xue			
ü	yu							nü	lü								ju	qu	xu			
ueng	weng																					
uang	wang												zhuang	chuang	shuang					guang	kuang	huang
un	wen					dun	tun		lun	zun	cun	sun	zhun	chun	shun	run				gun	kun	hun
uan	wan					duan	tuan	nuan	luan	zuan	cuan	suan	zhuan	chuan	shuan	ruan				guan	kuan	huan
ui	wei					dui	tui			zui	cui	sui	zhui	chui	shui	rui				gui	kui	hui
uai	wai												zhuai	chuai	shuai					guai	kuai	huai
uo	wo					duo	tuo	nuo	luo	zuo	cuo	suo	zhuo	chuo	shuo	ruo				guo	kuo	huo
ua	wa												zhua	chua	shua					gua	kua	hua
u	wu	bu	pu	mu	fu	du	tu	nu	lu	zu	cu	su	zhu	chu	shu	ru				gu	ku	hu
iong	yong																jiong	qiong	xiong			
ing	ying	bing	ping	ming		ding	ting	ning	ling								jing	qing	xing			
iang	yang							niang	liang								jiang	qiang	xiang			
in	yin	bin	pin	min				nin	lin								jin	qin	xin			
ian	yan	bian	pian	mian		dian	tian	nian	lian								jian	qian	xian			
iu	you			miu		diu		niu	liu								jiu	qiu	xiu			
ie	ye	bie	pie	mie		die	tie	nie	lie								jie	qie	xie			
iao	yao	biao	piao	miao		diao	tiao	niao	liao								jiao	qiao	xiao			
ia	ya					dia			lia								jia	qia	xia			
i	yi	bi	pi	mi		di	ti	ni	li								ji	qi	xi			
ong						dong	tong	nong	long	zong	cong	song	zhong	chong		rong				gong	kong	hong
eng	eng	beng	peng	meng	feng	deng	teng	neng	leng	zeng	ceng	seng	zheng	cheng	sheng	reng				geng	keng	heng
ang	ang	bang	pang	mang	fang	dang	tang	nang	lang	zang	cang	sang	zhang	chang	shang	rang				gang	kang	hang
en	en	ben	pen	men	fen	den		nen		zen	cen	sen	zhen	chen	shen	ren				gen	ken	hen
an	an	ban	pan	man	fan	dan	tan	nan	lan	zan	can	san	zhan	chan	shan	ran				gan	kan	han
ou	ou		pou	mou	fou	dou	tou	nou	lou	zou	cou	sou	zhou	chou	shou	rou				gou	kou	hou
ao	ao	bao	pao	mao		dao	tao	nao	lao	zao	cao	sao	zhao	chao	shao	rao				gao	kao	hao
ei	ei	bei	pei	mei	fei	dei		nei	lei	zei			zhei		shei					gei	kei	hei
ai	ai	bai	pai	mai		dai	tai	nai	lai	zai	cai	sai	zhai	chai	shai					gai	kai	hai
-i	er									zi	ci	si	zhi	chi	shi	ri						
ê	ê																					
e	e			me		de	te	ne	le	ze	ce	se	zhe	che	she	re				ge	ke	he
o	o	bo	po	mo	fo																	
a	a	ba	pa	ma	fa	da	ta	na	la	za	ca	sa	zha	cha	sha					ga	ka	ha

Chinese characters, known as Han characters or *hànzì*, form a unique logographic writing system with the longest history to date. Chinese characters are also known as ideographs, or graphic symbols that represent a thing or an idea, and the Chinese writing system is known as ideography. This writing system is a key to open the door of Chinese language and culture.

A famous ancient Chinese legend says that a man named *Cāngjié* created Chinese characters according to the tracks of birds and animals on the ground. Although it is just a legend, pictographs are important parts of the development of Chinese characters. Here are some examples of inscriptions made on tortoise shells over 3, 000 years ago, found in the Henan Province of China at the end of the 19th century.

Pair Work

With a partner, try to guess the meaning of each of the characters that appears above.

造字法   Chinese Character Types

Liùshū 六书 (the Six Categories of Chinese Characters) is the traditional Chinese theory devised by ancient scholars regarding the six different types of Chinese characters. Two of the categories refer to how the characters are used, but more importantly, four of these categories refer to the building of the characters.

1. Xiàngxíng 象形

Pictographs convey their meanings through their resemblance to certain objects. For example:

Guess the meanings of the following characters.

2. Zhǐshì 指事

Ideograms are graphic symbols that represent an idea or a concept. This type of character may also be created by adding a symbol to a pictograph. For example:

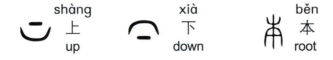

3. Huìyì 会意

Ideogrammic compounds combine two or more pictographs or ideographs to create a character. For example:

Connect each character with its proper meaning based on its shape.

cóng 从	forest
míng 明	many people
lín 林	to follow
zhòng 众	bright

4. Xíngshēng 形声

Phonograms combine two parts to create a compound character with one part indicating the meaning and the other indicating the pronunciation. This is the most common type of Chinese character. For example:

Meaning	Pronunciation	Character
心→忄 xīn = heart	+ 青 qīng = blue, green →	qíng 情 feeling
水→氵 shuǐ = water	+ 可 kě = to be able to →	hé 河 river
言→讠 yán = to speak; speech	+ 吾 wú = I →	yǔ 语 language, speech

Use the chart on pages 46~47 and find the meaning part of each character.

 fāng 芳 fragrant

 pǎo 跑 to run

chī 吃 to eat

字体　Script of Chinese Characters

The script of Chinese characters has changed during the long history.

	jiǎgǔwén 甲骨文 **Oracle**	zhuànshū 篆书 **Seal Character**	lìshū 隶书 **Official Script**	kǎishū 楷书 **Regular Script**
shān 山	⛰	山	山	山
shuǐ 水			水	水
rén 人			人	人
yáng 羊		羊	羊	羊
zhōu 舟			舟	舟
chē 车		車	车	车

结构和部件　Structure and Components

Chinese characters should demonstrate the following properties: well-balanced, square, and upright. There are two types of structure: single-element characters (e.g. 人, 木, 羊) and compound characters (e.g. 从, 休, 洋).

Compound characters are made up of various components, the basic structural units of Chinese characters. For example, 明 is made up of the components 日 and 月, and 河 is made up of 氵 and 可. The different types of compound characters include:

1. Left-right Structure
nǐ 你　　míng 明

2. Upper-lower Structure
zì 字　　shì 是

3. Semi-enclosed Structure
zhè 这　　tīng 厅

4. Total-enclosed Structure
yīn 因　　guó 国

5. Structure Like 品
pǐn 品　　zhòng 众

6. Left-middle-right Structure
zuò 做　　shù 树

With a partner, name the structure type of each of the following characters.

liù 六　　guò 过　　wèn 问　　tā 他　　jiā 家　　hú 湖　　jīng 晶　　sī 司　　rì 日　　kùn 困

部首 Radicals

The radical is used as the primary organizer in traditional Chinese dictionaries because the same radical is used to form many characters. The radical usually indicates the classified meaning of characters. Some radicals have several different forms, which help to keep the structure of each character well-balanced and easy to write.

Radical	Classified Meaning	Variations	Characters
kǒu 口	related to mouth	口	chī 吃 (to eat), hē 喝 (to drink), tūn 吞 (to swallow)
rén 人	related to people	人，亻	mìng 命 (life), tā 他 (he), zuò 做 (to do)
xīn 心	related to thinking	心，忄	wàng 忘 (to forget), rěn 忍 (to suffer), qíng 情 (feeling)
shuǐ 水	related to water	水，氵	quán 泉 (spring), hǎi 海 (sea), kě 渴 (thirsty)
shǒu 手	related to hand	手，扌，龵	zhǎng 掌 (palm), dǎ 打 (to hit), kàn 看 (to look)
huǒ 火	related to fire	火，灬	kǎo 烤 (to toast), tàng 烫 (scalding), rè 热 (hot)

Observe the following characters, then guess their meanings according to the pictures.

hǎn	hàn	yōu	nù	yī
喊	汗	忧	怒	依

pāi	wò	zhǔ	sǎn
拍	握	煮	伞

笔画 Strokes

While Chinese characters may appear to be complicated drawings, they are really just a series of strokes. Each Chinese character is made up of one or more of the eight basic strokes that you must learn in order to properly write Chinese characters.

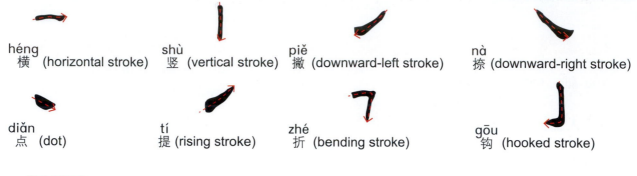

héng
横 (horizontal stroke)

shù
竖 (vertical stroke)

piě
撇 (downward-left stroke)

nà
捺 (downward-right stroke)

diǎn
点 (dot)

tí
提 (rising stroke)

zhé
折 (bending stroke)

gōu
钩 (hooked stroke)

Pair Work

A. In pairs, take turns reading the names of the strokes in Chinese while the other writes it down.
B. Try to count the number of the strokes of the following characters.

干　生　市　永　早　习　买　远　邹

笔顺 Stroke Order

It is important to learn the correct stroke order in order to write Chinese characters. The general principles are as follows.

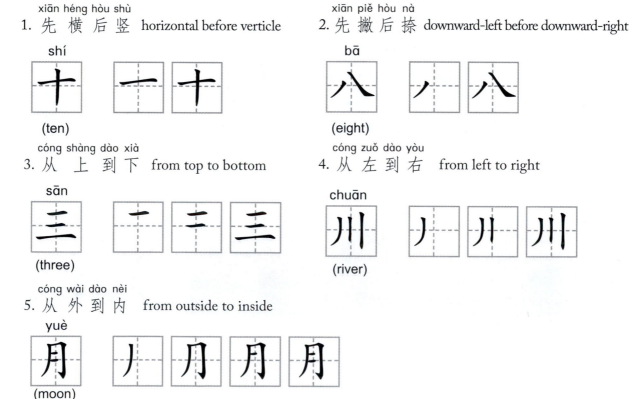

xiān héng hòu shù
1. 先 横 后 竖 horizontal before verticle

shí
十　一　十
(ten)

xiān piě hòu nà
2. 先 撇 后 捺 downward-left before downward-right

bā
八　丿　八
(eight)

cóng shàng dào xià
3. 从 上 到 下 from top to bottom

sān
三　一　二　三
(three)

cóng zuǒ dào yòu
4. 从 左 到 右　from left to right

chuān
川　丿　川　川
(river)

cóng wài dào nèi
5. 从 外 到 内　from outside to inside

yuè
月　丿　月　月　月
(moon)

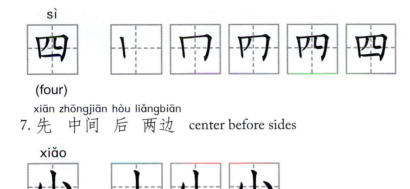

cóng wài dào nèi zài fēngkǒu
6. 从 外 到 内 再 封 口 from outside to inside then enclose

sì
四 | 丨 冂 冂 四 四
(four)

xiān zhōngjiān hòu liǎngbiān
7. 先 中间 后 两边 center before sides

xiǎo
小 丨 小 小
(small)

Pair Work
Using the rules you just learned, try to determine the correct stroke order of the following characters.

丁 中 习 区 车 回 办 心 牛 风 走 万

简体字和繁体字 Simplified and Traditional Characters

For this course, you will be required to learn simplified Chinese characters. Simplified characters are typically used in the mainland of China, Singapore, Thailand, Malaysia, Japan, South Korea and the United Nations. Traditional characters are used in three areas of China, which are Taiwan, Hong Kong and Macau. Simplified characters are easier for beginners to learn; however, it is necessary to learn both traditional and simplified characters in order to have a deep understanding of Chinese language and culture.

	Simplified	Traditional
Zhōngguó (China)	中国	中國
Hànyǔ (Chinese)	汉语	漢語

字和词 Characters and Words

In ancient Chinese, a character usually stands alone as an individual word. However, in modern Chinese, some of these characters can no longer be used independently. For example, xí 习 means "to practice" in ancient Chinese, but in order to appear in modern Chinese, it must combine with another character to form a word such as xuéxí 学习 or liànxí 练习.

Some ancient Chinese characters, such as tiān 天, may be used as an independent word or combined with other characters to form other words. For example:

tiān		tiānkōng	tiānzhēn	jīntiān	Xīngqītiān
天	→	天空	天真	今天	星期天
sky		sky	innocent	today	Sunday

中国书法 Chinese Calligraphy

The art of Chinese calligraphy is an important part of traditional Chinese culture which requires great skill. The *bǐ* 笔 (writing brush), *mò* 墨 (ink stick), *zhǐ* 纸 (paper), and *yàn* 砚 (ink stone) are considered the "four treasures of the study". With a writing brush and China ink, as well as all of the rules mentioned above and countless flexible changes, Chinese calligraphy becomes a special art.

With its shape taken in the Han Dynasty, Chinese calligraphy is widely practiced and revered in the countries that use Chinese characters, such as Japan, South Korea, and Vietnam. Many different types of script that have appeared throughout history can be found in Chinese calligraphic works and there are many famous calligraphers, including Wang Xizhi, Yan Zhenqing, Liu Gongquan, Ouyang Xun, Su Shi and Zhao Mengfu.

Wang Xizhi's Handwriting

In China, many people enjoy the art of calligraphy as a hobby. Some people even practice calligraphy in parks, using the water as "ink" and the concrete roads as "paper". This is called *shuǐshū* 水书, which means "writing with water".

50 Common Radicals of Chinese Characters

Radical	Name of Radical	General Meaning	Example
人	人字头 rénzìtóu	human	命 mìng (fate)
口	口字旁 kǒuzìpáng	mouth	唱 chàng (to sing)
大	大字头 dàzìtóu	big or good	太 tài (too)
囗	国字框 guózìkuàng	a certain range	国 guó (country)
门	门字框 ménzìkuàng	door	闭 bì (to close)
山	山字旁 shānzìpáng	mountain	岛 dǎo (island)
女	女字旁 nǚzìpáng	woman	姐 jiě (elder sister)
王	王字旁 wángzìpáng	jade	玩 wán (to play)
贝	贝字旁 bèizìpáng	treasure	财 cái (treasure)
木	木字旁 mùzìpáng	wood	林 lín (woods)
日	日字旁 rìzìpáng	sun	晴 qíng (sunny)
车	车字旁 chēzìpáng	car	辆 liàng (measure word for vehicles)
目	目字旁 mùzìpáng	eye or vision	眼 yǎn (eye)
牛	牛字旁 niúzìpáng	cow or ox	物 wù (things)
马	马字旁 mǎzìpáng	horse	驰 chí (to run quickly)
月	月字旁 yuèzìpáng	body	脸 liǎn (face)
火	火字旁 huǒzìpáng	fire	炉 lú (oven)

Radical	Name of Radical	General Meaning	Example
心	心字旁 xīnzìpáng	heart or feeling	想 xiǎng (to think)
石	石字旁 shízìpáng	stone	岩 yán (stone)
禾	禾字旁 hézìpáng	crop	稻 dào (rice)
鸟	鸟字旁 niǎozìpáng	bird	鸡 jī (chicken)
鱼	鱼字旁 yúzìpáng	fish	鲸 jīng (whale)
虫	虫字旁 chóngzìpáng	insect	蛇 shé (snake)
米	米字旁 mǐzìpáng	rice	粮 liáng (grain)
身	身字旁 shēnzìpáng	body	躲 duǒ (to hide)
广	广字旁 guǎngzìpáng	house	库 kù (warehouse)
雨	雨字头 yǔzìtóu	rain	雷 léi (thunder)
耳	耳字旁 ěrzìpáng	ear	聊 liáo (to chat)
亻	单人旁 dānrénpáng	people	你 nǐ (you)
彳	双人旁 shuāngrénpáng	walk	行 xíng (to walk)
冫	两点水 liǎngdiǎnshuǐ	water	冷 lěng (cold)
氵	三点水 sāndiǎnshuǐ	water or liquid	汗 hàn (sweat)
讠	言字旁 yánzìpáng	language or speech	词 cí (word)
忄	竖心旁 shùxīnpáng	mind or feeling	情 qíng (feeling)
扌	提手旁 tíshǒupáng	hand	打 dǎ (to beat)
辶	走之 zǒuzhī	walk	远 yuǎn (far away)
纟	绞丝旁 jiǎosīpáng	silk	线 xiàn (wire)
饣	食字旁 shízìpáng	food	饭 fàn (rice, food)
犭	反犬旁 fǎnquǎnpáng	animal	狗 gǒu (dog)
艹	草字头 cǎozìtóu	plant	草 cǎo (grass)
灬	四点底 sìdiǎndǐ	fire	热 rè (hot)
礻	示字旁 shìzìpáng	hints from God	神 shén (God)
衤	衣字旁 yīzìpáng	clothes	衬衫 chènshān (shirt)
宀	宝盖头 bǎogàitóu	house	家 jiā (home)
钅	金字旁 jīnzìpáng	metal	铁 tiě (iron)
土	提土旁 títǔpáng	soil	地 dì (ground)
疒	病字头 bìngzìtóu	illness	疼 téng (painful)
刂	立刀旁 lìdāopáng	knife	刻 kè (to carve)
𥫗	竹字头 zhúzìtóu	bamboo	笔 bǐ (pen, brush)
𧾷	足字旁 zúzìpáng	foot	跳 tiào (to jump)

Unit 1　第一单元
Dì-yī dānyuán

Meeting Each Other

Jiàn miàn hán xuān
见面寒暄

Sometimes people meet each other by chance, and then they become friends or families. In Chinese, the word *yuánfèn* 缘分 (fate) is used to describe this "special relationship arranged by destiny". Our story unfolds with twins Bill and Jenny studying Chinese in China and the U.S., respectively. Both of them have experienced *yuánfèn* 缘分 in two different contexts.

In this unit, you will learn:

FUNCTION

☐ to greet each other: 你好！见到你很高兴。/我也很高兴。

☐ to introduce yourself: 我是比尔。

☐ to ask someone's name: 你姓什么？/你叫什么名字？

☐ to give a compliment: 你的汉语很好。

☐ to ask for a phone number: 你的电话号码是多少？

GRAMMAR

☐ word order in Chinese sentences

☐ to express judgement using the verb 是

☐ to confirm information using Yes-no questions ending with 吗

☐ to use the adverb 很 in sentences with an adjectival predicate

CULTURE

☐ how Chinese people respond to compliments

☐ how Chinese people greet each other

☐ Chinese name order

🖊 听与说 Listen and Speak 🎧

Listen to the recording and read silently. Listen again and repeat the sentences after you hear them, and then practice the conversation in pairs.

At the Airport

Bill arrives in China for a year-long Chinese study program at Peking University. Li Li, a sophomore from the same university, picks him up from the airport.

Bǐ' ěr: Nǐ hǎo!
比尔：你好！

Lǐ Lì: Nǐ hǎo!
李丽：你好！

Bǐ' ěr: Wǒ shì Bǐ' ěr, nǐ shì Lǐ Lì ma?
比尔：我是比尔，你是李丽吗[1]？

Lǐ Lì: Wǒ shì Lǐ Lì. Jiàndào nǐ hěn gāoxìng.
李丽：我是李丽。见到 你很 高兴。

Bǐ' ěr: Wǒ yě hěn gāoxìng.
比尔：我也很 高兴。

Lǐ Lì: Nǐ de Hànyǔ hěn hǎo.
李丽：你的汉语 很 好。

Bǐ' ěr: Nǎli nǎli.
比尔：哪里哪里[2]。

Bill: Hi!
Li Li: Hi!
Bill: I'm Bill. Are you Li Li?
Li Li: I'm Li Li. Glad to see you.
Bill: Glad to see you too.
Li Li: Your Chinese is pretty good.
Bill: I'm flattered.

---

[1] 吗 occurs at the end of a sentence as a question particle to show it's a question. For example: *Bǐ' ěr de Hànyǔ hǎo ma*? 比尔的汉语好吗？

[2] 哪里 here indicates modesty in response to compliments. The original meaning of 哪里 is "where".

Required Words and Expressions

	nǐ	
你		you
好	hǎo	good
我	wǒ	I, me
是	shì	to be
吗	ma	(a question particle)
见到	jiàndào	to have seen
很	hěn	very
高兴	gāoxìng	glad
也	yě	too
你的	nǐ de	your
汉语	Hànyǔ	Chinese
哪里哪里	nǎli nǎli	it's not that nice, I am flattered

ℬ 个人练习 Self-practice

Word Order: Create sentences by arranging the following words in the appropriate order.

1. ① 好 _{hǎo} ② 你 _{nǐ}   ②① _____

2. ① 比尔 _{Bǐ'ěr} ② 我 _{wǒ} ③ 是 _{shì} _____

3. ① 见到 _{jiàndào} ② 高兴 _{gāoxìng} ③ 你 _{nǐ} ④ 很 _{hěn} _____

4. ① 我 _{wǒ} ② 高兴 _{gāoxìng} ③ 很 _{hěn} ④ 也 _{yě} _____

5. ① 很 _{hěn} ② 好 _{hǎo} ③ 你的 _{nǐ de} ④ 汉语 _{Hànyǔ} _____

𝒞 二人练习   Pair Work

Meeting Each Other: With a partner, practice greeting each other and introducing yourselves.

A：你好，我 是 比尔。
_{Nǐ hǎo, wǒ shì Bǐ'ěr.}

B：你好，比尔。
_{Nǐ hǎo, Bǐ'ěr.}

我 是 李丽。
_{Wǒ shì Lǐ Lì.}

A：见到 你 很 高兴 。
_{Jiàndào nǐ hěn gāoxìng.}

B：我也 很 高兴 。
_{Wǒ yě hěn gāoxìng.}

𝒟 小组活动   Group Work

Name Game: Make a circle with your classmates. Introduce yourself and then say the names of the classmates that have come before you.

A：我 是 比尔。
_{Wǒ shì Bǐ'ěr.}

B：我 是 李丽，他 是 比尔。
_{Wǒ shì Lǐ Lì, tā shì Bǐ'ěr.}

C：我 是 珍妮，她 是 李丽，他 是 比尔。
_{Wǒ shì Zhēnnī, tā shì Lǐ Lì, tā shì Bǐ'ěr.}

Expanded Words and Expressions

他 _{tā}	he, him
她 _{tā}	she, her

Expanded Words and Expressions

shuài	帅	handsome
měi	美	beautiful
kě'ài	可爱	lovely, cute
tián	甜	sweet
tāmen	他们	they, them
bàng	棒	wonderful

听与说　Listen and Speak

Listen to the recording and read silently. Listen again and repeat the sentences after you hear them.

Tā shì Láng Lǎng.
他 是 郎 朗 。

Tā hěn shuài.
他 很 帅 。

Tā de qínshēng hěn měi.
他 的 琴声 很 美。

He is Lang Lang.
He is handsome.
His piano sound is magnificent.

Tā shì Lín Miàokě.
她 是 林 妙可[1]。

Tā hěn kě'ài.
她 很 可爱。

Tā de xiàoróng hěn tián.
她 的 笑容 很 甜[2]。

She is Lin Miaoke.
She is cute.
Her smile is sweet.

Tāmen hěn bàng.
他们[3] 很 棒。
They are wonderful.

Stars at the 2008 Beijing Olympic Opening Ceremony

---

[1] You can find more information about Lang Lang and Lin Miaoke by searching online. Don't forget to try your search in Chinese.

[2] 甜 here means pleasant and beautiful.

[3] 他们 is masculine and 她们 is feminine. However, 他们 is used when men and women are both included.

03 句型操练 Sentence Patterns

A 听与说 Listen and Speak 🎧

Listen to the recording and read silently. Listen again and repeat the sentences after you hear them.

pron. + 是 + name	pron. + 很 + adj.
Nǐ shì Bǐ'ěr ma? A: 你是 比尔 吗？	Nǐ hěn bàng. 你 很 棒 。
Wǒ shì Bǐ'ěr. B: 我 是 比尔。	Tā hěn shuài. 他 很 帅 。
Nǐ shì Lǐ Lì ma? A: 你是 李丽 吗？	Tā hěn kě'ài. 她 很 可爱。
Wǒ bú shì Lǐ Lì. B: 我 不 是 李丽。	

B 选择 Choose the correct answer.

Choose the correct words in parentheses to complete the conversation. Then practice with your partner.

(Tā / Tā) shì Yáo Míng.
A：_____（他 / 她）是 姚 明。

Yáo Míng　　　　(shì / hěn) bàng.
B：姚 明 _____（是 / 很）棒 。

(Tāmen / Tāmen) shì S.H.E.
A：_____（他们 / 她们）是 S.H.E[1]。

S.H.E　　　(shì / hěn) kě'ài.
B：S.H.E _____（是 / 很）可爱。

C 班级活动 Class Activity

Famous Classmates: Think of a celebrity and write his or her name on a piece of paper. Fold the paper and put it in the bag supplied by your teacher. You will be asked to draw a random name out of the bag and then find the student who corresponds with that name by greeting each other.

Nǐ hǎo, nǐ shì Brad Pitt ma?
A：你好，你是 Brad Pitt 吗？

Wǒ bú shì Brad Pitt.
B：我不是 Brad Pitt。

Nǐ hǎo, nǐ shì Brad Pitt ma?
A：你好，你是 Brad Pitt 吗？

Wǒ shì Brad Pitt.　Jiàndào nǐ hěn gāoxìng.
C：我是 Brad Pitt。 见到 你很 高兴 。

Wǒ yě hěn gāoxìng.　Nǐ hěn bàng.
A：我也很 高兴 。你很 棒 。

Brad Pitt

Tā shì Yáo Míng. Tā hěn gāo.
他是姚 明。他很 高。

[1]　S.H.E is a famous singing group from Taiwan, China. Its members are three girls named Selina, Hebe and Ella.

听与说 Listen and Speak

Listen to the recording and read silently. Listen again and repeat the sentences after you hear them, and then practice the conversation in pairs.

In the Classroom

As Jenny greets new classmates and updates the class phone book, she meets Wang Damin, an American-born Chinese student.

Zhēnnī: Qǐngwèn, nǐ xìng shénme?
珍妮：请问，你 姓 什么？

Wáng Dàmín: Wǒ xìng Wáng.
王 大民：我 姓 王。

Zhēnnī: Nǐ jiào shénme míngzi?
珍妮：你 叫 什么 名字？

Wáng Dàmín: Wǒ jiào Wáng Dàmín.
王 大民：我 叫 王 大民。

Zhēnnī: Nǐ de diànhuà hàomǎ shì duōshao?
珍妮：你的 电话 号码 是 多少[1]？

Wáng Dàmín: Liù wǔ bā qī qī èr èr. Nǐ de hànzì hěn
王 大民：6 5 8 7 7 2 2。你的 汉字 很

piàoliang!
漂亮！

Zhēnnī: Méiyǒu méiyǒu.
珍妮：没有 没有。

Jenny: May I ask what's your surname?
Wang: My surname is Wang.
Jenny: What's your name?
Wang: My name is Wang Damin.
Jenny: What's your phone number?
Wang: 6587722. Your Chinese handwriting is very beautiful!
Jenny: I am flattered.

Required Words and Expressions

qǐngwèn	请问	May I ask...?
xìng	姓	surname; to be surnamed
shénme	什么	what
jiào	叫	to name, to call
míngzi	名字	name
diànhuà	电话	phone
hàomǎ	号码	number
duōshao	多少	how many/much
hànzì	汉字	Chinese character
piàoliang	漂亮	beautiful
méiyǒu	没有	not have

[1] 多少 here means "what". It also means "how many/much" when it is used to ask for information of quantity.

B 个人练习 Self-practice

Word Order: Create sentences by arranging the following words in the appropriate order.

1. ① 姓 (xìng) ② 什么 (shénme) ③ 请问 (qǐngwèn) ④ 你 (nǐ)   ③④①②

2. ① 王 (Wáng) ② 姓 (xìng) ③ 我 (wǒ)   _____

3. ① 什么 (shénme) ② 叫 (jiào) ③ 名字 (míngzi) ④ 你 (nǐ)   _____

4. ① 我 (wǒ) ② 大民 (Dàmín) ③ 王 (Wáng) ④ 叫 (jiào)   _____

5. ① 多少 (duōshao) ② 电话 号码 (diànhuà hàomǎ) ③ 的 (de) ④ 你 (nǐ) ⑤ 是 (shì)   _____

C 二人练习 Pair Work

What's your name? With a partner, practice asking each other's names.

A： 请问 , 你 姓 什么 ? (Qǐngwèn, nǐ xìng shénme?)

B： 我 姓 王 。 (Wǒ xìng Wáng.)

A： 你 叫 什么 名字 ? (Nǐ jiào shénme míngzi?)

B： 我 叫 王 丽 。 (Wǒ jiào Wáng Lì.)

D 小组活动 Group Work

Social Networking: Ask new friends in the class for their names and phone numbers. Make a class phone book for yourself and enjoy networking with others. Don't forget to ask them in Chinese!

A： 请问 , 你 姓 什么 ? (Qǐngwèn, nǐ xìng shénme?)

B： 我 姓李 。 (Wǒ xìng Lǐ.)

A： 你 叫 什么 名字 ? (Nǐ jiào shénme míngzi?)

B： 我 叫李军 。 (Wǒ jiào Lǐ Jūn.)

A： 你的 电话 号码 是 多少 ? (Nǐ de diànhuà hàomǎ shì duōshao?)

B： ……

李 军 Li Jun

电话(Tel)：78015524

手机(Cell phone)：14633970206

05 姓名　Chinese Name

A 听与说　Listen and Speak 🎧

Listen to the recording and read silently. Listen again and repeat the names after you hear them.

Zhāng Lì	Wáng Jūn	Liú Mǐn	Yáng Dàmín
① 张 丽	② 王 军	③ 刘 敏	④ 杨 大民

Chén Fāng	Zhào Xiǎoqiáng	Lǐ Xiǎowēi
⑤ 陈 芳	⑥ 赵 小强	⑦ 李 小薇

B 班级活动　Class Activity

Find Your Chinese Name: Seek your teacher's help to find yourself a Chinese name. Then make a name card in Chinese for yourself.

☺ 休息一下　Break Time

Practice writing the following two characters using the proper stroke order indicated below.

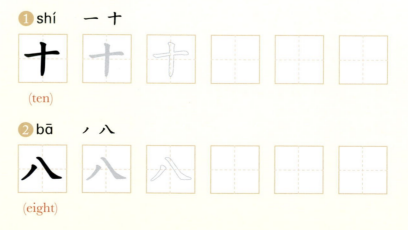

① shí　一 十

十 十 十 □ □ □

(ten)

② bā　ノ 八

八 八 八 □ □ □

(eight)

Culture Box

Common Surnames in China[1]

Some of the most common surnames in China:

Wáng	Lǐ	Zhāng	Liú	Chén
王	李	张	刘	陈

Yáng	Zhōu	Huáng	Zhào	Sūn
杨	周	黄	赵	孙

Common Names in China

Some of the most common given names in China:

♂
jūn	wěi
军 (army)	伟 (great)
qiáng	mín
强 (strong)	民 (people)

♀
lì	mǐn
丽 (beautiful)	敏 (swift)
wēi	fāng
薇 (rose)	芳 (fragrant)

---

[1] There is an ancient book named *Hundred Family Surnames* (*Bǎijiāxìng* 百家姓) in China which lists about five hundred common surnames. These are some of the most common.

06 数字　Numbers 0-10

𝒜 听与说　Listen and Speak 🎧

Listen to the recording and read silently. Listen again and repeat the numbers after you hear them.

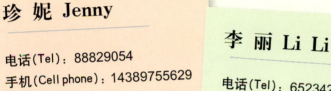

⓪	①	②	③	④	⑤	⑥	⑦	⑧	⑨	⑩
líng	yī	èr	sān	sì	wǔ	liù	qī	bā	jiǔ	shí
零	一[1]	二	三	四	五	六	七	八	九	十

ℬ 二人练习　Pair Work

Phone Number: Practice Jenny and Li Li's phone numbers in pairs, taking turns reading the numbers and checking each other's accuracy.

珍 妮 Jenny

电话(Tel)：88829054
手机(Cell phone)：14389755629

李 丽 Li Li

电话(Tel)：65234235
手机(Cell phone)：19522337200

𝒞 听力练习　Listening 🎧

Bill and Li Li are making a list of classmates' phone numbers. Listen and complete the list.

  Nǐ hǎo!　Wǒ shì Bǐ'ěr.　Jiàndào nǐ hěn gāoxìng.
A：你好！我是比尔。见到 你 很 高兴。
  Nǐ hǎo!　Wǒ shì Lǐ Lì.　Jiàndào nǐ wǒ yě hěn gāoxìng.
B：你好！我是李丽。见到 你我 也 很 高兴。
  Nǐ de diànhuà hàomǎ shì duōshao?
A：你的 电话 号码 是 多少？
  Liù wǔ èr sān sì èr sān wǔ.
B：6 5 2 3 4 2 3 5 。

  ……

Name	Phone number	Name	Phone number
Lǐ Lì 李丽	65234235	Liú Fāng 刘 芳	
Bǐ'ěr 比尔		Chén Xiǎowēi 陈 小薇	
Wáng Dàmín 王 大民		Zhōu Dàwěi 周 大伟	

---

[1] In oral Chinese, *yī* 一 is often read as *yāo* when talking about phone and room numbers.

07 问好 Saying Hello

听与说 Listen and Speak

Listen to the recording and read silently. Listen again and repeat the sentences after you hear them, then practice the conversations in pairs.

1. A: Hello!
   B: Hello!
2. A: Good morning!
   B: Good morning!
3. A: Going out?
   B: Yeah.
4. A: Did you have the meal?
   B: Yes, I did.

1.
   Nín hǎo!
   A：您 好！
   Nǐ hǎo!
   B：你 好！

2.
   Zǎoshang hǎo!
   A：早上 好！
   Zǎoshang hǎo!
   B：早上 好！

3.
   Chūqu a?
   A：出去 啊[1]？
   Chūqu.
   B：出去。

4.
   Chīle ma?
   A：吃了吗？
   Chī le.
   B：吃了。

Expanded Words and Expressions

nín 您	you (polite form)	
zǎoshang 早上	(early) morning	
chūqu 出去	to go out	
a 啊	(a modal particle)	
chī 吃	to eat	
le 了	(a modal particle indicating the event already happened)	

---

[1] 啊 is typically used at the end of an exclamatory sentence to express strong feelings or just following a declarative sentence to make sure about something. For example: *Zhēn hǎo a*! 真好啊！(How nice!) *Chūqu a*? 出去啊？ (Are you going out?)

☺ 休息一下 Break Time

Listen to the recording and read silently. Listen again and repeat the sentences after you hear them. Then compete with a partner, trying to say the two sentences as quickly and accurately as you can.

Pay attention to the pronunciation of the four consonants *d*, *t*, *b* and *p* while repeating the sentences. When you pronounce *p* and *t*, the breath is stronger than *b* and *d*.

Dùzi bǎo le.
肚子饱了。
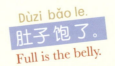
Full is the belly.

Tùzi pǎo le.
兔子跑了。
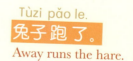
Away runs the hare.

08 文化掠影　Culture Snapshot

☐ In *Episodes 1 & 2*, you have learned two phrases used for **giving compliments:** 你的汉语很好 and 你的汉字很漂亮. Compliments are often used in greeting others, both in Chinese and English contexts. In English, the proper reply is usually "thank you" or "I'm flattered". In Chinese, however, people treat compliments slightly differently. Jenny and Bill know the Chinese way so well that they respond humbly, saying 哪里哪里 and 没有没有 meaning "no, it's not that good". It may sound to you as if Chinese people are refusing your compliments, but this is not the case. They are actually happy, but culture dictates that they act with humility. Don't give in to the temptation to accept compliments too easily because this implies that you agree wholeheartedly with the complimentary assessment. Rather, use the phrases that you've learned from Jenny and Bill to humbly express your thanks. Also, don't hesitate to compliment your Chinese friends and acquaintances, even though you might experience culture shock in hearing their responses. Just use the vocabulary in the *Spotlight*!

☐ In **Saying Hello**, you learned four different ways of greetings other than 你好. Sometimes, you might even hear Chinese friends ask, *Nǐ qù nǎr?* 你去哪儿? (Where are you going?) as a polite way of greeting. If someone asks you this, you should not say "It's none of your business". When you hear Chinese people greet you in the above ways, don't feel surprised or annoyed. Just like Americans often say "How's everything?", you are not obligated to tell everything that has happened to you. These are habitual ways of greeting in China. Just do as the Chinese do, and you will thrive in the Chinese culture!

☐ In **Chinese Name**, please note that one's surname always comes first, and the given name comes next.

Nín guìxìng? 您贵姓? (What's your honorable surname?) is a polite way of asking someone's surname. When you meet a Chinese person for the first time, it is considered polite to ask his/her surname only, rather than his/her full name. When answering the question 您贵姓, one can either give one's surname by saying *wǒ xìng Wáng* 我姓王, or give one's full name by saying *wǒ xìng Wáng, jiào Wáng Dàmín* 我姓王, 叫王大民. *Nǐ xìng shénme*? 你姓什么? (What's your surname?) is an informal way of asking someone's surname. It is appropriate when an adult is speaking to a child, or when young people are talking with each other.

百家姓				
赵	冯	朱	孔	
钱	陈	秦	曹	
孙	褚	尤	严	
李	卫	许	华	
周	蒋	何	金	
吴	沈	吕	魏	
郑	韩	施	陶	
王	杨	张	姜	

09 语法要点 Grammar Kit

1 Word Order in Chinese Sentences

The main characteristic of Chinese grammar is that it generally lacks changes in person, tense, gender, number, and case. The word order, however, is very important to convey different grammatical meanings. The subject of a sentence is usually placed before the predicate.

(1) Hello!

Nǐ hǎo.
(1) 你好。

(2) He is very handsome.

Tā hěn shuài.
(2) 他 很 帅 。

2 Expressing Judgement Using the Verb 是

In a 是 sentence, the verb 是 is used to connect the subject and the object of the sentence. It means " to be" and has no changes in person or tense.

(1) A: Are you Li Li ?
    B: I am Li Li.

Nǐ shì Lǐ Lì ma?
(1) A：你是 李丽 吗?

Wǒ shì Lǐ Lì.
    B：我 是 李丽。

Its negative form is made by putting 不[1] before the verb 是.

(2) He is Wang Damin.
(3) He is not Bill.

Tā shì Wáng Dàmín.
(2) 他 是 王 大民。

Tā bú shì Bǐ'ěr.
(3) 他 不 是 比尔。

3 Confirming Information Using Yes-no Questions Ending with 吗

A declarative sentence can be changed into a Yes-no question by adding the question particle 吗 at the end of the sentence.

(1) A: Are you Bill?
    B: I am Bill.
    C: I am not Bill.

Nǐ shì Bǐ'ěr ma?
(1) A：你 是 比尔 吗?

Wǒ shì Bǐ'ěr.
    B：我 是 比尔。

Wǒ bú shì Bǐ'ěr.
    C：我 不 是 比尔。

---

[1] The original tone of 不 is a 4th tone. However, when followed by another 4th tone syllable, *bù* changes to 2nd tone *bú*, as in *bú shì* 不是. See *Pinyin Step 6* for more information on tone changes of *bù* 不.

(2)　A：你叫李丽吗？
Nǐ jiào Lǐ Lì ma?

　　B：我叫李丽。
Wǒ jiào Lǐ Lì.

　　C：我不叫李丽。
Wǒ bú jiào Lǐ Lì.

(2) A: Is your name Li Li?
B: My name is Li Li.
C: My name is not Li Li.

4 Using the Adverb 很 in Sentences with an Adjectival Predicate

In sentences with an adjectival predicate, the verb 是 is not neccesary. Instead, an adverb like 很 is used before the adjective it modifies. The meaning of 很 here is "very", but more importantly, its role is to make the declarative sentence complete.

Lín Miàokě hěn kě'ài.
(1)　林 妙可 很 可爱。

Tā de xiàoróng hěn tián.
(2)　她的 笑容 很 甜。

(1) Lin Miaoke is very lovely.
(2) Her smile is very sweet.

Sentences with an adjectival predicate cannot appear without putting an adverb like 很 before the adjective unless the speakers want to make a comparison.

Yáo Míng gāo,　Bǐ'ěr bù gāo.
(3)　姚 明 高，比尔 不高。

(3) Yao Ming is tall, but Bill is not tall.

10 语法练习　Grammar Practice

1 Make complete sentences following the examples given.

Nǐ hǎo!
❶ 你好！
nín
您

Wǒ shì Bǐ'ěr.
❷ 我是比尔。
tā　Láng Lǎng
他　郎 朗
tā　Lín Miàokě
她 林 妙可

Nǐ hěn gāo.
❸ 你 很 高。
tā　　shuài
他　　帅
tā　　kě'ài
她　　可爱
tā de Hànyǔ　hǎo
他的汉语　好
tā de hànzì　piàoliang
她的汉字　漂亮

④ **我** 姓 王 。 **我** 叫 **王 大民** 。
Wǒ xìng Wáng. Wǒ jiào Wáng Dàmín.

他 赵 他 赵 小强
tā Zhào tā Zhào Xiǎoqiáng

她 李 她 李丽
_tā Lǐ tā Lǐ Lì_

2 **Complete the following sentences with the words given.**

贵姓[1]	叫	多少	是	很	也
guìxìng	jiào	duōshao	shì	hěn	yě

① 你 ＿＿＿ 李丽 吗？
_Nǐ Lǐ Lì ma?_

② 你 ＿＿＿ 什么 名字？
Nǐ shénme míngzi?

③ 请问 ，您 ＿＿＿ ？
Qǐngwèn, nín ?

④ 你的 电话 号码 是 ＿＿＿ ？
Nǐ de diànhuà hàomǎ shì ?

⑤ 你的 汉语 ＿＿＿ 好 。你的
Nǐ de Hànyǔ hǎo. Nǐ de

汉字 ＿＿＿ 很 漂亮 。
hànzì hěn piàoliang.

3 **Rewrite the following sentences in the form indicated.**

① 我 是李丽 。 Make a sentence using 不.
Wǒ shì Lǐ Lì.

_____

② 他 是 郎 朗 。 Make a question using 吗.
Tā shì Láng Lǎng.

_____

③ 她 是 林 妙可 。 Make a question using 吗.
Tā shì Lín Miàokě.

_____

④ 珍妮 很 漂亮 。 Make a question using 吗.
Zhēnnī hěn piàoliang.

_____

⑤ 珍妮 的 汉语 很 好 。 Make a sentence using 不.
Zhēnnī de Hànyǔ hěn hǎo.

_____

---

[1] Remember that 您贵姓 is a polite way to ask someone's surname.

Tā bú xìng Wáng, tā xìng Lǐ.

⑥ 他 不 姓 王，他 姓 李。 Make a question using 什么.

Tā bú jiào Bǐ'ěr, tā jiào Wáng Dàmín.

⑦ 他 不 叫 比尔，他 叫 王 大民。 Make a question using 什么.

Wǒ de diànhuà hàomǎ shì bā sì bā èr wǔ qī liù jiǔ.

⑧ 我 的 电话 号码 是 8 4 8 2 5 7 6 9。 Make a question using 多少.

11 语音提示 Pronunciation Tips

1 汉语四声 Chinese Tones

Read the following syllables and pay attention to their tones.

qǐngwèn	guìxìng	gāoxìng	jiàndào
请问	贵姓	高兴	见到
diànhuà	méiyǒu	Hànyǔ	hànzì
电话	没有	汉语	汉字
nǐ	wǒ	tā	nín
你	我	他	您

Tip

Yìshēng píng,
一声 平，
Èrshēng yáng,
二声 扬，
Sānshēng qūzhé,
三声 曲折，
Sìshēng jiàng.
四声 降。

1st tone is high and level,
2nd tone rises,
3rd tone falls then rises,
4th tone falls down.

2 轻声 Neutral Tone

Practice reading the following words with neutral tone.

nǐ de	shénme	míng zi
你的	什么	名字
duōshao	shì ma	
多少	是 吗	

Tip

Qīngshēng 轻声 (neutral tone) is not the 5th tone, but rather a change of the four tones. Neutral syllables should be pronounced shorter and softer than the original tone.

3 三声变调 The Changes of the 3rd Tone

Listen to your teacher and try to find the actual changes of the 3rd tone.

Nǐ hǎo! Jiàndào nǐ hěn gāoxìng!

A：你 好！ 见到 你 很 高兴！

Wǒ yě hěn gāoxìng.

B：我 也 很 高兴。

Tip

The 3rd tone can change in two ways:
- into the 2nd tone before another 3rd tone syllable;
- into the semi-3rd tone before the 1st, the 2nd or the 4th tone syllable.

 汉字书写 Writing Chinese Characters

1 笔画 Strokes

Strokes are the smallest structural units of Chinese characters. Some stroke types include:

(horizontal stroke)	一			(downward-left stroke)	丿		
héng 横	一	二	三	piě 撇	八	人	木
(vertical stroke)	丨			(downward-right stroke)	乀		
shù 竖	十	上	王	nà 捺	大	天	夫

2 笔顺 Stroke Order

When writing a Chinese character, it is important to follow the correct stroke order. The general principles are as follows.

xiān héng hòu shù
先 横 后 竖   horizontal before vertical

 eg.
shí
十
(ten)
一 十

xiān piě hòu nà
先 撇 后 捺   downward-left before downward-right

eg.
bā
八
(eight)
丿 八

You can write it!

Practice writing the following Chinese characters. Don't forget to follow the correct stroke order!

yī 一
一 一
(one)

dà 一 ナ 大
大 大
(big)

wáng 一 二 千 王
王 王
(king)

shàng 丨 卜 上
上 上
(up)

rén 丿 人
人 人
(people)

mù 一 十 才 木
木 木
(wood)

3 汉字的演变 Evolution of Chinese Characters

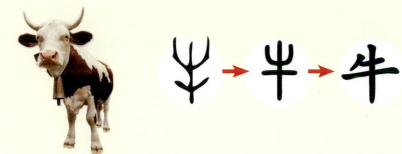

13 综合练习 Integrative Practice

Listening

1 Listen to the following words and mark the missing tones.

ni hao	gaoxing	mingzi	dianhua haoma	piaoliang
你 好	高兴	名字	电话 号码	漂亮

2 Listen to the following conversation and complete the sentences with the correct characters in parentheses.

Nǐ hǎo! Wǒ shì (Wáng Bǐ'ěr / Huáng Bǐ'ěr). Nǐ jiào shénme míngzi?
A：你好! 我 是＿＿＿(a.王 比尔 / b. 黄 比尔)。你 叫 什么 名字?

Nǐ hǎo! Wǒ xìng Wáng, jiào (Wáng Yīmín / Wáng Yīmǐn). Jiàndào nǐ hěn
B：你好! 我 姓 王，叫＿＿＿(a.王 一民 / b.王 一敏)。见到 你 很 ＿＿＿

(gāoxìng / piàoliang).
(a. 高兴 / b. 漂亮)。

Wǒ yě hěn gāoxìng.
A：我 也 很 高兴。

Nǐ de diànhuà hàomǎ shì duōshao?
B：你 的 电话 号码 是 多少 ?

Wǒ de diànhuà hàomǎ shì jiǔ bā bā èr sān èr sān. Nǐ de ne?
A：我 的 电话 号码 是 9 8 8 2 3 2 3 。你 的 呢? (What about you?)

Wǒ de diànhuà hàomǎ shì (bā bā bā yāo yāo wǔ jiǔ bā/
B：我 的 电话 号码 是＿＿＿(a. 8 8 8 1 1 5 9 8 /

bā bā bā yāo yāo jiǔ wǔ bā). Nǐ de Hànyǔ hěn (hǎo/ měi).
b. 8 8 8 1 1 9 5 8)。你的 汉语 很 ＿＿＿(a.好/ b.美)。

Nǎli nǎli.
A：哪里 哪里。

3 Listen to the recording and decide whether the following statements are true or false.

T   F

①   Tā xìng Lín, jiào Lín Miàokě.
a. 她 姓 林，叫 林 妙可。 ☐ ☐

Tā hěn piàoliang, yě hěn kě'ài.
b. 她 很 漂亮，也 很 可爱。 ☐ ☐

Tā de xiàoróng bù tián.
c. 她的 笑容 不 甜。 ☐ ☐

Tā de diànhuà hàomǎ shì sì wǔ liù qī bā jiǔ sì wǔ.
d. 她的 电话 号码 是 4 5 6 7 8 9 4 5。 ☐ ☐

②   Tā shì Láng Lǎng.
a. 他 是 郎 朗。 ☐ ☐

Tā bú shuài, yě bú bàng.
b. 他 不 帅，也 不 棒。 ☐ ☐

Tā de qínshēng hěn měi.
c. 他的 琴声 很 美。 ☐ ☐

Tā de diànhuà hàomǎ shì èr wǔ èr líng yāo sì qī bā.
d. 他的 电话 号码 是 2 5 2 0 1 4 7 8。 ☐ ☐

Speaking

1 With a partner, read the following conversation aloud.

Lǐ Mín: Nǐ hǎo.
李 民：你 好。

Wáng Měilì: Nǐ hǎo.
王 美丽：你 好。

Lǐ Mín: Jiàndào nǐ hěn gāoxìng.
李 民：见到 你 很 高兴。

Wáng Měilì: Wǒ yě hěn gāoxìng. Qǐngwèn, nǐ guìxìng?
王 美丽：我 也 很 高兴。请问，你 贵姓？

Lǐ Mín: Wǒ xìng Lǐ, jiào Lǐ Mín. Nǐ ne?
李 民：我 姓 李，叫 李 民。你 呢？

Wáng Měilì: Wǒ xìng Wáng, jiào Wáng Měilì.
王 美丽：我 姓 王，叫 王 美丽。

Lǐ Mín: Nǐ de míngzi hěn hǎo.
李 民：你的 名字 很 好。

Wáng Měilì: Nǎli nǎli. Nǐ de míngzi yě hěn hǎo.
王 美丽：哪里哪里。你的 名字 也 很 好。

Lǐ Mín: Nǐ de diànhuà hàomǎ shì duōshao?
李 民：你的 电话 号码 是 多少？

Wáng Měilì: Wǒ de diànhuà hàomǎ shì yāo sì èr wǔ sān liù qī bā.
王 美丽：我的 电话 号码 是 1 4 2 5 3 6 7 8。

2 Take turns answering the following questions with a partner.

① How does Li Min greet Wang Meili?

② How does Wang Meili answer Li Min's greeting?

③ How does Wang Meili ask for Li Min's name?

④ What does Li Min think of Wang Meili's name?

⑤ How does Li Min ask Wang Meili's phone number?

3 Now practice the conversation from Activity 1 with your partner, substituting your own information where you can.

Reading

Read the information on Lin Mu's profile and answer the questions that follow.

Gèrén xìnxī
个人信息 Personal Information

Xìngmíng: Lín Mù
姓名   ：林木

Shēngrì:
生日 ：1981-03-23

Chéngshì: Shànghǎi
城市   ：上海

Zuì xǐ'ài de míngxīng: Chéng Lóng   kù
最喜爱的 明星 ：成 龙 ¹—酷 (cool)

Zuì xǐ'ài de dòngwù: xióngmāo   kě'ài
最喜爱的 动物 ： 熊猫 (panda) —可爱

Zuì xǐ'ài de diànshì jiémù: Kuàilè Dàběnyíng
最喜爱的 电视 节目：快乐 大本营²

Liánxì xìnxī
联系信息 Contact Information

Diànzǐ yóuxiāng :
电子 邮箱 ： mumu@hotmail.com

Diànhuà: yāo sān bā yāo líng líng líng qī liù yāo líng
电话 ： 1 3 8 1 0 0 0 7 6 1 0

1 What's Lin Mu's surname? What's her given name?

2 How old is she?

3 Where does she live?

4 Who is her favorite star? Why?

5 What's her favorite animal? Why?

6 What's her phone number?

7 What do *Shànghǎi* 上海, *diànzǐ yóuxiāng* 电子邮箱 and *kuàilè* 快乐 mean?

Expanded Words and Expressions

xìngmíng 姓名	full name
shēngrì 生日	birthday
chéngshì 城市	city
zuì xǐ'ài de 最喜爱的	favorite
míngxīng 明星	star
dòngwù 动物	animal
diànshì jiémù 电视 节目	TV program

---

¹ *Chéng Lóng* 成龙 is Jackie Chan.
² *Kuàilè Dàběnyíng* 快乐大本营 is a famous TV program in China.

Writing

Create your own profile by filling in the blanks. You can write the names of 城市，明星，动物，电视节目 in English.

Gèrén xìnxī
个人信息 Personal Information

Xìngmíng:
姓名：_____

Shēngrì:
生日：_____

Chéngshì:
城市：_____

Zuì xǐ'ài de míngxīng:
最喜爱的明星：_____

Zuì xǐ'ài de dòngwù:
最喜爱的动物：_____

Zuì xǐ'ài de diànshì jiémù:
最喜爱的电视节目：_____

Liánxì xìnxī
联系信息 Contact Information

Diànzǐ yóuxiāng:
电子邮箱：_____

Diànhuà:
电话：_____

Word List of Unit 1

Required Words and Expressions
(For Comprehension and Both Oral and Written Communication)

Míngcí 名词 (Nouns)

电话	diànhuà	phone
汉语	Hànyǔ	Chinese
汉字	hànzì	Chinese character
号码	hàomǎ	number
名字	míngzi	name

Dòngcí 动词 (Verbs)

见到	jiàndào	to have seen
叫	jiào	to name, to call
请问	qǐngwèn	May I ask...?
是	shì	to be

Jiānlèicí 兼类词 (Conversion Word)

姓	xìng	n./v.	surname; to be surnamed

Xíngróngcí 形容词 (Adjectives)

高兴	gāoxìng	glad
好	hǎo	good
漂亮	piàoliang	beautiful

Dàicí 代词 (Pronouns)

多少	duōshao	how many/ much
你	nǐ	you
什么	shénme	what

我	wǒ	I, me

Fùcí 副词 (Adverbs)

很	hěn	very
没有	méiyǒu	not have
也	yě	too

Yǔqìcí 语气词 (Modal Particle)

吗	ma	(a question particle)

Chángyòng biǎodá 常用表达 (Expressions)

哪里哪里	nǎli nǎli	it's not that nice, I am flattered
你的	nǐ de	your

选 Expanded Words and Expressions
(For Comprehension and Oral Communication)

Míngcí 名词 (Nouns)

城市	chéngshì	city
电视节目	diànshì jiémù	TV program
动物	dòngwù	animal
明星	míngxīng	star
生日	shēngrì	birthday
姓名	xìngmíng	full name
早上	zǎoshang	(early) morning

Dòngcí 动词 (Verbs)

吃	chī	to eat
出去	chūqu	to go out

Xíngróngcí 形容词 (Adjectives)

棒	bàng	wonderful
高	gāo	tall
可爱	kě'ài	lovely, cute
美	měi	beautiful
帅	shuài	handsome
甜	tián	sweet

Dàicí 代词 (Pronouns)

您	nín	you (polite form)
他	tā	he, him
他们	tāmen	they, them
她	tā	she, her
她们	tāmen	they, them

Fùcí 副词 (Adverb)

不	bù	not

Zhùcí 助词 (Auxiliary Word)

了	le	(a modal particle indicating the event already happened)

Yǔqìcí 语气词 (Modal Particle)

啊	a	(a modal particle)

Chángyòng biǎodá 常用表达 (Expression)

最喜爱的	zuì xǐ'ài de	favorite

荐 Suggested Words and Expressions
(For Comprehension Only)

Míngcí 名词 (Nouns)

电子邮箱	diànzǐ yóuxiāng	e-mail address
琴声	qínshēng	piano sound
上海	Shànghǎi	Shanghai
笑容	xiàoróng	smile
熊猫	xióngmāo	panda

Xíngróngcí 形容词 (Adjectives)

酷	kù	cool
快乐	kuàilè	happy, joyful

Unit 2

Dì-èr dānyuán

第二单元

Gifts and Courtesy

Lǐ   shàng   wǎng   lái

礼尚往来

How would you respond to a friend from another culture if they asked you about your age? If you wanted to give them a gift or accept a gift from them, what would you say? Please keep in mind these questions as you watch how Jenny and Bill deal with these situations and the differences between the East and the West.

In this unit, you will learn:

FUNCTION

☐ to name objects: 这是什么？
☐ to give and accept gifts: 送给你。／谢谢。
☐ to introduce people to each other: 珍妮，这是我妈妈。
☐ to ask someone's age: 珍妮今年多大了？

GRAMMAR

☐ to use the proximal demonstrative pronoun 这
☐ to ask what-questions with the interrogative pronoun 什么
☐ to use the adverbs of range 也 and 都

CULTURE

☐ Chinese small-talk topics such as age, marriage and salary
☐ how Chinese people give and accept gifts
☐ how Chinese people express and reciprocate courtesy

听与说 Listen and Speak

Listen to the recording and read silently. Listen again and repeat the sentences after you hear them, and then practice the conversation in pairs.

At the Welcome Party

One Friday evening, Wang Damin hosts a new student welcome party at his house where he introduces Jenny to his mother.

Wáng Dàmín:
王大民： 珍妮，这是我妈妈。

Māma, zhè shì wǒ péngyou Zhēnnī.
妈妈，这是我朋友珍妮。

Zhēnnī: Āyí hǎo! Āyí zhēn piàoliang!
珍妮： 阿姨好！阿姨真漂亮！

Jīntiān jiàndào nín zhēn gāoxìng.
今天见到您真高兴。

Wáng māma: Nǎli nǎli, nǐ yě hěn piàoliang.
王妈妈： 哪里哪里，你也很漂亮。

Jiàndào nǐ wǒ yě hěn gāoxìng.
见到你我也很高兴。

Wáng Dàmín: Nǐmen dōu hěn piàoliang.
王大民： 你们都很漂亮。

Wáng māma: Zhēnnī jīnnián duō dà le?
王妈妈： 珍妮今年多大了[1]？

Zhēnnī: Wǒ jīnnián èrshí suì.
珍妮： (hesitates for a second) 我今年20岁。

Wang: Jenny, this is my mom. Mom, this is my friend Jenny.

Jenny: Hello! You are so beautiful, auntie! It's so nice to meet you today.

Wang's mom: I'm flattered. You are also very beautiful. It's so nice to meet you, too.

Wang: Both of you are very beautiful!

Wang's mom: How old are you, Jenny?

Jenny: (hesitates for a second) I'm 20 years old this year.

---

[1] When used at the end of a sentence, 了 indicates how things are going until that point.

Required Words and Expressions

zhè	这	this
māma	妈妈	mother
péngyou	朋友	friend
āyí	阿姨	aunt
zhēn	真	really, truly
jīntiān	今天	today
nǐmen	你们	you (plural)
dōu	都	all
jīnnián	今年	this year
duō dà	多大	how old
le	了	(a particle)
suì	岁	year (of age)

B 个人练习 Self-practice

Word Order: Create sentences by arranging the following words in the appropriate order.

1. ① 妈妈 māma ② 这 zhè ③ 是 shì ④ 我 wǒ _____

2. ① 阿姨 āyí ② 漂亮 piàoliang ③ 真 zhēn _____

3. ① 多大 duō dà ② 今年 jīnnián ③ 了 le _____

4. ① 很 hěn ② 漂亮 piàoliang ③ 也 yě ④ 你 nǐ _____

C 二人练习 Pair Work

Meeting a New Friend: Work with your partner using the sentences in the box to complete the conversation, then practice the conversation together.

李丽: Lǐ Lì: 比尔，这是 小军，这是 小芳 。
Bǐ'ěr, zhè shì Xiǎojūn, zhè shì Xiǎofāng.

比尔: Bǐ'ěr: _____。

小军: Xiǎojūn: 我 也 是。
Wǒ yě shì.

比尔: Bǐ'ěr: 你 贵姓 ？
Nǐ guìxìng?

小军: Xiǎojūn: _____，叫 李 小军 。
jiào Lǐ Xiǎojūn.

小芳: Xiǎofāng: 李丽，_____。
Lǐ Lì,

李丽: Lǐ Lì: 哪里哪里，_____。
Nǎli nǎli,

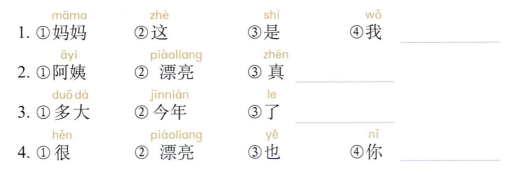

① 你 今天 真 漂亮 。
Nǐ jīntiān zhēn piàoliang.

② 你 也 很 漂亮 。
Nǐ yě hěn piàoliang.

③ 很 高兴 认识 你们。
Hěn gāoxìng rènshi nǐmen.

④ 我 姓 李。
Wǒ xìng Lǐ.

D 小组活动 Group Work

Party Time: Imagine that you and your classmates are at a party. Practice the conversation from Activity C, using your own information where possible. Then introduce your friends to know each other. Don't forget to compliment each other in Chinese!

Expanded Words and Expressions

认识 rènshi to know

02 数字 Numbers 10-100

A 听与说 Listen and Speak

Listen to the recording and read silently. Listen again and repeat the numbers after you hear them.

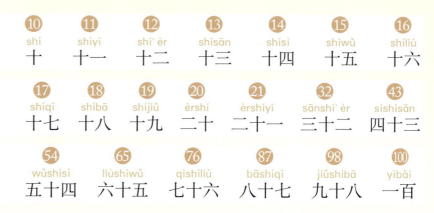

⑩ shí 十	⑪ shíyī 十一	⑫ shí' èr 十二	⑬ shísān 十三	⑭ shísì 十四	⑮ shíwǔ 十五	⑯ shíliù 十六
⑰ shíqī 十七	⑱ shíbā 十八	⑲ shíjiǔ 十九	⑳ èrshí 二十	㉑ èrshíyī 二十一	㉜ sānshí' èr 三十二	㊸ sìshísān 四十三
(54) wǔshísì 五十四	(65) liùshíwǔ 六十五	(76) qīshíliù 七十六	(87) bāshíqī 八十七	(98) jiǔshíbā 九十八	(100) yībǎi 一百	

B 二人练习 Pair Work

Guess Their Ages: Look at the pictures in Activity C, then use the following model to discuss how old you think each person is.

Chéng Lóng jīnnián duō dà le?
A：成 龙 今年 多 大 了？

Wǒ cāi tā sìshí suì.
B：我 猜 他 40 岁。

Zhēn de ma? Wǒ cāi tā wǔshí suì.
A：真 的[1]吗？我 猜 他 50 岁。

Chéng Lóng
成 龙

Expanded Words and Expressions

cāi
猜 to guess

Culture Box

Age is generally not a secret among Chinese people. However, for reasons you can probably guess, more and more Chinese women and successful people prefer not to talk about their age.

C 听力练习 Listening

Listen to the recording and find out the exact ages of the people below. Then compare your answers and see who has the best guess.

Liú Déhuá
刘 德华 ______

Cài Yīlín
蔡依林 ______

Xú Jìnglěi
徐静蕾[2] ______

1 *Zhēn* 真 means "really". Like *hěn* 很, it can be used as an adverb that occurs before an adjective or a verb. *Zhēnde* 真的 indicates "it's true" and can also be used as an independent sentence.

2 They are all famous stars in China. Liu comes from HongKong, Cai comes from Taiwan and Xu comes from Beijing.

03 句型操练 Sentence Patterns

𝒜 听与说 Listen and Speak 🎧

Listen to the recording and read silently. Listen again and repeat the sentences after you hear them.

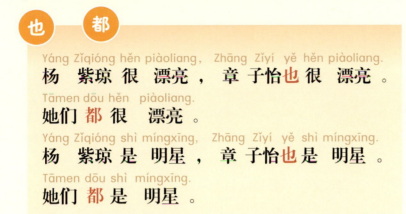

也　　都

Yáng Zǐqióng hěn piàoliang,　Zhāng Zǐyí yě hěn piàoliang.
杨 紫琼 很 漂亮 ， 章 子怡也很 漂亮 。
Tāmen dōu hěn piàoliang.
她们 都 很 漂亮 。
Yáng Zǐqióng shì míngxīng,　Zhāng Zǐyí yě shì míngxīng.
杨 紫琼 是 明星 ， 章 子怡也是 明星 。
Tāmen dōu shì míngxīng.
她们 都 是 明星 。

Tāmen dōu shì míngxīng.
她们 都 是 明星 。

ℬ 选择 Choose the correct answer.

Choose the correct words in parentheses to complete the conversations. Then practice with your partner.

Zhè shì Ānnà,　tā　　　(shì / hěn) niánqīng.
1. A：这 是 安娜，她 _____（是 / 很） 年轻 。
Mǎlì　　　(yě / dōu / shì) hěn niánqīng.
 B：玛丽_____（也 / 都 / 是） 很 年轻 。
Tāmen　　　(yě / dōu / shì) hěn niánqīng.
 A：她们_____（也 / 都 / 是） 很 年轻 。

Nǐ hǎo,　wǒ jiào Wáng Lì.　Qǐngwèn,　nín guìxìng?
2. A：你 好，我 叫 王 丽。请问 ，您 贵姓？
Wǒ　　　(yě / dōu) xìng Wáng,　wǒ jiào Wáng Jūn.
 B：我_____（也 / 都） 姓 王，我 叫 王 军。
Zhēn hǎo!　Wǒmen　　　(yě / dōu) xìng Wáng.
 A：真 好！我们_____（也 / 都） 姓 王。

Expanded Words and Expressions

niánqīng
年轻　　　young

☺ 休息一下 Break Time

Practice writing the following two characters using the proper stroke order indicated below.

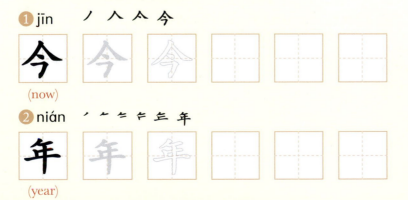

❶ jīn 　ノ 入 今 今
今
(now)

❷ nián 　ノ 𠂉 𠂉 年 年 年
年
(year)

✍ 听与说 Listen and Speak 🎧

Listen to the recording and read silently. Listen again and repeat the sentences after you hear them, and then practice the conversation in pairs.

At a Teahouse

Bill invites Li Li to go to a teahouse and offers to treat Li Li. She accepts Bill's invitation and brings him a special gift.

Bǐ'ěr:	Zhè shì shénme?	
比尔:	这是 什么？	
Lǐ Lì:	(hesitates for a second) Zhè shì Zhōngguó dìtú,	
李丽:	(hesitates for a second) 这是 中国 地图，	
	sònggěi nǐ. Xīwàng nǐ xǐhuan.	
	送给 你。希望 你 喜欢。	
Bǐ'ěr:	Xièxie! Wǒ hěn xǐhuan kàn dìtú.	
比尔:	谢谢！我 很 喜欢 看 地图。	
Lǐ Lì:	Bú kèqi.	
李丽:	不客气。	
Bǐ'ěr:	Nǐ hē shénme? Wǒ qǐngkè.	
比尔:	你喝 什么？我 请客。	
Lǐ Lì:	Wǒ xǐhuan hē chá, nǐ ne?	
李丽:	我喜欢 喝茶，你 呢¹？	
Bǐ'ěr:	Wǒ yě xǐhuan hē chá.	
比尔:	我 也 喜欢 喝茶。	
Lǐ Lì:	Hǎo de. Nà wǒmen dōu hē chá ba.	
李丽:	好的。那我们 都 喝茶 吧²。

Bill: What's this?

Li Li: (hesitates for a second) This is a map of China. It's a gift for you. I hope you will like it.

Bill: Thank you so much! I like studying maps.

Li Li: You're welcome.

Bill: What would you like to drink? It's my treat.

Li Li: I would like tea. What about you?

Bill: I would like tea, too.

Li Li: OK. Let's both have tea.

[1,2] 呢 indicates a question while 吧 usually means a suggestion or guess. They all appear at the end of a sentence. For example:

Nǐ ne? 你呢？ （How about you?）

Hē chá ba! 喝茶吧！ （Have some tea!）

Nǐ shì Lǐ Lì ba? 你是李丽吧？ （I guess you are Li Li.）

Required Words and Expressions

Zhōngguó 中国	China
dìtú 地图	map
sòng gěi 送 给	to send to, to give to
xīwàng 希望	hope; to hope
xǐhuan 喜欢	to like
xièxie 谢谢	thank you
kàn 看	to look
bù kèqi 不客气	you're welcome
hē 喝	to drink
qǐngkè 请客	to treat
chá 茶	tea
ne 呢	(a question particle)
hǎo de 好的	OK
ba 吧	(a suggestive particle)

ℬ 个人练习　Self-practice

Word Order: Create sentences by arranging the following words in the appropriate order.

1. ① 中国　②这　③是　④地图 ＿＿＿＿＿＿
   Zhōngguó　zhè　shì　dìtú

2. ①喝　② 什么　③你 ＿＿＿＿＿＿
   hē　shénme　nǐ

3. ①我　②喝　③茶　④喜欢　⑤也 ＿＿＿＿＿＿
   wǒ　hē　chá　xǐhuan　yě

𝒞 二人练习　Pair Work

Exchange Gifts: Exchange gifts with your partner by using the following pattern.

Zhè shì shénme?
A：这 是 什么？

Zhè shì Zhōngguó dìtú.
B：这 是 中国 地图。

Sòng gěi nǐ!
送 给 你！

Xièxie!
A：谢谢！

qiǎokèlì
巧克力　chocolate

zìdiǎn
字典　dictionary

huā
花　flower

𝒟 班级活动　Class Activity

Common Points: Use the question "*Nǐ ne? 你呢?*" to find out which classmates you have a lot in common with. Similarities may include the same surname, name, age and appearance.

Wǒ xìng Smith,　nǐ ne?
A：我 姓 Smith，你呢？

Wǒ yě xìng Smith.
B：我 也 姓 Smith。

Wǒmen dōu xìng Smith.
A：我们 都 姓 Smith。

Wǒ èrshíyī suì,　nǐ ne?
A：我 21 岁，你呢？

Wǒ yě èrshíyī suì.
B：我也 21 岁。

Wǒmen dōu èrshíyī suì.
A：我们 都 21 岁。

Culture Box

Some items are not good to give as gifts in Chinese culture, such as knives and clocks. Because these items are traditionally associated with death, many avoid giving them as gifts. However, nowadays, many young people are less concerned about following tradition in these matters.

05 精彩瞬间 Spotlight

1 2 3 4 5 6

① 相机 ② 护照 ③ 手机 ④ 钱包 ⑤ 书 ⑥ 笔

𝒜 听与说 Listen and Speak

Listen to the recording and read silently. Listen again and repeat the objects and sentences after you hear them.

Zhè shì shénme?
这¹是 什么？

Zhè shì wǒ de xiàngjī.
这 是 我 的 相机。

Zhè shì tā de hùzhào.
这 是 他 的 护照。

Zhè shì tā de shǒujī.
这 是 她 的 手机。

Zhè shì tā de qiánbāo.
这 是 她 的 钱包。

Zhèxiē shì shénme?
这些²是 什么？

Zhèxiē shì wǒmen de shū.
这些 是 我们 的 书。

Zhèxiē shì tāmen de bǐ.
这些 是 他们 的 笔。

What is this?
    This is my camera.
    This is his passport.
    This is her cell phone.
    This is her wallet.
What are these?
    They're our books.
    They're their pens.

ℬ 听力练习 Listening

Listen to the recording to find out what Bill and Li Li have in their bags. Write the numbers of the objects in the picture above as you hear them.

1. Bill's bag: _____

2. Li Li's bag: _____

Expanded Words and Expressions

xiàngjī	
相机	camera
hùzhào	
护照	passport
shǒujī	
手机	cell phone
qiánbāo	
钱包	wallet
shū	
书	book
bǐ	
笔	pen

[1,2] *Zhè* 这 means "this" or "these". However, *zhèxiē* 这些 only means "these".

06 喜欢和不喜欢　Likes and Dislikes

𝒜 听与说　Listen and Speak 🎧

Listen to the recording and read silently. Listen again and repeat the phrases after you hear them.

Xiǎolì 小丽				Dàwěi 大伟			
xǐhuan 喜欢 LIKE		bù xǐhuan 不 喜欢 DISLIKE		xǐhuan 喜欢 LIKE		bù xǐhuan 不 喜欢 DISLIKE	
gòuwù 购物	to go shopping	zuòfàn 做饭	to cook	shuìjiào 睡觉	to sleep	xiě bókè 写博客	to write a blog
shuìjiào 睡觉	to sleep	dǎ diànwán 打 电玩	to play video games	chànggē 唱歌	to sing	zuòfàn 做饭	to cook
chànggē 唱歌	to sing	kàn shū 看 书	to read	dǎ diànwán 打 电玩	to play video games	gòuwù 购物	to go shopping

ℬ 二人练习　Pair Work

Happiness Index: Xiaoli and Dawei are getting married. Among their friends, some believe they will make a great couple, but others don't. They decided to have a serious talk about whether they should marry or not based on their knowledge of the couple's likes and dislikes. With a partner, use the following model to create more reasons why Xiaoli and Dawei's relationship might or might not work.

Student A:
Dàwěi xǐhuan shuìjiào,　Xiǎolì yě xǐhuan shuìjiào,　tāmen dōu xǐhuan shuìjiào.
大伟 喜欢 睡觉 ，小丽 也 喜欢 睡觉 ，他们 都 喜欢 睡觉 。

Student B:
Dàwěi xǐhuan dǎ diànwán,　Xiǎolì bù xǐhuan dǎ diànwán.
大伟 喜欢 打 电玩 ，小丽 不 喜欢 打 电玩 。

Happiness index ★★☆☆☆

07 礼尚往来 Gifts and Courtesy

听与说 Listen and Speak 🎧

Listen to the recording and read silently. Listen again and repeat the sentences after you hear them, then practice the conversations in pairs.

1. A: This is a small gift for you.
   B: How nice!

2. A: Please accept it.
   B: You are so kind.

3. A: You are so humorous!
   B: Well, you said so.

4. A: You are great!
   B: I'm flattered.

1. Zhè shì wǒ de yìdiǎnr xīnyì.
   A：这是我的一点儿心意。
   Nǐ tài kèqi le.
   B：你太客气了。

2. Qǐng nín shōuxià.
   A：请您收下。
   Nǐ tài jiànwài le.
   B：你太见外了。

3. Nǐ zhēn yōumò.
   A：你真幽默。
   Guòjiǎng, guòjiǎng.
   B：过奖，过奖。

4. Nǐ zhēn bàng!
   A：你真棒！
   Mǎmǎ hūhū.
   B：马马虎虎[1]。

休息一下 Break Time 🎧

Listen to the recording and read silently. Listen again and repeat the sentence after you hear it.

Pay attention to the pronunciation of the two initials *s* and *sh* and the tones of *i* while repeating the sentence. Then compete with a partner, trying to say the sentence as quickly and accurately as you can.

Sì shì sì, shí shì shí; shísì shì shísì, sìshí shì sìshí.
四是四，十是十；十四是十四，四十是四十。
Four is four and ten is ten; fourteen is fourteen and forty is forty.

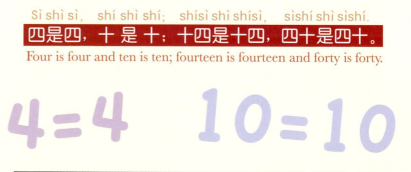

Expanded Words and Expressions

yìdiǎnr	一点儿	a little, a bit
xīnyì	心意	regard
kèqi	客气	polite, courteous
qǐng	请	please
shōuxià	收下	to accept
guòjiǎng	过奖	to overpraise, to flatter

[1] The original meanings of *mǎ* 马 (horse) and *hǔ* 虎 (tiger) are two kinds of animals, however, the meaning of *mǎmǎ hūhū* 马马虎虎 is "just so-so" or "careless". In oral Chinese, it is often read as *mǎmǎ hūhū* 马马虎虎. The pronunciation of 虎 has been changed into the first tone.

文化掠影 **Culture Snapshot**

☐ In *Episode 1*, Wang's mother **asked** Jenny her **age**. Jenny, feeling very uneasy for a moment, but fearing that Wang's mother would think she was rude, came up with a response. In China, the elderly express their care by asking young people questions about their age, marital status and even their salary level. We know that some of the above topics are too sensitive to ask about in Western culture. While you might feel averse to such probes into your privacy, keep in mind that this is a normal occurrence in Chinese culture, and you should not feel offended.

☐ ***Exchanging gifts*** can have different connotations in different cultures with regard to both the type and the value of gifts. Americans, for instance, prefer to open the gifts right on spot to show appreciation while Chinese usually wait to unwrap the gifts after the occasion. Americans consider exchanging gifts more as social interaction or bonding regardless of the value of the gifts while Chinese sometimes seem to care more about the value and/or practical utility

of the gifts, especially among friends and relatives. Either way, there is no absolute rule which is more appropriate among people from diverse cultures. So people make different choices and decisions based on their level of comfort and with an understanding of each other's expectations.

☐ By learning ***Gifts and Courtesy***, you might have been able to give feedback to compliments in Chinese way. There is an old Chinese saying *lǐshàngwǎnglái* 礼尚往来 (courtesy demands reciprocity), meaning that one should treat others in the same way which he/she receives. Chinese people consider it a basic principle of interpersonal communication. It also means one should be modest in replying to others' compliments with some friendly words. It would be good to return a few complimentary words to the one who has been so courteous to you. In doing so, everyone will end the conversation on a happy note.

1 The Proximal Demonstrative Pronoun 这[1]

这 is the most commonly used demonstrative pronoun in Chinese. It can be used with 是 to form 这是. The objects that follow can be singular or plural nouns. 这 is often pronounced as *zhèi* in oral Chinese, especially in the north of China.

A: What is this?
B: It is a gift.
A: Are these books?
B: No, they are not books. They are maps.

Zhè shì shénme?
A：这 是 什么？

Zhè shì lǐwù.
B：这 是 礼物。

Zhè shì shū ma?
A：这 是 书 吗？

Zhè bú shì shū. Zhè shì yìxiē dìtú.
B：这 不 是 书。这 是 一些 地图。

Expanded Words and Expressions

lǐwù
礼物   gift, present

yìxiē
一些   some

2 Asking What-questions with the Interrogative Pronoun 什么

The interrogative pronoun 什么 inquires about something when it is used in an interrogative sentence. The word order in Chinese what-questions is usually different from that in English. In Chinese, the question word occurs where the expected answer would be rather than at the beginning of the sentence.

A: What is your name? (You are called what name?)
B: My name is Li Li.
A: What is this? (This is what?)
B: It is a map of China.

Nǐ jiào shénme míngzi?
A：你 叫 什么 名字？

Wǒ jiào Lǐ Lì.
B：我 叫 李丽。

Zhè shì shénme?
A：这 是 什么？

Zhè shì Zhōngguó dìtú.
B：这 是 中国 地图。

3 The Adverbs of Range 也 and 都

In Chinese, adverbs, especially one-syllable adverbs like 也 and 都 normally appear after subjects and in front of verbs.
也 basically means "too" or "also". It can occur whether the subject concerns an individual or collective concept.

---

[1] The proximal demonstrative pronoun 这 indicates things or people, while the common distal demonstrative pronoun in Chinese is "*nà* 那". For example:
Zhè shì Lǐ Lì. Nà shì Zhēnnī.这是李丽。那是珍妮。
This is Li Li. That is Jenny.

Wǒ xìng Wáng.
A：我 姓 王 。

Wǒ yě xìng Wáng.
B：我 也 姓 王 。

Tāmen yě xìng Wáng.
C：他们 也 姓 王 。

都 means "both" or "all" and indicates inclusiveness. Don't use 都 when the subject concerns an individual concept.

Lǐ Lì piàoliang ma?
A：李丽 漂亮 吗?

Lǐ Lì hěn piàoliang.
B：李丽很 漂亮 。

Zhēnnī ne?
A：珍妮 呢?

Zhēnnī yě hěn piàoliang. Tāmen dōu hěn piàoliang.
B：珍妮 也 很 漂亮 。 她们 都 很 漂亮 。

When 也 and 都 occur in the same environment, they have different meanings.

Wǒmen yě xǐhuan Hànyǔ.
(1) 我们 也 喜欢 汉语。

Wǒmen dōu xǐhuan Hànyǔ.
(2) 我们 都 喜欢 汉语。

A: My surname is Wang.
B: My surname is Wang, too.
C: Their surname is Wang, too.

A: Is Li Li beautiful?
B: Yes, she is very beautiful.
A: How about Jenny?
B: She is beautiful, too. They are both very beautiful.

(1) We love Chinese, too. (Some people mentioned love Chinese.)
(2) We all love Chinese. (Everyone of us loves Chinese.)

10 语法练习 Grammar Practice

1 Make complete sentences following the examples given.

❶
Zhè shì shénme?
A：这 是 什么 ?

Zhè shì bǐ.
B：这 是 笔。

zhè shǒujī
这 手机

zhè hùzhào
这 护照

❷
Nǐ duō dà le?   Wǒ èrshíwǔ suì.
A：你 多大了?   B：我 25 岁。

tā   èrshíbā
他   28

tāmen   sānshí
他们   30

Xiǎoqiáng   shíwǔ
小强   15

③   A：我 喜欢 购物，你 呢?
Wǒ xǐhuan gòuwù, nǐ ne?

     B：我 不 喜欢 购物，我 喜欢 打 电玩。
Wǒ bù xǐhuan gòuwù, wǒ xǐhuan dǎ diànwán.

kàn shū	*chànggē*
看 书	唱歌
zuòfàn	*shuìjiào*
做饭	睡觉

2 Complete the following sentences with the words given.

ne	*yě*	*dōu*	*shénme*	*zhè*	*duō dà*
呢	也	都	什么	这	多大

① A：我 喜欢 看 书，你 _____ ?
Wǒ xǐhuan kàn shū, nǐ _____ ?

   B：我 不 喜欢，我 喜欢 睡觉。
Wǒ bù xǐhuan, wǒ xǐhuan shuìjiào.

② A：你 _____ 了? B：我 19 岁。
Nǐ _____ le?   *Wǒ shíjiǔ suì.*

③ A：你 喝 _____ ? B：我 喝 茶。
Nǐ hē _____ ?   *Wǒ hē chá.*

④ 我们 _____ 喝茶。
Wǒmen _____ hē chá.

⑤ _____ 是 你的 相机 吗?
_____ shì nǐ de xiàngjī ma?

⑥ 我 喜欢 写 博客，我 妈妈 _____ 喜欢 写 博客。
Wǒ xǐhuan xiě bókè, wǒ māma _____ xǐhuan xiě bókè.

3 Rewrite the following sentences in the form indicated.

① 这 是 钱包 。Make a question using 什么.
Zhè shì qiánbāo.

_____

② 我 喜欢 唱歌 。Make a question using 吗.
Wǒ xǐhuan chànggē.

_____

③ 我 喝 茶。Make a question using 呢.
Wǒ hē chá.

_____

④ 我 喜欢 做饭，你 喜欢 做饭 吗? Make a question using 呢.
Wǒ xǐhuan zuòfàn, nǐ xǐhuan zuòfàn ma?

_____

⑤ 他 写 博客。我 写 博客。 Make a sentence using 也.
Tā xiě bókè. Wǒ xiě bókè.

_____

Wǒ hē kělè,   tā yě hē kělè.

⑥ 我 喝可乐，他也 喝可乐。Make a sentence using **都**.

Tā qī suì.

⑦ 他七岁。Make a question using **多大**.

Expanded Words and Expressions

kělè
可乐   cola

---

11 语音提示   Pronunciation Tips

1 Initials *z, c, s* and *zh, ch, sh*

Read the following syllables.

zè—zhě	zì—zhì	zǎo—zhǎo	zài—zhài
cū—chū	cāi—chāi	cí—chí	cā—chā
sēn—shēn	suì—shuì	sì—shì	sū—shū

Tip

Put the tip of the tongue behind the upper front teeth, with the teeth closed, release the tongue slightly to let the air flow through the narrow space between the tongue and teeth to say *z, c, s*. Then keep the same formation, curl the tongue back and say *zh, ch, sh*.

2 Words with *z, c, s* and *zh, ch, sh*

Read the following words focusing on the syllables with *z, c, s* or *zh, ch, sh*.

zhè	shì	shénme	suì
这	是	什么	岁
hē chá	**zì**	**zhēn**	**kàn shū**
喝茶	字	真	看书
shǒujī	**hùzhào**	**shuìjiào**	**shōuxià**
手机	护照	睡觉	收下

3 Intonation of the interrogative sentences

Repeat the following sentences after your teacher. Pay special attention to the intonation.

Zhè shì shénme? Zhè shì Zhōngguó dìtú ma?

1. 这是 什么？这是 中国 地图吗？

Nǐ hē shénme?

2. 你喝 什么？

Wǒ hē chá, nǐ ne?

3. 我喝茶，你呢？

Tip

In Chinese, interrogative sentences are read in natural rising intonations. The intonation goes a little higher when question particles like 吗 or 呢 appears at the end of a sentence.

12 汉字书写 Writing Chinese Characters

1 笔画 Strokes

Strokes are the smallest structural units of Chinese characters. You have already learned four stroke types in Unit 1. Four more stroke types include:

(dot)	、	、	、	、	(bending stroke)	ㄱ	ㄷ	ㄱ	一
diǎn 点	六	主	太	外	zhé 折	口	九	书	客
(upward stroke)	✓	╯	✓	╱	(hook)	亅	ㄴ	亅	ㄱ
tí 提	次	打	江	习	gōu 勾	手	我	子	的

2 笔顺 Stroke Order

When writing a Chinese character, it is important to follow the correct stroke order. The general principles are as follows.

cóng shàng dào xià
从　上　到　下　from top to bottom

eg. sān
三 （three）　一　二　三

cóng zuǒ dào yòu
从　左　到　右　from left to right

eg. chuān
川 （river）　丿　川　川

You can write it!

Practice writing the following Chinese characters. Don't forget to follow the correct stroke order!

zhōng 丨口口中
中　中
(center)

shū ㄱ乛书书
书　书
(book)

bù 一丆不不
不　不
(not)

wǒ 亅二于手我我我
我　我
(I, me)

tài 一ナ大太
太　太
(too)

lǐ 丶ㄱ礻礼礼
礼　礼
(gift)

3 汉字的演变 Evolution of Chinese Characters

巛 → 屾 → 山

13 综合练习　Integrative Practice

Listening

1 Listen to the following words and mark the missing tones. 🎧

liwu	Zhongguo	ditu	song	zhe	jinnian	duo da	sui
礼物	中国	地图	送	这	今年	多大	岁

2 Listen to the following conversations and complete the sentences with the correct characters in parentheses. 🎧

❶ 　Míngming, nǐ jīnnián duō dà le?
A：明明，你 今年 多 大 了？
　　Yéye, wǒ jīnnián　　　　(shísì suì / shíqī suì).
B：爷爷，我 今年 _____（a. 14 岁 / b. 17 岁）。

❷ 　Zhè shì shénme?
A：这 是 什么？
　　Zhè shì　　　　(hùzhào / qiánbāo).
B：这 是 _____（a.护照 / b. 钱包 ）。

❸ 　Nǐ hē shénme?
A：你 喝 什么？
　　Wǒ hē kělè.　Nǐ ne?
B：我 喝可乐。你呢？
　　Wǒ　　　　(yě / bù) hē kělè.
A：我 _____（a.也 / b.不) 喝可乐。

3 Listen to the recording and decide whether the following statements are true or false. 🎧

T   F

Mǎlì hěn piàoliang, tā xǐhuan chī
① 玛丽 很 漂亮 ，她 喜欢 吃
bǐsà, bù xǐhuan hē kāfēi.
比萨，不 喜欢 喝 咖啡。 ☐ ☐

Xiǎoměi hěn kě'ài, tā xǐhuan chī bǐsà,
② 小美 很 可爱，她 喜欢 吃比萨，
bù xǐhuan xiě bókè.
不 喜欢 写 博客。 ☐ ☐

Dàwěi hěn gāo, tā xǐhuan kàn shū, bù
③ 大伟 很 高，他 喜欢 看 书，不
xǐhuan chànggē.
喜欢 唱歌 。 ☐ ☐

Fēifei hěn gāo, tā xǐhuan hē chá, bù
④ 飞飞 很 高，他 喜欢 喝 茶，不
xǐhuan kàn shū.
喜欢 看 书。 ☐ ☐

Expanded Words and Expressions

bǐsà
比萨   pizza

kāfēi
咖啡   coffee

Speaking

1 With a partner, practice the following conversation.

(At a Restaurant)

Míngming: Ānnà, nǐ hē kělè háishi kāfēi?
明明 ：安娜，你 喝 可乐 还是 咖啡？

Ānnà: Wǒ hē kāfēi.
安娜：我 喝 咖啡。

Míngming: Hǎo de. Fúwùyuán, wǒmen dōu hē
明明 ：好 的。服务员，我们 都 喝
kāfēi.
咖啡。

Ānnà: Nǐ kàn, nàge rén zhēn shuài!
安娜：你 看，那个 人 真 帅 ！

Míngming: Èng, tā kànqǐlai hěn kù.
明明 ：嗯，他 看起来 很 酷。

Ānnà: Nǐ cāi tā duō dà le?
安娜：你 猜 他 多 大 了？

Míngming: Wǒ cāi tā èrshí suì le.
明明 ：我 猜 他 20 岁 了。

2 Take turns answering the following questions with a partner.

① What do Mingming and Anna drink?
② Who are they talking about?
③ Why do they mention that person?
④ How old is that person?
⑤ What do *fúwùyuán* 服务员 and *kànqǐlai* 看起来 mean?

3 Now practice the conversation from Activity 1 with your partner, substituting your own information where you can.

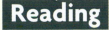

Reading

Read the text about Wang Jun and his girlfriend, then answer the questions that follow.

Zhè shì Wáng Jūn,   tā jīnnián èrshí suì,   tā hěn shuài.   Tā xǐhuan dǎ diànwán,   yě
这 是 王 军，他 今年 20 岁，他 很 帅。他 喜欢 打 电玩，也
xǐhuan chànggē.
喜欢 唱歌。

Zhè shì Wáng Jūn de nǔpéngyou Lǐ Fāng.   Tā jīnnián yě shì èrshí suì,   tā hěn kě'ài.   Tā
这是 王 军的 女朋友 李芳。她 今年 也是 20 岁，她 很 可爱。她
xǐhuan kàn shū,   xiě bókè.
喜欢 看 书、写博客。

Tāmen rènshi yì nián le.   Wáng Jūn hěn xǐhuan Lǐ Fāng,   Lǐ Fāng yě hěn xǐhuan Wáng Jūn.
他们 认识 一 年 了。王 军 很 喜欢 李芳，李芳 也 很 喜欢 王 军。

Jīntiān shì Lǐ Fāng de shēngrì,   Wáng Jūn sòng gěi tā yí gè lǐwù.   Tā hěn kāixīn.
今天 是 李芳 的 生日，王 军 送 给 她 一个 礼物。她 很 开心。

1. How old is Wang Jun?
2. What does Li Fang like to do?
3. How long have they known each other?
4. Why does Wang Jun give a gift to Li Fang today?
5. Guess the meanings of *nǔpéngyou* 女朋友 and *kāixīn* 开心.

Writing

Zhè shì Màikè.
这 是 迈克。
Tā hěn
他 很 _____，
yě hěn
也 很 _____。
Tā jīnnián èrshíyī
他 今年 21 _____。
Tā xǐhuan
他 喜欢 _____。

Zhè shì Mòlì.
这 是 茉莉。
Tā hěn
她 很 _____，
yě hěn
也 很 _____。
Tā xǐhuan
她 喜欢 _____。

Word List of Unit 2

Míngcí 名词 (Nouns)

阿姨	āyí	aunt
茶	chá	tea
地图	dìtú	map
今年	jīnnián	this year
今天	jīntiān	today
妈妈	māma	mother
朋友	péngyou	friend
中国	Zhōngguó	China

Dòngcí 动词 (Verbs)

喝	hē	to drink
看	kàn	to look
请客	qǐngkè	to treat
喜欢	xǐhuan	to like
谢谢	xièxie	thank you

Jiānlèicí 兼类词 (Conversion Word)

希望	xīwàng	n./v.	hope; to hope

Dàicí 代词 (Pronouns)

你们	nǐmen	you (plural)

这	zhè	this

Fùcí 副词 (Adverbs)

都	dōu	all
真	zhēn	really, truly

Liàngcí 量词 (Measure Word)

岁	suì	year (of age)

Yǔqìcí 语气词 (Modal Particles)

吧	ba	(a suggestive particle)
了	le	(a particle)
呢	ne	(a question particle)

Chángyòng biǎodá 常用表达 (Expressions)

不客气	bù kèqi	you're welcome
多大	duō dà	how old
好的	hǎo de	OK
送给	sòng gěi	to send to, to give to

Míngcí 名词 (Nouns)

比萨	bǐsà	pizza
笔	bǐ	pen
护照	hùzhào	passport
咖啡	kāfēi	coffee
可乐	kělè	cola
礼物	lǐwù	gift, present
钱包	qiánbāo	wallet
手机	shǒujī	cell phone
书	shū	book
相机	xiàngjī	camera
心意	xīnyì	regard

Dòngcí 动词 (Verbs)

猜	cāi	to guess
过奖	guòjiǎng	to overpraise, to flatter

请	qǐng	please
认识	rènshi	to know
收下	shōuxià	to accept

Xíngróngcí 形容词 （Adjectives）

客气	kèqi	polite, courteous

年轻	niánqīng	young

Chángyòng biǎodá 常用表达 （Expressions）

一点儿	yīdiǎnr	a little, a bit
一些	yīxiē	some

Suggested Words and Expressions
(For Comprehension Only)

Míngcí 名词 （Nouns）

服务员	fúwùyuán	waiter, waitress
花	huā	flower
女朋友	nǚpéngyou	girlfriend
巧克力	qiǎokèlì	chocolate
字典	zìdiǎn	dictionary

Dòngcí 动词 （Verbs）

唱歌	chànggē	to sing
购物	gòuwù	to go shopping
见外	jiànwài	to regard somebody as an outsider
看起来	kànqǐlai	seem to be

睡觉	shuìjiào	to sleep
做饭	zuòfàn	to cook

Xíngróngcí 形容词 （Adjectives）

开心	kāixīn	happy
马马虎虎	mǎmǎ hǔhǔ (mǎmǎ hūhū)	just so-so; careless
幽默	yōumò	humorous

Chángyòng biǎodá 常用表达 （Expressions）

打电玩	dǎ diànwán	to play video games
看书	kàn shū	to read
写博客	xiě bókè	to write a blog

Unit 3

Feel at Home Wherever You Are

Sì hǎi wéi jiā

四海为家

Many young people enjoy traveling around the world, meeting new people, and seeking out enriching experiences. They feel as if they belong to the worldwide family. When mutual trust is established among these new "family members", it is common for them to bring the topic of their own families into conversations about their own interests and experiences.

In this unit, you will learn:

FUNCTION

☐ to ask about and tell time: 现在几点了？/现在八点。

☐ to ask about and give information about nationality：你是哪国人？/我是日本人。

☐ to talk about family members：这是我的全家福。我家有四口人：爸爸、妈妈、哥哥和我。

☐ to ask about and give information about work：他们做什么工作？/我爸爸是医生。我妈妈在学校工作，她是老师。

GRAMMAR

☐ how to tell time

☐ to ask which-questions with the interrogative pronoun 哪

☐ to ask others to confirm information using 吗 or verb+不+verb questions

CULTURE

☐ about culture integration

☐ how Chinese people address others

☐ about respecting seniority

听与说 Listen and Speak

Listen to the recording and read silently. Listen again and repeat the sentences after you hear them, and then practice the conversation in pairs.

In the Admissions Office

Both Bill and Yamada[1] are new arrivals at Peking University in a Study Abroad Program. They come across each other at the Admissions Office.

比尔： Qǐngwèn, xiànzài jǐ diǎn le?
请问，现在几点了？

山田： Xiànzài bā diǎn.
现在八点。

比尔： Xièxie. Nǐ yě shì liúxuéshēng ma?
谢谢。你也是留学生吗？

山田： Shì, wǒ shì Rìběnrén. Nǐ shì nǎ guó rén?
是，我是日本人。你是哪国人？

比尔： Wǒ shì Měiguórén. Nǐ jiào shénme míngzi?
我是美国人。你叫什么名字？

山田： Wǒ jiào Shāntián. Dàjiā dōu jiào wǒ
我叫山田。大家都叫我
"xiǎo Běijīng".
"小[2]北京"。

比尔： Zhège míngzi hěn yǒuyìsi. Wǒ jiào Bǐ'ěr,
这个[3]名字很有意思。我叫比尔，
hěn gāoxìng rènshi nǐ.
很高兴认识你。

山田： Wǒ yě shì. Zàijiàn!
我也是。再见！

比尔： Zàijiàn!
再见！

Bill: Excuse me, what time is it now?
Yamada: Eight o'clock.
Bill: Thank you. Are you also an international student?
Yamada: Yeah, I'm from Japan. What about you?
Bill: I am American. What's your name?
Yamada: My name is Yamada. They all call me "Little Beijing".
Bill: This name is very interesting. My name is Bill. Glad to meet you.
Yamada: Me too. Goodbye!
Bill: Bye-bye!

---

[1] Yamada is the Japanese pronunciation of 山田.

[2] The word *xiǎo* 小 is often used to indicate an affection to younger people.

[3] 个 is used very commonly in Chinese. It appears before people, things or ideas with certain numbers. For example: *yí gè rén* 一个人 (a person), *yí gè miànbāo* 一个面包 (a loaf of bread), *yí gè xiǎngfǎ* 一个想法 (an idea).

Required Words and Expressions

xiànzài 现在	now
jǐ 几	how many
diǎn 点	o'clock
liúxuéshēng 留学生	international student
Rìběn 日本	Japan
nǎ 哪	which
guó 国	country
rén 人	people
Měiguó 美国	the United States of America
dàjiā 大家	everybody
xiǎo 小	little
Běijīng 北京	Beijing
gè 个	(a commonly used measure word)
yǒuyìsi 有意思	interesting
zàijiàn 再见	goodbye

ℬ 个人练习　Self-practice

Word Order: Create sentences by arranging the following words in the appropriate order.

1. ①我 wǒ　②日本 Rìběn　③是 shì　④人 rén ＿＿＿＿＿＿
2. ①是 shì　②你 nǐ　③国 guó　④哪 nǎ　⑤人 rén ＿＿＿＿＿＿
3. ①都 dōu　②叫 jiào　③大家 dàjiā　④我 wǒ　⑤小北京 xiǎoBěijīng ＿＿＿＿＿＿
4. ①有意思 yǒuyìsi　②名字 míngzi　③很 hěn　④这个 zhège ＿＿＿＿＿＿

𝒞 二人练习　Pair Work

Nationality: With a partner, practice asking for and giving information about nationality.

A：你是哪国人？ Nǐ shì nǎ guó rén?
B：我是日本人。你呢？ Wǒ shì Rìběnrén. Nǐ ne?
A：我是美国人。 Wǒ shì Měiguórén.

Hánguó		Yìdàlì	
韩国	South Korea	意大利	Italy
Jiānádà		Fǎguó	
加拿大	Canada	法国	France
Mòxīgē		Yìndù	
墨西哥	Mexico	印度	India

𝒟 小组活动　Group Work

Who is it? Think of a student in the class. The other students in your class will ask Yes-no questions to guess which classmate you're thinking of.

他是 男同学 吗？ Tā shì nántóngxué ma? ／ 她是 女同学 吗？ Tā shì nǚtóngxué ma?

他姓 什么？ Tā xìng shénme? ／ 她姓 什么？ Tā xìng shénme?

他是哪国人？ Tā shì nǎ guó rén ／ 她是哪国人？ Tā shì nǎ guó rén

他高吗？ 帅 吗？ Tā gāo ma? Shuài ma? ／ 她 漂亮 吗？ 可爱吗？ Tā piàoliang ma? Kě'ài ma?

他喜欢 什么？ Tā xǐhuan shénme? ／ 她 喜欢 什么？ Tā xǐhuan shénme?

Expanded Words and Expressions

	nán	
男		male
	nǚ	
女		female
	tóngxué	
同学		classmate

听与说　Listen and Speak

Listen to the recording and read silently. Listen again and repeat the names of the countries after you hear them.

Top 10 Countries by GDP

Měiguó
1. 美国　United States

Éluósī
6. 俄罗斯　Russia

Zhōngguó
2. 中国　China

Yīngguó
7. 英国　United Kingdom

Rìběn
3. 日本　Japan

Bāxī
8. 巴西　Brazil

Yìndù
4. 印度　India

Fǎguó
9. 法国　France

Déguó
5. 德国　Germany

Yìdàlì
10. 意大利　Italy

2010 List by the CIA World Factbook

二人练习　Pair Work

Countries and Cities: Match the following cities with the correct countries from Activity A. Then try to say the names of the countries and their cities in Chinese. How many can you remember?

Bālí
a. 巴黎　Paris

Bólín
f. 柏林　Berlin

Huáshèngdùn
b. 华盛顿　Washington D. C.

Luómǎ
g. 罗马　Rome

Lúndūn
c. 伦敦　London

Dōngjīng
h. 东京　Tokyo

Lǐyuērènèilú
d. 里约热内卢　Rio de Janeiro

Xīndélǐ
i. 新德里　New Delhi

Mòsīkē
e. 莫斯科　Moscow

Běijīng
j. 北京　Beijing

03 时间 Time

A 听与说 Listen and Speak

Listen to the recording and read silently. Listen again and repeat the time after you hear them.

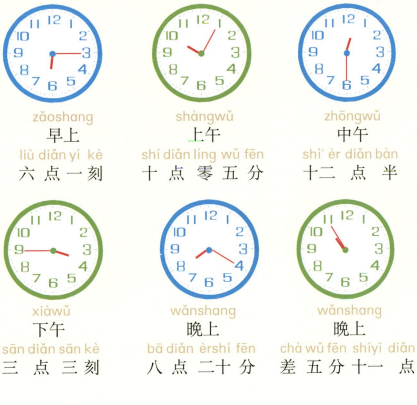

zǎoshang
早上
liù diǎn yí kè
六 点 一 刻

shàngwǔ
上午
shí diǎn líng wǔ fēn
十 点 零 五 分

zhōngwǔ
中午
shí' èr diǎn bàn
十二 点 半

xiàwǔ
下午
sān diǎn sān kè
三 点 三 刻

wǎnshang
晚上
bā diǎn èrshí fēn
八 点 二十 分

wǎnshang
晚上
chà wǔ fēn shíyī diǎn
差 五 分 十一 点

B 二人练习 Pair Work

What time is it? Look at the clocks above and practice.

Xiànzài jǐ diǎn?
A：现在 几 点？
Xiànzài liù diǎn yí kè.
B：现在 六 点 一 刻。

C 班级活动 Class Activity

Calling Friends Overseas: Wang Yi and Lin Mu are calling friends in different parts of the world. Listen to the conversation and complete the chart.

Name	Country	City	Time
Wáng Jūn 王 军			
Lǐ Xiǎowěi 李 小伟			

Expanded Words and Expressions

shàngwǔ	上午	morning
zhōngwǔ	中午	noon
xiàwǔ	下午	afternoon
wǎnshang	晚上	night
kè	刻	quarter (of an hour)
fēn	分	minute
bàn	半	half
chà	差	to be less than

Tip

Pay attention to the time changes for the different time zones. In Chinese, this is called *shíchā* 时差.

听与说　Listen and Speak

Listen to the recording and read silently. Listen again and repeat the sentences after you hear them, and then practice the conversation in pairs.

At Jenny's Home
Jenny holds a family photo and chats with her classmate, Wang Damin, about her family.

Zhēnnī:　Zhè shì wǒ de quánjiāfú.　Wǒ jiā yǒu sì
珍妮：这是我的全家福[1]。我家有四
kǒu rén:　bàba,　māma,　gēge hé wǒ.
口人：爸爸、妈妈、哥哥和我。

Wáng Dàmín:　Tāmēn zuò shénme gōngzuò?
王大民：他们做什么工作？

Zhēnnī:　Wǒ bàba shì yīshēng.　Wǒ māma
珍妮：我爸爸是医生。我妈妈
zài xuéxiào gōngzuò,　tā shì lǎoshī.
在学校工作，她是老师。

Wáng Dàmín:　Nǐ gēge ne?
王大民：你哥哥呢？

Zhēnnī:　Tā shì xuésheng,　xiànzài zài Běijīng Dàxué
珍妮：他是学生，现在在北京大学
xuéxí.
学习。

Wáng Dàmín:　Tā shuō bu shuō Hànyǔ?
王大民：他说不说汉语？

Zhēnnī:　Tā shì gè "Zhōngguótōng".
珍妮：他是个"中国通[2]"。

Wáng Dàmín:　Wǒ xǐhuan nǐ de jiārén.
王大民：我喜欢你的家人。

Jenny:　This is my family photo. There are four members in my family: my father, my mother, my elder brother and I.

Wang:　What do they do?

Jenny:　My father is a doctor. My mother works at a school. She is a teacher.

Wang:　What about your elder brother?

Jenny:　He is a student, and he is studying at Peking University now.

Wang:　Can he speak Chinese?

Jenny:　He is an expert on China.

Wang:　I like your family.

---

[1] *Quánjiāfú* 全家福 means "family photo".

[2] *Tōng* 通 means "to be an expert in some field".

Required Words and Expressions

jiā 家	home, family
kǒu 口	(a measure word for family members)
bàba 爸爸	father
gēge 哥哥	elder brother
hé 和	and
zuò 做	to do
gōngzuò 工作	job; to work
yīshēng 医生	doctor
zài 在	in
xuéxiào 学校	school
lǎoshī 老师	teacher
xuésheng 学生	student
dàxué 大学	university
xuéxí 学习	to study
shuō 说	to speak
jiārén 家人	family member

B 个人练习　Self-practice

Word Order: Create sentences by arranging the following words in the appropriate order.

1. ① 爸爸 bàba ② 我 wǒ ③ 医生 yīshēng ④ 是 shì ＿＿＿＿＿＿＿

2. ① 工作 gōngzuò ② 妈妈 māma ③ 你 nǐ ④ 什么 shénme
   ⑤ 做 zuò ＿＿＿＿＿＿＿

3. ① 北京 Běijīng ② 在 zài ③ 他 tā ④ 现在 xiànzài ＿＿＿＿＿＿＿

4. ① 中国通 Zhōngguótōng ② 他 tā ③ 个 gè ④ 是 shì ＿＿＿＿＿＿＿

C 二人练习　Pair Work

Family Members and Occupations: Tell your partner about your family and their jobs.

A：你 爸爸 做 什么 工作？
Nǐ bàba zuò shénme gōngzuò?
B：我 爸爸 是 医生。
Wǒ bàba shì yīshēng.

……

律师 lùshī	lawyer	商人 shāngrén	businessman
工程师 gōngchéngshī	engineer	心理学家 xīnlǐxuéjiā	psychologist
记者 jìzhě	journalist	护士 hùshi	nurse

D 小组活动　Group Work

Family Presentation: Make a presentation about your family members and present it to your group.

我 叫 张 小明，我 是 学生。
Wǒ jiào Zhāng Xiǎomíng, wǒ shì xuésheng.
我 爸爸 叫 张 文，他 是 医生。
Wǒ bàba jiào Zhāng Wén, tā shì yīshēng.
我 妈妈 叫 赵 丽，她 是 老师。
Wǒ māma jiào Zhào Lì, tā shì lǎoshī.

……

05 词汇扩展 **Word Power**

■ 听与说 **Listen and Speak** 🎧

Listen to the recording and read silently. Listen again and repeat the sentences after you hear them.

1. My grandpa is a doctor.
2. My grandma is a housewife.
3. My father is an office clerk.
4. My mother is a lawyer.
5. I am a student.

Yéye shì yīshēng.
1. 爷爷是 医生 。

Nǎinai shì jiātíng zhǔfù.
2. 奶奶 是 家庭 主妇。

Bàba shì gōngsī zhíyuán.
3. 爸爸 是 公司 职员 。

Māma shì lùshī.
4. 妈妈是律师。

Wǒ shì xuésheng.
5. 我是 学生 。

Expanded Words and Expressions

yéye
爷爷   grandpa (on the father's side)

nǎi nai
奶奶   grandma (on the father's side)

jiātíng zhǔfù
家庭主妇   housewife

gōngsī
公司   company

zhíyuán
职员   office clerk

☺ 休息一下 **Break Time**

Practice writing the following two characters using the proper stroke order indicated below.

❶ nán   丨 口 日 日 田 甼 男

男
(male)

❷ nǔ   乙 女 女

女
(female)

06 句型操练 Sentence Patterns

𝒜 听与说 Listen and Speak

Listen to the recording and read silently. Listen again and repeat the sentences after you hear them.

subj. + v. + obj. + 吗?	subj. + v. + 不 + v. + obj.?
Tā shuō Hànyǔ ma? 他 说 汉语 吗?	Tā shuō bu shuō Hànyǔ? 他 说 不 说 汉语?
Tā xǐhuan Běijīng ma? 她 喜欢 北京 吗?	Tā xǐhuan bu xǐhuan 她 喜欢 不 喜欢 Běijīng? 北京?

Nǐ xǐhuan bu xǐhuan Běijīng?
你 喜欢 不 喜欢 北京?

ℬ 选择 Choose the correct answer.

Choose the correct words in parentheses to complete the conversation. Then practice with your partner.

A：Nǐ gēge
你 哥哥 _____ (shì / bú shì) xuésheng ma?
（是 / 不是）学 生 吗?

B：Wǒ gēge shì xuésheng. Tā xiànzài zài Zhōngguó xuéxí.
我 哥哥 是 学生 。他 现在 在 中国 学习。

A：Tā shuō bu shuō Hànyǔ
他 说 不 说 汉语 _____ (－/ma)?
（－/吗）?

B：Tā shuō Hànyǔ, yě shuō Rìyǔ.
他 说 汉语 ，也 说 日语。

𝒞 二人练习 Pair Work

Occupations and Preferences: Talk with your partner regarding your family members' occupations, preferences, and so forth.

A：Nǐ jiějie shì bu shì lǎoshī?
你 姐姐 是 不 是 老师?

B：Bù, tā bú shì lǎoshī. Tā shì gōngsī zhíyuán.
不, 她 不 是 老师。她 是 公司 职员 。

A：Tā xǐhuan bu xǐhuan chànggē?
她 喜欢 不 喜欢 唱歌 ?

B：Tā xǐhuan chànggē, yě hěn xǐhuan zuòfàn.
她 喜欢 唱歌 ，也 很 喜欢 做饭。

A：Tā xǐ bu xǐhuan kàn shū?
她 喜 不 喜欢[1] 看 书?

B：Tā bù xǐhuan kàn shū.
她 不 喜欢 看 书。

---

[1] xǐ bu xǐhuan 喜不喜欢 = xǐhuan bu xǐhuan 喜欢不喜欢

Expanded Words and Expressions

jiějie 姐姐	elder sister
mèimei 妹妹	younger sister
dìdi 弟弟	younger brother

07 称呼 Titles

1. A: Hello, Mr. Zhang.
   B: Hello, Ms. Zhou.
2. A: Goodbye, Aunt Zhou and Uncle Zhang.
   B: Bye-bye.
3. A: Where are you going, Uncle Wang and Aunt Li?
4. A: How are you, Grandpa Wang and Grandma Li?

Expanded Words and Expressions

xiānsheng 先生	sir, mister
nǚshì 女士	lady
shūshu 叔叔	uncle
nǎr 哪儿	where

---

[1] *Bàibài* 拜拜 is commonly used by young people in China to say goodbye. The actual pronunciation of 拜拜 in oral Chinese is very similar to "bye-bye" in English. The original 4th tone pronunciation of this word is not used.

[2] *Nǎ* 哪 means "which" when it occurs before nouns. For example, *nǎ guó* 哪国 means "which country" and *nǎ nián* 哪年 means "which year". However, the basic meaning of *nǎr* 哪儿 is "where".

听与说　Listen and Speak

Listen to the recording and read silently. Listen again and repeat the sentences after you hear them, and then practice the conversations in pairs.

1. A：
   Zhāng xiānsheng,　nǐ hǎo!
   张　先生，你好!
   B：
   Zhōu nǚshì,　nǐ hǎo!
   周 女士，你好!

2. A：
   Zhōu āyí,　Zhāng shūshu,　zàijiàn!
   周 阿姨，张　叔叔，再见!
   B：
   Bàibài!
   拜拜[1]!

3. A：
   Wáng dàye,　Lǐ dàmā,　qù nǎr　a?
   王 大爷，李大妈，去哪儿[2]啊?

4. A：
   Wáng yéye,　Lǐ nǎinai,　nǐmen hǎo!
   王 爷爷，李奶奶，你们 好!

☺ 休息一下　Break Time

Listen to the recording and read silently. Listen again and repeat the sentences after you hear them.

Pay attention to the pronunciation of the two consonants *m* and *n*, and the tones of *a* and *iu* while repeating the sentences. Then compete with a partner trying to say the two sentences as quickly and accurately as you can.

Niūniu qí niú,　niú nìng,　niūniu niǔ niú.
妞妞 骑牛，牛 拧，妞妞 扭 牛。
Daughter rides a cow and twists it for its stubbornness.

Māma qí mǎ,　mǎ màn,　māma mà mǎ.
妈妈 骑马，马 慢，妈妈 骂马。
Mother rides a horse and curses it for its slow speed.

08 文化掠影 Culture Snapshot

☐ With its rapid economic development, **Beijing** has undeniably become one of the most viable global metropolitan cities, thus attracting a lot of international students. With global symbols, bilingual signs, modern transportation and the Internet, it does not come as a surprise that there are many non-native Chinese speakers in Beijing. Some of them can speak so fluently that they are easily mistaken for Beijing locals judging from their genuine Beijing accent.

☐ **Forms of address** are an important aspect of Chinese culture. It is common for relatives to address their elder male siblings as *gēge* 哥哥, and their younger male siblings as *dìdi* 弟弟. Likewise, you will always hear people call their elder female siblings *jiějie* 姐姐 or their younger female siblings *mèimei* 妹妹. Even among friends and colleagues, or even strangers, people use *dàgē* 大哥 or *xiǎodì* 小弟 to address older or younger males, respectively, and *dàjiě* 大姐 or *xiǎomèi* 小妹 to address older or younger females. *Dàye* 大爷 and *dàmā* 大妈 are used to address men and women who are older than your parents. *Yéye* 爷爷 and *nǎinai* 奶奶 are common ways to address elderly men and women whose ages are similar to your grandparents. Chinese usually add the surname before these titles, just like *Wáng dàye* 王大爷 and *Lǐ dàmā* 李大妈. In formal settings, Chinese use *xiānsheng* 先生 and *nǚshì* 女士 to refer to gentlemen and ladies, respectively. This is very different from the custom of addressing friends, siblings, or colleagues commonly used in the U.S.

☐ In China, **seniority** is very much respected. Usually you call people by their **titles or roles** in the family. It is pretty rare to call your boss by his or her first name, or to call your uncle or aunt by his or her first name.

1 Telling Time

In Chinese, there are equivalents to "o'clock", "quarter to/after" and "minute" in English. Please see the following examples.

3:00	three o'clock	3:00　三 点 （钟） sān diǎn (zhōng)
10:05	five minutes after ten	10:05　十 点 零 五 分 shí diǎn líng wǔ fēn
5:15	a quarter after five / five fifteen	5:15　五 点 一 刻/五 点 十五 分 wǔ diǎn yí kè/wǔ diǎn shíwǔ fēn
6:30	half past six / six thirty	6:30　六 点 半/六 点 三十 分 liù diǎn bàn/liù diǎn sānshí fēn
7:45	seven and three quarters / a quarter to eight / seven forty-five	7:45　七 点 三 刻/差 一 刻 八 点/七 点 四十 五 分 qī diǎn sān kè/chà yí kè bā diǎn/qī diǎn sìshíwǔ fēn
8:55	five to nine / eight fifty-five	8:55　差 五 分 九 点/八 点 五十五 分 chà wǔ fēn jiǔ diǎn/bā diǎn wǔshíwǔ fēn

Word Order

早上 ／ 上午 / 中午 /下午/ 晚上 ＋时间
zǎoshang/shàngwǔ/zhōngwǔ/xiàwǔ/wǎnshang+shíjiān

early morning/morning/noon/afternoon/evening+time

早上 七 点 半
zǎoshang qī diǎn bàn

half past seven in the morning

下午 四 点 二十 分
xiàwǔ sì diǎn èrshí fēn

four twenty in the afternoon

A：现在 几 点 ？
Xiànzài jǐ diǎn?

A: What time is it now?

B：现在 中午 十 二 点 半。
Xiànzài zhōngwǔ shí' èr diǎn bàn.

B: It's 12:30.

2 Asking Which-questions with the Interrogative Pronoun 哪

哪 is an interrogative pronoun. The word order of 哪 sentences is the same as declarative sentences. However, in this case 哪 indicates a question, and these sentences should be spoken with natural rise in intonation or keep level intonation, stressing 哪.

(1) A：你 是 哪 国 人？
Nǐ shì nǎ guó rén?

(1) A: Where are you from?

B：我 是 美国人。
Wǒ shì Měiguórén.

B: I am American.

(2) A：你 是 哪个 学校 的 学生 ？
Nǐ shì nǎge xuéxiào de xuésheng?

(2) A: Which university do you study in?

B：我 是 北京 大学 的 学生 。
Wǒ shì Běijīng Dàxué de xuésheng.

B: I am a student from Peking University.

3 Asking Others to Confirm Information Using 吗 or Verb+不+Verb Questions

You have already learned that a declarative sentence can be changed into a Yes-no question by adding the question particle 吗 at the end of it.

Nǐ shì Bǐ'ěr ma?
A：你 是 比尔 吗？

Wǒ shì Bǐ'ěr.
B：我 是 比尔。

Wǒ bú shì Bǐ'ěr.
C：我 不 是 比尔。

A: Are you Bill?
B: I am Bill.
C: I am not Bill.

Verb+不+verb questions repeat the negative form of the verb just after the affirmative form. Answering verb+不+verb questions is the same as answering questions with particles, like those with 吗. The subject and the object of the question can be omitted from the answer.

Tā shuō bu shuō Hànyǔ?
(1) A：他 说 不 说 汉语？

(Tā) bù shuō (Hànyǔ), tā shuō Rìyǔ.
B：(他) 不 说 (汉语)，他 说 日语。

Nǐ rèn(shi) bú rènshi tā?
(2) A：你 认(识) 不 认识 他？

(Wǒ) rènshi (tā). Tā shì Bǐ'ěr.
B：(我) 认识 (他)。他 是 比尔。

(1) A: Can he speak Chinese?
   B: He cannot speak Chinese.
      He can speak Japanese.
(2) A: Do you know him?
   B: Yes, I do. He is Bill.

Remember that when you ask questions in the verb+不+verb model, you do not add 吗 at the end of the sentences.

10 语法练习 Grammar Practice

1 Make complete sentences following the examples given.

Xiànzài jǐ diǎn?
❶ A：现在几点？
Xiànzài bā diǎn.
B：现在八点。

7:30
12:55
21:15

Nǐ shì nǎ guó rén?
❷ A：你 是 哪 国 人？
Wǒ shì Měiguórén.
B：我 是 美国人。

tā   Zhōngguórén
他   中国人
tā   Rìběnrén
她   日本人
tāmen Yīngguórén
他们 英国人

Nǐ zuò shénme gōngzuò?
❸ A：你 做 什么 工作？
Wǒ shì yīshēng.
B：我 是 医生。

tā   jìzhě
她   记者
tāmen   gōngsī zhíyuán
他们   公司 职员
tāmen   hùshi
她们   护士

2 **Complete the following sentences with the words given.**

nǎ	jiào	shénme	nǎr	jǐ
哪	叫	什么	哪儿	几

Tāmen ___ wǒ māma Wáng tàitai.
① 她们 _____ 我 妈妈 王 太太。

Nǐ zuò ___ gōngzuò?
② A：你 做 _____ 工作 ？

Wǒ shì lǎoshī.
B：我 是 老师。

Nǐ zài ___ xuéxí?
③ A：你 在 _____ 学习？

Wǒ zài Běijīng Dàxué xuéxí.
B：我 在 北京 大学 学习。

Xiànzài ___ diǎn le?
④ A：现在 _____ 点 了？

Xiànzài wǔ diǎn.
B：现在 五 点 。

Nǐ shì ___ guó rén?
⑤ A：你 是 _____ 国 人？

Wǒ shì Déguórén.
B：我 是 德国人 。

3 **Rewrite the following sentences in the form indicated.**

Xiànzài bā diǎn.
① 现在 八点 。 Make a question about the underlined words.

_____

Wǒ shì Fǎguórén.
② 我是 法国人 。 Make a question about the underlined words.

_____

Wǒ xǐhuan hē kāfēi.
③ 我 喜欢 喝 咖啡 。 Make a question using the form verb + 不 + verb.

_____

Tā jiào Měiměi.
④ 她 叫 美美 。 Make a question about the underlined words.

_____

Tā zài Zhōngguó.
⑤ 他 在 中国 。 Make a question about the underlined words.

_____

11 语音提示 Pronunciation Tips

1 How to Pronounce *r*

Read the following syllables, paying special attention to their initials.

zhī	chī	shī	rì
Rìběn	Rìyǔ	rénshēng	rénrén

Tip

The consonant *r* in Chinese is similar to the first consonant of English word "round". However, as you pronounce the sound, the tongue should be curled back toward the roof of the mouth just like when you say *zh*, *ch* and *sh*.

2 How to Pronounce the Titles of Family Members

Read the following words and try to find their common characteristics.

bàba	māma	gēge
爸爸	妈妈	哥哥
shūshu	yéye	nǎinai
叔叔	爷爷	奶奶

Tip

These words are all used to address family members. The second syllable of each of these titles is a neutral tone.

3 Pauses in a Sentence

Read the sentences and find the right pause points in each sentence.

Wǒ jiā yǒu sì kǒu rén: bàba, māma, gēge hé wǒ.
1. 我家有四口人：爸爸、妈妈、哥哥和我。

Tā xiànzài zài Běijīng xuéxí.
2. 他现在在北京学习。

Tā shuō bu shuō Hànyǔ?
3. 他说不说汉语？

Tip

Pauses are determined by meaningful chunks or phrases of a sentence.
For instance:
Tā xiànzài zài Běijīng xuéxí.
他|现在|在北京|学习。
Tā shuō bu shuō Hànyǔ?
他|说不说|汉语？

12 汉字书写 Writing Chinese Characters

1 笔画复习 Stroke Review

In Units 1 and 2, you have learned that Chinese characters have eight main types of strokes. Please write the following character and explain each stroke.

yǒng

永
(forever)

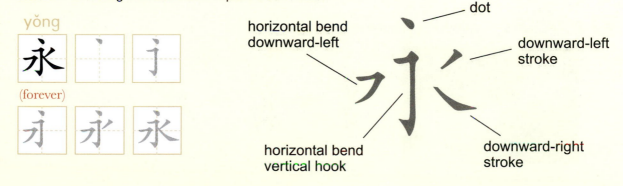

horizontal bend downward-left

dot

downward-left stroke

horizontal bend vertical hook

downward-right stroke

When writing a Chinese character, it is important to follow the correct stroke order. The general principles are as follows.

xiān wài hòu lǐ
先 外 后 里 from outside to inside

eg. 问 `wèn`
(to ask)

丶 丨 门 门 问 问

xiān wài hòu lǐ zài fēngkǒu
先 外 后 里再 封 口 from outside to inside then enclose

eg. 国 `guó`
(country)

丨 冂 冂 冃 用 国 国 国

xiān zhōngjiān hòu liǎngbiān
先 中间 后 两边 center before sides

eg. 小 `xiǎo`
(small)

丨 小 小

You can write it!

Practice writing the following Chinese characters. Don't forget to follow the correct stroke order!

`yǒng` 丶 乛 ⺈ 永 永				
永	永			

(forever)

`wèn` 丶 丨 门 问 问				
问	问			

(to ask)

`guó` 丨 冂 冂 冃 用 国 国 国				
国	国			

(country)

`zài` 一 ナ 才 右 在 在				
在	在			

(in)

`jǐ` 丿 几				
几	几			

(how many)

`diǎn` 丨 卜 占 占 点 点 点 点				
点	点			

(o'clock)

3 汉字的演变 **Evolution of Chinese Characters**

 → 水

13 综合练习　Integrative Practice

Listening

1 Listen to the following words and mark the missing tones. 🎧

Meiguo	xianzai	jiao	mama	gongzuo	he kafei	laoshi	xuesheng
美国	现在	叫	妈妈	工作	喝咖啡	老师	学生

2 Listen to the following conversation and match the questions to their responses. 🎧

Nǐ shì nǎ guó rén?
① 你是哪国人?

Nǐ jiào shénme míngzi?
② 你叫什么名字?

Nǐ zuò shénme gōngzuò?
③ 你做什么工作?

Wǒ jiào Mǎkè.
a. 我叫马克。

Wǒ shì lǎoshī.
b. 我是老师。

Wǒ shì Jiānádàrén.
c. 我是加拿大人。

3 Listen to the recording and decide whether the following statements are true or false. 🎧

T　F

Xiànzài shì Dōngjīng shíjiān zǎoshang bā diǎn sìshíwǔ fēn.
① 现在是东京时间早上八点四十五分。　□　□

Xiànzài shì Bólín shíjiān wǎnshang jiǔ diǎn bàn.
② 现在是柏林时间晚上九点半。　□　□

Xiànzài shì Běijīng shíjiān zhōngwǔ shíyī diǎn wǔshíwǔ fēn.
③ 现在是北京时间中午十一点五十五分。　□　□

Speaking

1 With a partner, read the following conversation aloud.

(Mark runs into Tony in the subway.)

Mǎkè: Hēi, Tuōní!
马克：嘿，托尼!

Tuōní: Nǐ hǎo, Mǎkè!
托尼：你好，马克!

Mǎkè: Hěn gāoxìng jiàndào nǐ.
马克：很高兴见到你。

Tuōní: Wǒ yě shì. Nǐ xiànzài zài nǎr gōngzuò?
托尼：我也是。你现在在哪儿工作?

Mǎkè: Wǒ zài Běijīng Dàxué gōngzuò.
马克：我在北京大学工作。

Expanded Words and Expressions

qīzi
妻子　wife

nǚ'ér
女儿　daughter

érzi
儿子　son

Tuōní: Nǐ de jiārén yě zài Běijīng ma?
托尼： 你的家人也在北京吗？

Mǎkè: Shìde, wǒ de qīzi hé liǎng gè nǚ'ér yě zài Běijīng Dàxué gōngzuò. Wǒmen dōu shì
马克： 是的，我的妻子和两个女儿也在北京大学工作。我们都是

lǎoshī. Nǐ ne?
老师。你呢？

Tuōní: Wǒ shì gōngchéngshī, zài IBM de Běijīng gōngsī gōngzuò. Wǒ qīzi yě zài Běijīng, tā
托尼： 我是工程师，在IBM的北京公司工作。我妻子也在北京，她

shì lǜshī. Wǒ érzi zài Rìběn gōngzuò.
是律师。我儿子在日本工作。

Nǐ xiànzài zài nǎr gōngzuò?
你现在在哪儿工作？

2 Take turns answering the following questions with a partner.

Tāmen zài nǎge chéngshì?
1. 他们在哪个城市？

Mǎkè jiā yǒu jǐ kǒu rén?
2. 马克家有几口人？

Mǎkè de jiārén zuò shénme gōngzuò?
3. 马克的家人做什么工作？

Tuōní zuò shénme gōngzuò?
4. 托尼做什么工作？

Tuōní de érzi zài nǎr?
5. 托尼的儿子在哪儿？

1. Which city are they in?
2. How many people are there in Mark's family?
3. What do Mark's family members do?
4. What does Tony do?
5. Where is Tony's son?

3 Now practice the conversation from Activity 1 with your partner, substituting your own information where you can.

Reading

Answer the following questions after reading the article carefully.

Bǐ'ěr de bókè
比尔的博客 Bill's Blog

首页　博文　图片　关于我

个人资料

Bill
20岁
美国人

📺 播客　🌀 微博
🏠 进入我的空间

加好友　发纸条
写留言　加关注

博客等级：**22**
博客积分：**806**
博客访问：**5,631,496**

正文

Jīntiān zǎoshang wǒ rènshile yí gè
今天 早上 我 认识了一个
péngyou, tā shì Rìběnrén, jiào Shāntián. Tā
朋友，他是 日本人，叫 山田。他
hěn shuài, tā de Hànyǔ yě hěn hǎo, dàjiā dōu
很 帅，他的 汉语 也 很 好，大家 都
jiào tā "xiǎoBěijīng". Tāmen jiā yǒu sì kǒu rén:
叫 他 "小北京"。他们 家 有 四 口 人：
tā de bàba shì gōngsī jīnglǐ, māma shì
他的 爸爸 是 公司 经理，妈妈 是
jiātíng zhǔfù, jiějie shì yīshēng, Shāntián
家庭 主妇，姐姐 是 医生，山田
xiànzài yě shì Běijīng Dàxué de
现 在 也 是 北 京 大 学 的
liúxuéshēng. Rènshi tā wǒ hěn gāoxing.
留学生。认识 他 我 很 高兴。

Expanded Words and Expressions

jīnglǐ
经理　manager

Jīntiān zǎoshang Bǐ'ěr rènshile shéi?
1. 今天 早上 比尔认识了 谁？

Shāntián jiā yǒu jǐ kǒu rén?
2. 山田 家有几口 人？

Shāntián de bàba zuò shénme gōngzuò?
3. 山田 的爸爸做 什么 工作？

Shāntián de jiějie zuò shénme gōngzuò?
4. 山田 的姐姐做 什么 工作？

Bǐ'ěr hé Shāntián dōu shì liúxuéshēng
5. 比尔和 山田 都 是 留学生
ma?
吗？

1. Who did Bill meet this morning?
2. How many people are there in Yamada's family?
3. What does Yamada's father do?
4. What does Yamada's elder sister do?
5. Are Bill and Yamada both international students?

Writing

Use some of the words you have learned in Units 1-3 to write a blog in Chinese introducing a friend you met recently. Feel free to add more information at the end of the blog as well.

首页　博文　图片　关于我

个人资料

_____ 岁
_____ 人

正文

Wǒ rènshile yí gè péngyou, tā / tā jiào _____, tā / tā shì
我认识了一个 朋友，他/她 叫_____，他 /她 是_____
rén. Tā / Tā hěn _____, yě hěn _____.
人。他/她 很 _____，也 很_____。
Tā / Tā jiā yǒu _____ kǒu rén: bàba shì _____, zài _____ gōngzuò;
他/她家 有 _____ 口 人：爸爸 是_____，在_____ 工作；
māma shì _____ ...
妈妈 是_____……

Word List of Unit 3

Míngcí 名词 (Nouns)

爸爸	bàba	father
北京	Běijīng	Beijing
大学	dàxué	university
哥哥	gēge	elder brother
国	guó	country
家	jiā	home, family
家人	jiārén	family member
老师	lǎoshī	teacher
留学生	liúxuéshēng	international student
美国	Měiguó	the United States of America
人	rén	people
日本	Rìběn	Japan
现在	xiànzài	now
学生	xuésheng	student
学校	xuéxiào	school
医生	yīshēng	doctor

Dòngcí 动词 (Verbs)

说	shuō	to speak
学习	xuéxí	to study
再见	zàijiàn	goodbye
做	zuò	to do

Jiānlèicí 兼类词 (Conversion Word)

| 工作 | gōngzuò | *n. / v.* job; to work |

Xíngróngcí 形容词 (Adjective)

| 小 | xiǎo | little |

Dàicí 代词 (Pronouns)

| 大家 | dàjiā | everybody |
| 哪 | nǎ | which |

Jiècí 介词 (Preposition)

| 在 | zài | in |

Liáncí 连词 (Conjunction)

| 和 | hé | and |

Shùcí 数词 (Numeral)

| 几 | jǐ | how many |

Liàngcí 量词 (Measure Words)

点	diǎn	o'clock
个	gè	(a commonly used measure word)
口	kǒu	(a measure word for family members)

Chángyòng biǎodá 常用表达 (Expression)

| 有意思 | yǒuyìsi | interesting |

Míngcí 名词 (Nouns)

弟弟	dìdi	younger brother
儿子	érzi	son
公司	gōngsī	company
家庭主妇	jiātíng zhǔfù	housewife
姐姐	jiějie	elder sister
经理	jīnglǐ	manager
妹妹	mèimei	younger sister
奶奶	nǎinai	grandma (on the father's side)

女儿	nǚ'ér	daughter
女士	nǚshì	lady
妻子	qīzi	wife
上午	shàngwǔ	morning
叔叔	shūshu	uncle
同学	tóngxué	classmate
晚上	wǎnshang	night
下午	xiàwǔ	afternoon
先生	xiānsheng	sir, mister
爷爷	yéye	grandpa (on the father's side)
职员	zhíyuán	office clerk
中午	zhōngwǔ	noon

Dòngcí 动词 (Verb)

差	chà	to be less than

Xíngróngcí 形容词 (Adjectives)

男	nán	male
女	nǚ	female

Dàicí 代词 (Pronoun)

哪儿	nǎr	where

Shùcí 数词 (Numeral)

半	bàn	half

Liàngcí 量词 (Measure Words)

分	fēn	minute
刻	kè	quarter (of an hour)

Suggested Words and Expressions
(For Comprehension Only)

Míngcí 名词 (Nouns)

大妈	dàmā	(the title of a woman older than your parents)
大爷	dàye	(the title of a man older than your parents)
法国	Fǎguó	France
工程师	gōngchéngshī	engineer
韩国	Hánguó	South Korea
护士	hùshi	nurse
记者	jìzhě	journalist

加拿大	Jiānádà	Canada
律师	lǜshī	lawyer
墨西哥	Mòxīgē	Mexico
全家福	quánjiāfú	family photo
商人	shāngrén	businessman
心理学家	xīnlǐxuéjiā	psychologist
意大利	Yìdàlì	Italy
印度	Yìndù	India
中国通	Zhōngguótōng	an expert on China

Dòngcí 动词 (Verb)

拜拜	bàibài (baibai)	bye-bye

01 语音营　Pronunciation Kit

A Read the following characters and words, and group them according to the tones.

多　好　岁　这　吗　真　也　很　和
姓　是　的　都　您　叫　茶　了　几

声调 (Tones)	字 (Characters)
━（一声）	多
╱（二声）	您
╲╱（三声）	好
╲（四声）	这
·（轻声）	吗

你好　什么　认识　中国　请客　希望　号码
地图　年轻　汉语　哪里　没有　学习　喜欢
漂亮　名字　朋友　今年　钱包　谢谢　老师
工作　电话　今天　妈妈

声调 (Tones)	词 (Words)
━ ＋ ━/╱/╲╱/╲	中国
╱ ＋ ━/╱/╲╱/╲	年轻
╲╱ ＋ ━/╱/╲╱/╲	请客
╲ ＋ ━/╱/╲╱/╲	地图
━/╱/╲╱/╲ ＋ ·	什么

B Listen to the recording, and read the following poem with a partner, paying close attention to the pronunciation of each syllable as well as the flow of each line. 🎧

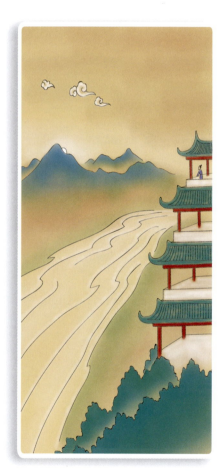

On the Stork Tower

Wang Zhihuan (Tang Dynasty)

The sun beyond the mountains glows;
The Yellow River seawards flows.
You can enjoy a grander sight
By climbing to a greater height.

(Translated by Xu Yuanchong)

Dēng Guànquè Lóu
登 鹳雀 楼
Wáng Zhīhuàn (Táng)
王 之涣 （唐）
Báirì yī shān jìn,　　Huáng Hé rù hǎi liú.
白日依山尽，　黄 河入海流。
Yù qióng qiān lǐ mù,　Gèng shàng yì céng lóu.
欲穷 千里目，更 上 一层楼。

Group the following words with similar patterns or functions.

哥哥　　高兴　　地图　　喝茶　　中国　　书

美　　看书　　老师　　美国　　弟弟　　妹妹

护照　　睡觉　　购物　　医生　　俄罗斯　　可爱

律师　　钱包　　漂亮　　日本　　姐姐　　商人

Who is she/he?

How is she/he?

What's in your bag?

What would you like to do in your leisure time?

Which country do you want to visit most?

What kind of work do you want to do?

03 见字知意 Understanding the Meanings of the Chinese Characters

A Complete the sentences by filling in the blanks with the most appropriate word.

1. tā nǐ yě tā shén zuò
    他 你 也 她 什 做

(1) 我 （　　） 喜欢喝茶。

(2) （　　） 叫李丽，很漂亮。

(3) 你妈妈 （　　） 什么工作？

2. ma ba ne jiào hé kǒu
    吗 吧 呢 叫 和 口

(1) 我是中国人，你 （　　） ？

(2) 我们都喝茶 （　　） 。

(3) 我家有爸爸、妈妈 （　　） 我。

3. méi hàn míng péng piào wǎn
    没 汉 明 朋 漂 晚

(1) A：你的 （　　） 语很好。

    B：（　　） 有，（　　） 有。

(2) 我和我的好 （　　） 友 （　　）
    天 （　　） 上见。

4. duō dà duōshao shénme
    多大 多少 什么

(1) 你的电话号码是 （　　） ？

(2) 你今年 （　　） ？

(3) 你喝 （　　） ？

B Listen to the dialogues and select the correct answers. 🎧

❶ ☐ A．我也是美国人。

   ☐ B．他也是美国人。

❷ ☐ A．我哥哥在医院工作，他是医生。

   ☐ B．我哥哥是学生，他现在在美国学习。

❸ ☐ A．他喝茶。

   ☐ B．我喝茶。

❹ ☐ A．现在早上九点半。

   ☐ B．现在下午五点半。

❺ ☐ A．三口，爸爸、妈妈和我。

   ☐ B．四口，爸爸、妈妈、哥哥和我。

C List all the characters you know that have the following radicals.

口：叫 名 _____ 亻：你 他 _____

D Write the equivalent to each number using Chinese characters.

13893327284   一三八九三三二七二八四

3:05   三点零五

010-57193248   _____

京G43657   _____

12:30   _____

14:45   _____

04 语法实练 Grammar Workshop

A Complete the chart by adding the appropriate questions or responses as needed.

	我是英语老师，在北京大学工作。
你喜不喜欢喝茶？	
	我是美国人。
	我的电话是3470791。
现在几点了？ 你的汉语很好。	
	这是李丽送给我的礼物。

B Pair Work

Question and Answer: With a partner, take turns asking questions and providing answers from the chart in Activity A.

C Team Work

Creating a Dialogue: In groups of four, write a dialogue using all or some of the questions and answers that appear in Activity A. You may add more information as needed.

D Present your dialogue for the rest of the class.

Complete the dialogues.

1.
　Dàshān, nǐ hǎo!
大山，你好！

　　Dàshān, nǐ hǎo!
　A：大山，你好！

　B：……！

　　Jiàndào nǐ hěn gāoxìng.
　A：见到 你 很 高兴。

　　…. Zhè shì wǒ de Zhōngguó péngyou.
　B：……。这 是 我 的 中国　朋友。

　　Nǐ hǎo, wǒ xìng Zhōu, jiào Zhōu Péng.
　C：你好，我 姓 周，叫 周 朋。

　　Nǐ hǎo, wǒ xìng …, jiào …, rènshi nǐ hěn gāoxìng.
　A：你好，我 姓……，叫……，认识 你 很 高兴。

　Zhè shì wǒ de míngpiàn.　　　Zhōu Péng, Huáměi Gōngsī jīnglǐ, diànhuà shì
　C：这 是 我 的 名片 (business card)。周 朋，华美 公司 经理，电话 是

　　bā bā bā bā yāo bā yāo jiǔ.
　　8 8 8 8 1 8 1 9。

　　Xièxie, zhè shì wǒ de míngpiàn, …..
　A：谢谢，这 是 我 的 名片，……。

2.
　Nǐ hěn shuài!
你 很 帅！

　　Xiǎomíng, shēngrì kuàilè!
　A：小明，生日 快乐！

　Xièxie!
　B：谢谢！

　　Zhè shì sòng gěi nǐ de lǐwù!
　A：这 是 送 给 你 的 礼物！

　B：……！

　　Nǐ hěn shuài!
　A：你 很 帅！

　　….
　B：……。

　　Nǐ de xiàoróng …!
　A：你 的 笑容 ……！！

　　….
　B：……。

　　Nǐ gēge …!
　A：你 哥哥 ……！

　　….
　B：……。

　　Nǐ māma …!
　A：你 妈妈 ……！

　B：……。

3.
　Rènshi nín hěn gāoxìng!
认识 您 很 高兴！

　　Nín hǎo! Nín shì … ma?
　A：您 好！您 是……吗？

　Shì.
　B：是。

　　Nín hǎo! Rènshi nín hěn gāoxìng!
　A：您 好！认识 您 很 高兴！

　　….　　Nǐ jiào shénme míngzi?
　B：……。你 叫 什么 名字？

　　Wǒ jiào …
　A：我 叫……。

　　… ?
　B：……？

　　Wǒ … suì.
　A：我……岁。

　　Nǐ de diànhuà hàomǎ shì duōshao?
　B：你 的 电话 号码 是 多少？

　　Wǒ de diànhuà hàomǎ shì …..
　A：我 的 电话 号码 是……。

Nǐ zuò shénme gōngzuò?
4. 你 做 什么 工作？

A：…… , nǐ jiā yǒu jǐ kǒu rén?
……，你家有几口人？

B：Wǒ jiā yǒu … kǒu rén, nǐ jiā ne?
我家有……口人，你家呢？

A：Wǒ jiā yǒu … kǒu rén.
我家有……口人。

B：Nǐ zuò shénme gōngzuò?
你 做 什么 工作？

A：… shì … , zài … gōngzuò.
……是……，在…… 工作 。

B：Nǐ … ne?
你……呢？

A：Wǒ … shì … , … zài … gōngzuò.
我……是……，……在…… 工作 。

06 妙笔生花 Writing Project

A Make your own business card according to the sample.

中国华美公司

周 朋 经理

电话(Tel)：010-88881819
电子邮件(E-mail)：zhoupeng@gmail.com

B Write a short description of your family members to introduce them to your classmates. Don't forget to mention each family member's name, profession and age, along with any other details you would like to include.

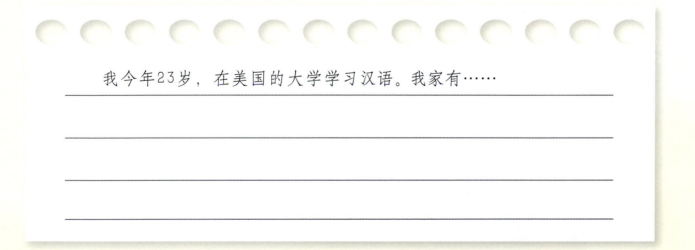

我今年23岁，在美国的大学学习汉语。我家有……

Unit 4 Dì-sì dānyuán 第四单元

In and Out of Class

Kè nèi kè wài
课内课外

Socializing with friends and classmates in Chinese is a great opportunity for you to use Chinese outside the classroom. By using Chinese to initiate an activity or event such as going to see a movie, you will be able to practice and learn the basic conversational vocabulary and grammatical patterns necessary to make, accept and decline invitations.

In this unit, you will learn:

FUNCTION

☐ to make plans: 我去上中国文化课。

☐ to make, accept and decline invitations, to make excuses:
  下课以后我们去KTV唱歌，怎么样？／好主意！

☐ to ask about and give information about time and location:
  我们什么时候见面？在哪儿？

GRAMMAR

☐ to express the time of an event or action using time phrases as adverbial phrases

☐ to give a suggestion or request using the sentence final modal particle 吧

☐ to form wh-questions using question words 谁，什么，什么时候，哪儿，哪个

CULTURE

☐ Chinese youth life

☐ Chinese way of declining invitations

☐ attitudes toward cultural differences

🖋 听与说 Listen and Speak 🎧

Listen to the recording and read silently. Listen again and repeat the sentences after you hear them, and then practice the conversation in pairs.

On Campus

Yamada runs into Bill on campus one day. They chat about a class on Chinese culture, and make plans for activities in the evening.

Shāntián: Nǐ jīntiān xiàwǔ zuò shénme?
山田：你今天下午做什么？

Bǐ ěr: Wǒ qù shàng Zhōngguó wénhuà kè.
比尔：我去上 中国 文化 课。

Shāntián: Wǒ kěyǐ qù pángtīng ma?
山田：我可以去 旁听 吗？

Bǐ ěr: Dāngrán kěyǐ. Wǒmen xiànzài qù zhàn zuò ba.
比尔：当然可以。我们 现在 去 占 座吧。

Shāntián: Zǒu ba. Xiàkè yǐhòu wǒmen qù KTV
山田：走吧。下课 以后 我们 去KTV[1]

chànggē, zěnmeyàng?
唱歌 ，怎么样？

Bǐ ěr: Hǎo zhǔyì! Wǒmen jiào Lǐ Lì yìqǐ qù ba.
比尔：好 主意[2]! 我们 叫 李 丽一起去 吧。

Shāntián: Hǎo. Wǒmen xiàkè hòu qù túshūguǎn zhǎo
山田：好。我们 下课 后 去 图书馆 找

tā ba.
她 吧。

Required Words and Expressions

qù 去	to go	
shàngkè 上课	to have a class	
wénhuà 文化	culture	
kěyǐ 可以	may	
pángtīng 旁听	to audit	
dāngrán 当然	of course	
zhàn zuò 占 座	to get a seat	
zǒu 走	to walk, to go	
xiàkè 下课	to dismiss a class	
yǐhòu 以后	after	
zěnmeyàng 怎么样	how, how about	
zhǔyi 主意	idea	
yìqǐ 一起	together	
túshūguǎn 图书馆	library	
zhǎo 找	to find	

Yamada: What are you going to do this afternoon?
Bill: I have a Chinese culture class.
Yamada: May I audit the class?
Bill: Sure. Let's go to get a seat.
Yamada: OK. Let's go to KTV after class, shall we?
Bill: Good idea! Shall we invite Li Li to come with us?
Yamada: Yeah, we will go to look for her at the library after class.

---

[1] KTV is the abbreviation of Karaoke TV, a place that provides Karaoke equipment and some snacks and drinks.

[2] *zhǔyi*主意 is usually read as *zhúyi* in oral Chinese.

B 个人练习 Self-practice

Word Order: Create sentences by arranging the following words in the appropriate order.

1. ① 下午 xiàwǔ ② 我 wǒ ③ 中国 Zhōngguó ④ 文化 课 wénhuà kè ⑤ 上 shàng _____

2. ① 可以 kěyǐ ② 去 qù ③ 我 wǒ ④ 旁听 pángtīng ⑤ 吗 ma _____

3. ① 我们 wǒmen ② 占 座 zhàn zuò ③ 现在 xiànzài ④ 吧 ba ⑤ 去 qù _____

4. ① 她 tā ② 我们 wǒmen ③ 吧 ba ④ 下课后 xiàkè hòu ⑤ 图书馆 túshūguǎn
   ⑥ 去 qù ⑦ 找 zhǎo _____

C 二人练习 Pair Work

Talk about Plans: With a partner, practice asking about his or her plans.

A：你 下午 做 什么？
Nǐ xiàwǔ zuò shénme?

B：我 下午 去 上 中国 文化 课。
Wǒ xiàwǔ qù shàng Zhōngguó wénhuà kè.

A：你 晚上 做 什么？
Nǐ wǎnshang zuò shénme?

B：我 晚上 去 KTV 唱歌。
Wǒ wǎnshang qù KTV chànggē.

D 小组活动 Group Work

Plans for Weekend: In a small group, take turns talking about your plans for the weekend. Try to comment on each other's plans and decide which one sounds more interesting.

精彩瞬间 Spotlight

听与说 Listen and Speak

Listen to the recording and read silently. Listen again and repeat the sentences after you hear them.

dàxuéshēng
大学生

Nǐ báitiān máng ma?
A：你 白天 忙 吗？

Hěn máng. Wǒ zǎoshang bā diǎn qù shàngkè,
B：很 忙。我 早上 八点 去 上课，

zhōngwǔ shí' èr diǎn qù chīfàn, xiàwǔ qù dǎgōng.
中午 十二 点 去 吃饭，下午 去 打工。

Nǐ shénme shíhou xuéxí?
A：你 什么 时候 学习？

Wǒ měi tiān wǎnshang bā diǎn qù jiàoshì xuéxí,
B：我 每 天 晚上 八 点 去 教室 学习，

shíyī diǎn huí sùshè shuìjiào.
十一点 回 宿舍 睡觉。

báilǐng
白领

Nǐ báitiān zuò shénme?
A：你 白天 做 什么？

Shàngwǔ jiǔ diǎn kāishǐ gōngzuò,
B：上午 九 点 开始 工作，

gōngzuò dào xiàwǔ liù diǎn.
工作 到 下午 六点。

Wǎnshang ne?
A：晚上 呢？

Wǎnshang hé péngyou yìqǐ qù KTV chànggē.
B：晚上 和 朋友 一起 去 KTV 唱歌。

zìyóu zhíyè zhě
自由职业者

Nǐ báitiān zuò shénme?
A：你 白天 做 什么？

Wǒ báitiān shàngwǎng.
B：我 白天 上网。

Nǐ shénme shíhou gōngzuò?
A：你 什么 时候 工作？

Wǒ wǎnshang shí diǎn yǐhòu
B：我 晚上 十点 以后

gōngzuò.
工作。

Expanded Words and Expressions

dàxuéshēng	
大学生	undergraduate
báitiān	
白天	daytime
máng	
忙	busy
dǎgōng	
打工	to do a part-time job
huí	
回	to return
sùshè	
宿舍	dormitory
báilǐng	
白领	white-collar
kāishǐ	
开始	to begin, to start
zìyóu zhíyè zhě	
自由职业者	freelancer
shàngwǎng	
上网	to surf the Internet
shíhou	
时候	moment, time

03 句型操练　Sentence Patterns

𝒜 听与说　Listen and Speak 🎧

Listen to the recording and read silently. Listen again and repeat the sentences after you hear them.

去 + action	去 + place + action
Nǐ jīntiān zuò shénme? 你 今天 做 什么？ Wǒ jīntiān qù chànggē. 我 今天 **去** 唱歌。	Nǐ jīntiān qù nǎr chànggē? 你 今天 **去** 哪儿 唱歌？ Wǒ jīntiān qù KTV chànggē. 我 今天 **去** KTV 唱歌。

ℬ 选择　Choose the correct answer.

Choose the correct words in parentheses to complete the conversations. Then practice with your partner.

Nǐ jīntiān xiàwǔ zuò shénme?
1. A：你 今天 下午 做 什么？
   Wǒ jīntiān xiàwǔ _____ (qù chànggē/ qù tiàowǔ).
   B：我 今天 下午 _____（去 唱歌 /去 跳舞）。
   Nǐ jīntiān qù _____ (nǎr / shénme) tiàowǔ?
   A：你 今天 去 _____（哪儿 / 什么）跳舞？
   Wǒ jīntiān qù jiǔbā tiàowǔ.
   B：我 今天 去 酒吧 跳舞。

Nǐ jīntiān qù hē kāfēi ma?
2. A：你 今天 去 喝 咖啡 吗？
   Wǒ jīntiān _____ (qù chànggē/ qù hē kāfēi).
   B：我 今天 _____（去 唱歌 /去 喝 咖啡）。
   Nǐ qù nǎr hē kāfēi?
   A：你 去 哪儿 喝 咖啡？
   Wǒ qù _____ (kāfēiguǎn /túshūguǎn) hē kāfēi.
   B：我 去 _____（咖啡馆 / 图书馆）喝咖啡。

Expanded Words and Expressions

tiàowǔ 跳舞	to dance
jiǔbā 酒吧	bar
kāfēiguǎn 咖啡馆	café

听与说　Listen and Speak

Listen to the recording and read silently. Listen again and repeat the sentences after you hear them, and then practice the conversation in pairs.

At Café off Campus

Wang Damin talks to Jenny on the cell phone, and invites her to a movie for the coming weekend.

Wáng Dàmín: Zhōuliù wǎnshang wǒmen qù kàn diànyǐng ba.
王大民：周六　晚上　我们去看　电影吧。

Zhēnnī: Hǎo a! Zuìjìn yǒu shénme hǎo diànyǐng?
珍妮：好啊！　最近　有什么好　电影？

Wáng Dàmín: Tīngshuō 《Kǒngzǐ》 hěn hǎokàn.
王大民：听说《孔子》[1] 很 好看。

Zhēnnī: Shéi shì zhǔyǎn? Shì bu shì Zhōu Rùnfā?
珍妮：谁是主演？是不是 周 润发[2]？

Wáng Dàmín: Shì tā! Tīngshuō nǐ shì tā de fěnsī.
王大民：是他！　听说 你是他的 粉丝[3]。

Zhēnnī: Duì ya! Wǒmen shénme shíhou jiànmiàn?
珍妮：对呀[4]！我们 什么 时候 见面？

Wáng Dàmín: Zhōuliù wǎnshang bā diǎn.
王大民：周六　晚上　八点。

Zhēnnī: Zài nǎr?
珍妮：在哪儿？

Wáng Dàmín: Diànyǐngyuàn ménkǒu hǎo ma?
王大民：电影院　门口　好吗？

Zhēnnī: Hǎo. Bújiàn búsàn!
珍妮：好。不见不散！

Wang: Shall we go to see a movie this Saturday evening?
Jenny: OK. What movies would you recommend?
Wang: I heard that *Confucius* is pretty good.
Jenny: Who's the leading actor? Is it Chow Yun-Fat?
Wang: Yes. I heard that you are a fan of his.
Jenny: Yeah. When shall we meet?
Wang: At 8 o'clock Saturday evening.
Jenny: Where?
Wang: At the entrance to the movie theater, OK?
Jenny: OK. See you there!

---

[1] 《孔子》 is a Chinese movie which was produced in 2010. Its English name is *Confucius*.

[2] 周润发 is a famous movie star from Hong Kong.

[3] Although 粉丝 is actually a type of Chinese food which looks like noodle, the term has come to be used like the English "fans" because of its similar pronunciation.

[4] 呀 is a particle that usually indicates confirmation, surprise or appreciation when it is used at the end of a sentence.

Required Words and Expressions

Zhōuliù 周六	Saturday	
diànyǐng 电影	movie	
zuìjìn 最近	recent	
tīngshuō 听说	it's said, people say	
shéi 谁	who	
zhǔyǎn 主演	starring actor/actress	
duì 对	correct	
ya 呀	(a particle)	
jiànmiàn 见面	to meet	
diànyǐngyuàn 电影院	movie theater	
ménkǒu 门口	gate, entrance	
bùjiàn bùsàn 不见不散	be there or be square	

B 个人练习　Self-practice

Word Order: Create sentences by arranging the following words in the appropriate order.

1. ① 晚上　② 看　③ 我们　④ 电影
   wǎnshang　*kàn*　*wǒmen*　*diànyǐng*

   ⑤ 去　⑥ 周六　⑦ 吧 ＿＿＿＿＿＿＿＿＿
   qù　*Zhōuliù*　*ba*

2. ① 有　② 电影　③ 最近　④ 好
   yǒu　*diànyǐng*　*zuìjìn*　*hǎo*

   ⑤ 什么 ＿＿＿＿＿＿＿＿＿
   shénme

3. ① 在　② 见面　③ 哪儿　④ 我们
   zài　*jiànmiàn*　*nǎr*　*wǒmen*

   ＿＿＿＿＿＿＿＿＿

C 二人练习　Pair Work

Invitation and Response: With a partner, practice inviting each other to do something interesting.

A：今天　晚上　我们 去 看 电影，好 吗?
   Jīntiān wǎnshang wǒmen qù kàn diànyǐng,　hǎo ma?

B：好啊。/ 对不起，今天 不行。
   Hǎo a.　/ *Duìbuqǐ,　jīntiān bùxíng.*

Expanded Words and Expressions	
duìbuqǐ 对不起	sorry
bùxíng 不行	will not do

D 小组活动　Group Work

What is your Chinese class like? In groups of three, take turns asking and answering the following questions. Then share the information with the rest of the class.

1. When is your Chinese class?
2. Where is your Chinese class?
3. Who is your Chinese teacher?
4. How is your Chinese teacher?
5. What does your teacher talk about in Chinese class?
6. Which part of your Chinese class do you enjoy most?

05 经理的一周　Manager's Week Schedule

听与说　Listen and Speak

Listen to the recording and read silently. Listen again and repeat the phrases after you hear them.

Zhōuyī 周一	Mon.	**kāihuì** 开会　have a meeting
Zhōu'èr 周二	Tue.	**jiàn lǎo kèhù** 见 老 客户　visit regular clients
Zhōusān 周三	Wed.	**shìchǎng diàoyán** 市场　调研　do some market research
Zhōusì 周四	Thu.	**qù Shànghǎi chūchāi** 去 上海　出差 go on a business trip to Shanghai
Zhōuwǔ 周五	Fri.	**wǎnshang hé gōngsī zhíyuán yìqǐ qù KTV** 晚上 和 公司 职员 一起去KTV go to KTV with the team members in the evening
Zhōuliù 周六	Sat.	**kàn fùmǔ** 看 父母　visit parents
Zhōurì 周日	Sun.	**hé nǚpéngyou qù kàn diànyǐng** 和 女朋友 去 看 电影 go to the movies with girlfriend

Expanded Words and Expressions

kāihuì
开会　to have a meeting

lǎo
老　old; regular

kèhù
客户　client

shìchǎng
市场　market

diàoyán
调研　to research

chūchāi
出差　to go on a business trip

fùmǔ
父母　parents

ānpái
安排　to make arrangements

chī fàn
吃饭　to have a meal

zhīdào
知道　to know

二人练习　Pair Work

Talking about the Schedule: Work with your partner to have a conversation, taking the following conversation between a boss and a secretary as an example.

Jīntiān shì Zhōuyī.
A：今天 是 周一。

Wǒ yǒu shénme ānpái?
B：我 有 什么 安排？

Nín jīntiān shàngwǔ kāihuì,　zhōngwǔ Liú jīnglǐ qǐng nín
A：您 今天 上午 开会，　中午 刘 经理 请 您
chīfàn,　wǎnshang nín qǐng kèhù Tuōní xiānsheng chīfàn.
吃饭，　晚上 您 请 客户托尼 先生 吃饭。

Hǎo de,　wǒ zhīdào le.
B：好的，我 知道 了。

06 用疑问代词的问句 Questions with an Interrogative Pronoun

𝒜 听与说 Listen and Speak 🎧

Listen to the recording and read silently. Listen again and repeat the sentences after you hear them.

Zuìjìn yǒu shénme hǎo diànyǐng?
① 最近 有 什么 好 电影？

Nà bù diànyǐng zěnmeyàng?
② 那部 电影 怎么样？

Shéi shì zhǔyǎn?
③ 谁 是 主演？

Wǒmen zài nǎr jiànmiàn?
④ 我们 在 哪儿 见面？

Wǒmen shénme shíhou kàn diànyǐng?
⑤ 我们 什么 时候 看 电影？

> **Tip**
>
> *Bù* 部 is a measure word for sets of books, volumes of works and movies, or groups of machines. You have already known that the pronoun *nà* 那 means "that" or "those", so *nà bù diànyǐng* 那部电影 means "that movie".

ℬ 选择 Choose the correct answer.

Choose the correct words in parentheses to complete the conversations. Then practice with your partner.

Jīntiān de Hànyǔ kè   (zěnmeyàng/shénme)?
1. A：今天 的 汉语 课 _____（怎么样 / 什么）？

    Jīntiān de Hànyǔ kè hěn yǒuyìsi.
    B：今天 的 汉语 课 很 有意思。

    Xiànzài wǎnshang qī diǎn le， wǒmen   (shénme shíhou / nǎr) qù chīfàn?
2. A：现在 晚上 七点 了，我们 _____（什么 时候 /哪儿）去 吃饭？

    Wǒmen xiànzài jiù qù ba.
    B：我们 现在 就 去 吧。

☺ 休息一下 Break Time

Practice writing the following two characters using the proper stroke order indicated below.

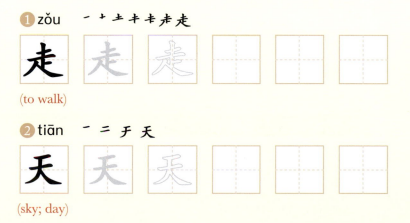

① zǒu 一 十 土 丰 丰 走 走

走

(to walk)

② tiān 一 二 于 天

天

(sky; day)

07 邀请 Invitation

1. A: May I invite you to dance?
   B: OK.
2. A: May I buy you a coffee?
   B: Sorry. I am not available.
3. A: Thanks for your help. May I treat you a meal?
   B: There is no need to be so courteous.
4. A: Please drop by our home when you have time.
   B: Sure. I would love to when I am free.

Expanded Words and Expressions

bēi	
杯	cup
yǒu yuē	
有 约	to have a date
gànmá	
干吗	why
yǒukòng	
有空	to have free time
wán	
玩	to play
yídìng	
一定	surely

Culture Box

It's common for Chinese to invite friends to have meals together at restaurants or at home. However, sometimes invitations may function more as greetings unless the host persists.

听与说   Listen and Speak

Listen to the recording and read silently. Listen again and repeat the sentences after you hear them, and then practice the conversations in pairs.

1. Kěyǐ qǐng nǐ tiàowǔ ma?
   A：可以 请 你 跳舞 吗?
   Hǎo a.
   B：好 啊。

2. Kěyǐ qǐng nǐ hē bēi kāfēi ma?
   A：可以 请 你 喝 杯 咖啡 吗?
   Duìbuqǐ, wǒ yǒu yuē le.
   B：对不起, 我 有 约 了。

3. Xièxie nǐ, wǒ qǐng nǐ chīfàn ba.
   A：谢谢 你, 我 请 你 吃饭 吧。
   Gànmá zhème kèqi?
   B：干吗 这么 客气?

4. Yǒukòng lái wǒmen jiā wán a.
   A：有空¹ 来 我们 家 玩² 啊。
   Hǎo, yǒukòng yídìng qù.
   B：好, 有空 一定 去。

☺ 休息一下 Break Time

Listen to the recording and read silently. Listen again and repeat the sentence after you hear it.

Pay attention to the pronunciation of the two consonants *p* and *t* and the tones of *u* and *ao* while repeating the sentence. Then compete with a partner, trying to say the sentence as quickly and accurately as you can.

Chī pútáo bù tǔ pútáopí, bù chī pútáo dào tǔ pútáopí.

吃 葡萄 不 吐 葡萄皮, 不 吃 葡萄 倒吐 葡萄皮。

Eat grapes without spitting out the skin, and spit out the skin without eating grapes.

[1,2] In oral Chinese, r-ending retroflexion usually happens to 有空 and 玩, which become *yǒukòngr* 有空儿 and *wánr* 玩儿.

08 文化掠影　Culture Snapshot

☐ **Chinese college students** are often known for their academic diligence. Many students spend the weekend studying in the classroom or library because they must receive high marks on their exams if they want to get a good job in a competitive job market. College students in the U.S. are also hard-working, but typically have a more balanced lifestyle, as evidenced by the commonly used phrase "Work hard, play hard."

☐ Hospitality is a universal concept, but different cultures have different ways of showing it. **Invitations**, for instance, are very culturally loaded. In China, an invitation is usually made verbally, spontaneously, and without much advance notice. For example, a friend might call you on Friday evening to invite you to lunch on Saturday. In American culture, on the other hand, invitations are usually more formal and are typically made with more advance notice. This is considered polite as it gives invitees time to prepare, to make plans, and to adjust their schedules. The refusal of invitations is also universal; however, Chinese are more likely to make an indirect refusal to save face and to avoid hurting anyone's feelings. Rather than saying, "I'm sorry, I can't make it due to a prior engagement", a Chinese person might say, "I'll come if I finish a pre-arranged event early", thus leaving room for possibilities.

☐ If you have the opportunity to study or work in China, you will notice many **cultural differences** in the ways that people speak and act. You may experience culture shock at first, but rather than viewing these differences as a threat, try to embrace the differences and learn from them. You will find it easier to acclimate so that you can act in a way that is more acceptable in the target culture.

1 Expressing the Time of an Event or Action Using Time Phrases as Adverbial Phrases

Some time phrases such as *jīntiān* 今天, *xiàwǔ* 下午 and *Zhōuyī* 周一 can function as adverbial phrases in a sentence to express the time of an event or action. These phrases can be put either in front of the subject or between the subject and the main predicate.

(1) A: Do you have time next Monday?

B: I will be very busy on Monday. I don't have time.

(2) A: What are you up to this afternoon?

B: I have a Chinese culture class this afternoon.

(3) A: Are you going to Beijing today?

B: No, I am going to Beijing tomorrow.

(1) A： Nǐ Zhōuyī yǒukòng ma?
你 周一 有空 吗？

B： Wǒ Zhōuyī hěn máng, méiyǒu shíjiān.
我 周一 很 忙，没有 时间。

(2) A： Xiàwǔ nǐ zuò shénme?
下午 你 做 什么？

B： Xiàwǔ wǒ shàng Zhōngguó wénhuà kè.
下午 我 上 中国 文化 课。

(3) A： Jīntiān nǐ qù Běijīng ma?
今天 你 去 北京 吗？

B： Bù, wǒ míngtiān qù Běijīng.
不，我 明天 去 北京。

2 Giving a Suggestion or Request Using the Sentence Final Particle 吧[1]

Ba 吧 is tagged onto a statement indicating a suggestion or request.

(1) A: Let's go and get seats.

B: Sure.

(2) A: Shall we go to a movie this Sunday evening?

B: Great idea!

(1) A： Wǒmen xiànzài qù zhàn zuò ba.
我们 现在 去 占 座 吧。

B： Zǒu ba.
走 吧。

(2) A： Zhōurì wǎnshang wǒmen yìqǐ qù kàn diànyǐng ba.
周日 晚上 我们 一起 去 看 电影 吧。

B： Hǎo zhǔyi!
好 主意！

---

[1] The intonation of sentences with 吧 tends to stay level or fall at the end when the speaker expresses a request. It rises slightly if the speaker wants to express a suggestion.

3 **Using Question Words to Form Wh-questions**

We have five "Wh" words to ask wh-questions. Following are their corresponding words in Chinese.

shénme	shéi	nǎ	nǎli / nǎr	nǎr	shénme shíhou
什么	谁	哪	哪里 / 哪儿		什么 时候
what	who	which	where		when

These words can be used to ask the following questions.

(1)　A： Tā shì shéi?
　　　 她是 谁？
　　 B： Tā shì wǒ de péngyou.
　　　 她是 我的 朋友 。
　　　A： Tā jiào shénme míngzi?
　　　 她叫 什么 名字？
　　 B： Tā jiào Zhēnnī.
　　　 她叫 珍妮。
　　　A： Tā shì nǎ guó rén?
　　　 她是 哪 国 人？
　　 B： Tā shì Měiguórén.
　　　 她是 美国人。
　　　A： Tā jiā zài nǎr?
　　　 她家在 哪儿？
　　 B： Tā jiā zài Huáshèngdùn.
　　　 她家在 华盛顿 。

(2)　A： Shéi shì Rìběn xuésheng?
　　　 谁是 日本 学生 ？
　　 B： Shāntián.
　　　 山田 。

(3)　A： Zhēnnī hé Wáng Dàmín shénme shíhou jiànmiàn?
　　　 珍妮 和 王 大民 什么 时候 见面 ？
　　 B： Zhōuliù wǎnshang bā diǎn.
　　　 周六 晚上 八 点 。

(1)　A: Who is she?
　　 B: She is my friend.
　　 A: What's her name?
　　 B: Her name is Jenny.
　　 A: Which country does she come from?
　　 B: She comes from the U.S.
　　 A: Where is her hometown?
　　 B: Washington D.C.

(2)　A: Who is the Japanese student?
　　 B: Yamada.

(3)　A: When will Jenny and Wang Damin meet?
　　 B: Saturday evening at 8 o'clock.

 语法练习　**Grammar Practice**

1 **Make complete sentences following the examples given.**

❶　Wǒ jīntiān xiàwǔ qù xuéxiào shàngkè.
　 我 今天 下午 去 学校 上课 。
　　 míngtiān shàngwǔ　KTV　chànggē
　　 明天 上午　KTV　唱歌
　　 jīntiān wǎnshang　kāfēiguǎn shàngwǎng
　　 今天 晚上　咖啡馆 上网
　　 hòutiān zhōngwǔ　túshūguǎn　kàn shū
　　 后天 中午　图书馆　看 书

Nǐ qù bu qù túshūguǎn?
② 你去不去 图书馆？

shàng Zhōngguó wénhuà kè
上 中国 文化 课

kàn diànyǐng
看 电影

chī fàn
吃 饭

2 Complete the following sentences with the words given.

hǎokàn	hǎochī	xuéxiào	ba	nǎr	shénme shíhou
好看	好吃	学校	吧	哪儿	什么 时候

Wǒmen míngtiān qù kàn diànyǐng
① 我们 明天 去 看 电影 _____。

Māma zuò de fàn zhēn
② 妈妈 做 的 饭 真 _____！

Zhè bù diànyǐng hěn
③ 这 部 电影 很 _____。

Nǐ qù zuò shénme?
④ A：你去 _____ 做 什么？

Wǒ qù kàn péngyou.
B：我 去 看 朋友。

Wǒmen qù zhǎo tā?
⑤ A：我们 去 _____ 找 她？

Wǒmen qù túshūguǎn zhǎo tā.
B：我们 去 图书馆 找 她。

Tāmen qù Zhōngguó?
⑥ A：他们 _____ 去 中国 ？

Míngtiān.
B：明天 。

3 Complete the following dialogue.

Jīntiān xiàwǔ nǐ zuò shénme?
A：今天 下午 你 做 什么？

B：_____

Xiàkè hòu wǒmen qù kàn diànyǐng, zěnmeyàng?
A：下课 后 我们 去 看 电影 ，怎么样？

B：_____

Shì Brad Pitt de diànyǐng, tīngshuō hěn hǎokàn.
A：是 Brad Pitt的 电影 ，听说 很 好看。

B：_____

Duì. Wǒ hěn xǐhuan tā de diànyǐng.
A：对。我 很 喜欢 他 的 电影 。

B：_____

Hǎo de, xiàkè jiàn.
A：好 的，下课 见。

11 语音提示 Pronunciation Tips

1 *j*, *q*, *x* and *zh*, *ch*, *sh*

Compare and pronounce.

jǐ – zhǐ   qī – chī   xí – shí
jiǎo – zhǎo   jiàn – zhàn   qíng – chéng

Tip

The palatal initials *j*, *q*, *x* are pronounced with a relaxed tongue, while the retroflex initials *zh*, *ch*, *sh* require the tongue to be curled back.

2 Words with Initials *j*, *q*, *x*

Read the following words and circle the syllables with initials *j*, *q*, *x*.

jīntiān	xiàwǔ	xiàkè	bùxíng
今天	下午	下课	不行
jiàoshì	xuéxí	zuìjìn	duìbuqǐ
教室	学习	最近	对不起

Tip

The initial *x* is a fricative, meaning that the upper and lower teeth are held close together while the air is forced through the small space between them.

3 Intonation of Wh- questions in Chinese

Repeat the following sentences after your teacher, paying attention to the intonation.

Zuìjìn yǒu shénme hǎo diànyǐng?
最近有 什么 好 电影？

Shéi shì zhǔyǎn?
谁 是 主演？

Wǒmen shénme shíhou jiànmiàn? Zài nǎr?
我们 什么 时候 见面 ？ 在哪儿？

Tip

In Chinese, the intonation of wh-questions is usually slightly lower than that of a Yes-no question. Wh-questions are usually stressed with a falling tone.

12 汉字书写 Writing Chinese Characters

1 笔顺 Stroke Order

When writing a Chinese character, it is important to follow the correct stroke order. The general principles are as follows.

Liǎng bāowéi jiégòu de shūxiě shùnxù
两 包围 结构 的 书写 顺序[1] The Stroke Order of Semi-enclosed Structure

Bāowéi 包围 means that in a Chinese character, some parts are enclosed by the other parts.

zuǒ shàng 、yòu shàng bāowéi, xiān wài hòu lǐ
左 上 、 右 上 包围 , 先 外 后 里 in a top-semi-enclosed structure, outside before inside

eg. 座 (seat)   zuò
` 宀 广 广 庐 庐 庑 庑 座 座

eg. 司 (department)   sī
㇆ ㇆ 司 司 司

[1] In Unit 3 you have learned that in a total-enclosed structure, you should write outside strokes before inside strokes, then closing.

zuǒ xià bāowéi, "辶"、"廴" de zì, xiān lǐ hòu wài
左 下 包 围, "辶"、"廴" 的 字, 先 里 后 外 in a bottom-semi-enclosed
structure, for characters with 辶 or 廴, inside before outside

eg.
zhè
这 丶 一 ナ 文 文 讠 这 这
(this)

zuǒ xià bāowéi, "辶"、"廴" yǐ wài de zì, xiān wài hòu lǐ
左 下 包 围, "辶"、"廴" 以 外 的 字, 先 外 后 里 in a bottom-semi-enclosed
structure, for characters not with 辶 or 廴, outside before inside

eg.
qǐ
起 一 十 土 キ キ 走 走 起 起 起
(to rise)

You can write it!

Practice writing the following Chinese characters. Don't forget to follow the correct stroke order!

hòu ノ 厂 厂 斤 后 后
后 后
(behind)

nián ノ 仁 仁 仁 年 年
年 年
(year)

yǐ ㇂ ㇂ 以 以
以 以
(by means of)

zhōu ノ 刀 月 月 円 用 周 周
周 周
(week)

yī 一
一 一
(one)

hòutiān
后 天
(the day after tomorrow)

tiān 一 二 于 天
天 天
(sky; day)

kě 一 丁 口 口 可
可 可
(may)

ài ノ 爫 爫 爫 爫 爫 岁 岁 爱 爱
爱 爱
(love)

mò 一 二 十 才 末
末 末
(end)

qǐ 一 十 土 キ キ 走 走 起 起 起
起 起
(to rise)

hòunián
后 年
(the year after next year)

kě'ài

可 爱 ☐ ☐ ☐

(lovely)

Zhōuyī

周 一 ☐ ☐ ☐

(Monday)

yīqǐ

一 起 ☐ ☐ ☐

(together)

kěyǐ

可 以 ☐ ☐ ☐

(may)

zhōumò

周 末 ☐ ☐ ☐

(weekend)

2 汉字的演变 Evolution of Chinese Characters

13 综合练习 Integrative Practice

Listening

1 Listen to the words and mark the missing tones. 🎧

xiake	tushuguan	changge	zhan zuo	dianyingyuan	zenmeyang
下课	图书馆	唱歌	占 座	电影院	怎么样

2 Listen to the following conversation and complete the sentences with the correct characters in parentheses. 🎧

Nǐ xiàwǔ zuò shénme?

A：你 下午 做 什么？

Wǒ xiàwǔ _____ (qù túshūguǎn kàn shū / qù kāfēitīng kàn shū).

B：我 下午 _____（a.去 图书馆 看 书 / b.去 咖啡厅 看 书）。

Nǐ míngtiān zuò shénme?

A：你 明天 做 什么？

Wǒ míngtiān qù gōngsī   (kāihuì / jiàn kèhù).
B：我 明天 去 公司 _____ (a. 开会 / b. 见 客户)。

Nǐ zhōumò zuò shénme?
A：你 周末 做 什么？

Wǒ zhōumò   (qù kàn fùmǔ / qù KTV chànggē).
B：我 周末 _____ (a. 去 看 父母 / b. 去KTV 唱歌)。

3 Listen to the recording and complete the following table. 🎧

Ǎn   (Ann)   de yì zhōu jìhuà
安 （Ann） 的 一 周 计划

Zhōuyī shàngwǔ 周一　上午	Zhōu'èr xiàwǔ 周二　下午	Zhōusān zhōngwǔ 周三　　中午	Zhōusì xiàwǔ 周四　下午	Zhōuwǔ wǎnshang 周五　　晚上
qù xuéxiào shàngkè 去 学校　上课				

qù kāfēiguǎn hē kāfēi
①去 咖啡馆 喝 咖啡

qù Mǎlì jiā dǎ diànwán
③去 玛丽家 打 电玩

qù KTV chànggē
②去KTV 唱歌

qù jiǔbā tiàowǔ
④去 酒吧 跳舞

Expanded Words and Expressions

jìhuà
计划　　　plan; to plan

méi wèntí
没 问题　　no problem

Speaking

1 With a partner, read the following conversation aloud.

Wáng Qiáng： Jīntiān wǎnshang qù jiǔbā, zěnmeyàng?
王 强 ： 今天 晚上 去 酒吧，怎么样？

Zhāng Xiǎopíng： Bùxíng, wǒ wǎnshang yào qù shàngkè.
张 小平： 不行，我 晚上 要 去 上课。

Wáng Qiáng： Nà Zhōuliù qù kàn diànyǐng zěnmeyàng?
王 强 ： 那[1] 周六 去 看 电影 怎么样？

Zhāng Xiǎopíng： Méi wèntí. Zuìjìn yǒu shénme hǎokàn de diànyǐng?
张 小平： 没 问题。最近 有 什么 好看 的 电影？

Wáng Qiáng： 《Gōngfu Xióngmāo Èr》.
王 强 ： 《功夫 熊猫 2》[2]。

Zhāng Xiǎopíng： Tīngshuō hěn hǎokàn.
张 小平： 听说 很 好看。

Wáng Qiáng： Nà wǒmen Zhōuliù wǎnshang qù kàn ba?
王 强 ： 那 我们 周六 晚上 去 看 吧？

Zhāng Xiǎopíng： Xíng, bā diǎn, diànyǐngyuàn ménkǒu jiàn.
张 小平： 行，八 点， 电影院 门口 见。

---

[1] Nà 那 here is a conjunction indicating "then".
[2] 《功夫熊猫2》＝Kung Fu Panda 2 (movie).

2 Take turns answering the following questions with a partner.

Tāmen jīntiān wǎnshang qù jiǔbā ma? Wèishénme?
1. 他们 今天 晚上 去酒吧吗？为什么？

Zhōumò tāmen zuò shénme?
2. 周末 他们 做 什么？

Tāmen shénme shíhou jiànmiàn? Zài nǎr jiànmiàn?
3. 他们 什么 时候 见面？在哪儿见面？

Zuìjìn yǒu shénme hǎo diànyǐng?
4. 最近有 什么 好 电影？

1. Are they going to the bar this evening? Why?
2. What are they going to do this weekend?
3. When and where are they going to meet?
4. Which movie is popular recently?

3 Now practice the conversation from Activity 1 with your partner, but substitute your own information where you can.

Reading

Where did you go last weekend?

Wáng Lì: Zhōuliù wǒ hé péngyou qù SweetHouse chī dàngāo,
王 丽： 周六我和 朋友 去Sweet House吃 蛋糕、
hē kāfēi. Wǒmen dōu xǐhuan nàr de dàngāo hé kāfēi.
喝咖啡。我们 都 喜欢那儿的 蛋糕 和咖啡。
Zhōurì wǒ xuéxí yújiā, wǒ de yújiā lǎoshī hěn bàng.
周日我 学习瑜伽，我的 瑜伽老师 很 棒。

Lǐ Xiǎojūn Zuìjìn wǒhěn máng, Xīngqīliù zài gōngsīgōngzuò. Xīngqītiān
李 小军： 最近我很 忙 ，星期六[1]在公司 工作。星期天[2]
wǒ qù lǎo jiē pāizhào. Wǒ zhēn xǐhuan zhège chéngshì.
我去老街 拍照。我 真 喜欢这个 城市 。

1 Fill in the blanks.

Wáng Lì Zhōuliù hé péngyou qù　　　　　dàngāo、
❶ 王 丽周六和 朋友 去 _____ 蛋糕、 _____ 。

Lǐ Xiǎojūn Xīngqīliù zài　　　　　, tā zuìjìn hěn
❷ 李 小军 星期六在 _____ ，他最近 很 _____ 。

2 Talk with your partner.

Nǐ zhīdào "dàngāo", "yújiā" hé "pāizhào" de yìsi ma?
1. 你 知道 "蛋糕"、"瑜伽"和 "拍照" 的意思吗？

Lǐ Xiǎojūn Xīngqītiān qù nǎr pāizhào le?
2. 李 小军 星期天 去哪儿 拍照 了？

Shéi de zhōumò gèng yǒuyìsi?
3. 谁 的 周末 更 有意思？

Nǐ shàng gè zhōumò qù nǎr le?
4. 你 上 个 周末 去哪儿了？

1,2 星期六=周六，星期天=周日

Expanded Words and Expressions

jiē
街　　　　　street

1. Do you know the meanings of dàngāo 蛋糕, yújiā 瑜伽 and pāizhào 拍照?
2. Where did Li Xiaojun go to take pictures last Sunday?
3. Whose weekend is more interesting?
4. Where did you go last weekend?

Writing

Make a schedule for Li Hua

Your Chinese friend Li Hua is coming to the U.S. for a short visit. You would like her to get to know your city. Make a schedule for her visit.

Xīngqīyī 星期一	Xīngqī'èr 星期二	Xīngqīsān 星期三	Xīngqīsì 星期四	Xīngqīwǔ 星期五	Xīngqīliù 星期六	Xīngqītiān 星期天
qù xuéxiào shàngkè 去 学校 上课						

Strongly Recommended!

túshūguǎn 图书馆 · jiǔbā 酒吧 · diànyǐngyuàn 电影院 · kāfēiguǎn 咖啡馆 · chāoshì 超市 · jiànshēnfáng 健身房

Word List of Unit 4

Required Words and Expressions
(For Comprehension and Both Oral and Written Communication)

Míngcí 名词 (Nouns)

电影	diànyǐng	movie
电影院	diànyǐngyuàn	movie theater
门口	ménkǒu	gate, entrance
图书馆	túshūguǎn	library
文化	wénhuà	culture
以后	yǐhòu	after
周六	Zhōuliù	Saturday
主演	zhǔyǎn	starring actor / actress
主意	zhǔyi (zhúyi)	idea
最近	zuìjìn	recent

Dòngcí 动词 (Verbs)

见面	jiànmiàn	to meet

可以	kěyǐ	may
旁听	pángtīng	to audit
去	qù	to go
上课	shàngkè	to have a class
听说	tīngshuō	it's said, people say
下课	xiàkè	to dismiss a class
找	zhǎo	to find
走	zǒu	to walk, to go

Xíngróngcí 形容词 (Adjective)

对	duì	correct

Dàicí 代词 (Pronouns)

谁	shéi	who
怎么样	zěnmeyàng	how, how about

Expanded Words and Expressions
(For Comprehension and Oral Communication)

Míngcí 名词 (Nouns)

白领	báilǐng	white-collar
白天	báitiān	daytime
杯	bēi	cup
大学生	dàxuéshēng	undergraduate
父母	fùmǔ	parents
街	jiē	street
酒吧	jiǔbā	bar
咖啡馆	kāfēiguǎn	café
客户	kèhù	client
时候	shíhou	moment, time
市场	shìchǎng	market
宿舍	sùshè	dormitory
自由职业者	zìyóu zhíyè zhě	freelancer

Dòngcí 动词 (Verbs)

安排	ānpái	to make arrangements
不行	bùxíng	will not do
吃饭	chīfàn	to have a meal
出差	chūchāi	to go on a business trip
打工	dǎgōng	to do a part-time job
调研	diàoyán	to research

对不起	duìbuqǐ	to be sorry
回	huí	to return
开会	kāihuì	to have a meeting
开始	kāishǐ	to begin, to start
上网	shàngwǎng	to surf the Internet
跳舞	tiàowǔ	to dance
玩	wán	to play
有空	yǒukòng	to have free time
知道	zhīdào	to know

Xíngróngcí 形容词 (Adjectives)

老	lǎo	old; regular
忙	máng	busy

Dàicí 代词 (Pronoun)

干吗	gànmá	why

Jiānlèicí 兼类词 (Conversion Word)

计划	jìhuà	*n. / v.*	plan; to plan

Fùcí 副词 (Adverb)

一定	yídìng	surely

Chángyòng biǎodá 常用表达 (Expressions)

没问题	méi wèntí	no problem
有约	yǒu yuē	to have a date

Suggested Words and Expressions
(For Comprehension Only)

Míngcí 名词 (Nouns)

超市	chāoshì	supermarket
蛋糕	dàngāo	cake
健身房	jiànshēnfáng	gymnasium
瑜伽	yújiā	yoga

Dòngcí 动词 (Verb)

拍照	pāizhào	to take pictures

Jiānlèicí 兼类词 (Conversion Word)

那	nà	*pron. /conj.*	that; then

Liàngcí 量词 (Measure Word)

部	bù	(a measure word for sets of books, volumes of works and movies, groups of machines)

Unit 5 第五单元
Dì-wǔ dānyuán

Shopping and Bargaining

讨价还价
Tǎo jià huán jià

Bargaining is an important skill to learn in order to understand Chinese culture. You can practice your bargaining skills at yard sales and small markets in the U.S., and in China you can use your bargaining skills to get a better price at free markets and corner shops. At the same time, you can practice your oral Chinese and experience the local culture. There is nothing like the satisfaction of using your language skills to get a good bargain in China!

In this unit, you will learn:

FUNCTION

☐ to ask about and describe goods and colors: 你们有红色的自行车吗？／你喜欢什么颜色？

☐ to ask about prices: 你这件衣服多少钱？

☐ to make comparisons: 迈克的衣服和你的一样。／我的衣服比他的贵。

☐ to bargain: 太贵了，便宜点儿吧。

GRAMMAR

☐ to express quantity using measure words

☐ to express comparison using the preposition 比

☐ different usages of 了

CULTURE

☐ bargaining

☐ colors in Chinese culture

听与说　Listen and Speak

Listen to the recording and read silently. Listen again and repeat the sentences after you hear them, and then practice the conversation in pairs.

In the Classroom

Yamada has noticed that Bill and Mike are both wearing the same jacket. Out of curiosity, he asks each of them where they bought it. To Bill's disappointment, Mike spent less money on the jacket than he did.

Shāntián：　Nǐ zhè jiàn yīfu duōshao qián?
山田：　你这件衣服多少 钱？

Bǐ'ěr：　Yìbǎi wǔshí yuán.
比尔：　150　元 [1]。

Shāntián：　Màikè de yīfu hé nǐ de yíyàng. Tā zhǐ huāle
山田：　迈克的衣服和你的一样。他只花了

yìbǎi kuài qián.
100 块 [2] 钱。

Bǐ'ěr：　Tā shì zài nǎr mǎi de?
比尔：　他是在哪儿买的？

Shāntián：　Zài Xiùshuǐ Jiē mǎi de.
山田：　在秀水街买的。

Bǐ'ěr：　Wǒ yě shì zài Xiùshuǐ Jiē mǎi de,　wèishénme wǒ
比尔：　我也是在 秀水街 [3] 买的，为什么 我

de yīfu bǐ tā de guì?
的衣服比他的贵？

Shāntián：　Yīnwèi Màikè huì kǎnjià ya.
山田：　因为迈克会砍价呀。

Yamada:　How much did your jacket cost?

Bill:　150 *yuan.*

Yamada:　Mike's jacket looks the same as yours. He bought it for only 100 *yuan.*

Bill:　Where did he buy it?

Yamada:　He bought it in Beijing's Silk Street market.

Bill:　I bought it there, too. How come mine is more expensive than his?

Yamada:　Because Mike is good at bargaining.

---

[1]　*Rénmínbì* 人民币 (RMB) is the currency of the People's Republic of China, and *yuán* 元 is its primary unit.

[2]　In oral Chinese, *yuán* 元 is usually called *kuài* 块.

[3]　*Xiùshuǐjiē* 秀水街 (Silk Street) is a very famous market in Beijing known for name-brand goods with very cheap price. Many people, especially foreigners, like to go there to test their bargaining skills.

Required Words and Expressions

jiàn 件	(measure word for clothes, things, etc.)
yīfu 衣服	clothes
qián 钱	money
yuán 元	*yuan*
yíyàng 一样	the same
zhǐ 只	just, only
huā 花	to spend (money or time)
kuài 块	*yuan* (spoken form)
mǎi 买	to buy
wèishénme 为什么	why
bǐ 比	than
guì 贵	expensive
yīnwèi 因为	because
huì 会	to be able to, can
kǎnjià 砍价	to bargain

B 个人练习 Self-practice

Word Order: Create sentences by arranging the following words in the appropriate order.

1. ① duōshao 多少 ② qián 钱 ③ nǐ de yīfu 你的衣服 _____

2. ① tā de yīfu 他的衣服 ② yíyàng 一样 ③ hé 和 ④ wǒ de yīfu 我的衣服

   _____

3. ① wǒ de yīfu 我的衣服 ② tā de 他的 ③ guì 贵 ④ bǐ 比

   ⑤ wèishénme 为什么 _____

C 二人练习 Pair Work

Talk about Shopping: With a partner, practice asking about his or her shopping.

A：Nǐ de yīfu shì zài nǎr mǎi de? 你的衣服是 在哪儿买 的?

B：Wǒ de yīfu shì zài shāngchǎng mǎi de. 我的衣服是 在 商场 买 的。

A：Duōshao qián? 多少 钱？

B：Yìbǎi bāshí kuài. 180 块。

Expanded Words and Expressions

shāngchǎng
商场   mall

D 小组活动 Group Work

Let's compare! Make comparisons with your classmates, expressing similarities with *yíyàng* 一样 and differences with *bǐ* 比 and *méiyǒu* 没有.

Tā de yīfu qībǎi kuài.
他 的衣服700 块。

Wǒ de yīfu bābǎi kuài.
我 的衣服800 块。

Wǒ de yīfu bǐ tā de yīfu guì.
我 的衣服比他的衣服贵。

Tā de yīfu méiyǒu wǒ de yīfu guì.
他 的衣服 没有 我 的衣服贵。

Wǒ èrshíyī suì.
我 21 岁。

Nǐ èrshíyī suì.
你 21 岁。

Wǒ hé nǐ yíyàng dà.
我和你 一样大。

Unit 5 第五单元   145

Spotlight

𝒜 听与说　Listen and Speak 🎧

Ms. Wang's Wardrobe: Ms. Wang, the Vice President of a high-tech company, went shopping and bought the following articles of clothing. Listen and repeat what Ms. Wang has bought.

	chènshān				pídài	
①	衬衫	blouse		⑥	皮带	belt
	T xùshān				wéijīn	
②	T恤衫	T-shirt		⑦	围巾	scarf
	wàitào				xīfú	
③	外套	coat		⑧	西服	suit
	fēngyī				yùndòngxié	
④	风衣	windbreaker		⑨	运动鞋	athletic shoes
	niúzǎikù				píxié	
⑤	牛仔裤	jeans		⑩	皮鞋	leather shoes

ℬ 选择　Choose the suitable clothes.

Complete the charts with the words from Activity A, placing each article of clothing in the appropriate box.

zhíyèzhuāng 职业装　Work Clothes		
yīfu 衣服	kùzi 裤子	xié 鞋

xiūxiánfú 休闲服　Casual Clothes		
yīfu 衣服	kùzi 裤子	xié 鞋

𝒞 二人练习　Pair Work

Find the Proper Measure Words: With a partner, practice matching each article of clothing in Activity A with the appropriate measure word below.

jiàn	tiáo	shuāng
件	条	双

Expanded Words and Expressions

T xùshān T恤衫	T-shirt	
niúzǎikù 牛仔裤	jeans	
kùzi 裤子	trousers	
xié 鞋	shoes	
tiáo 条	(measure word for something long and narrow)	
shuāng 双	(measure word for a pair)	

听与说 Listen and Speak 🎧

Listen to the recording and read silently. Listen again and repeat the sentences after you hear them.

A+比+B+adj.	A+没(有)+B+adj.	A+和+B+一样 (+adj.)
Wǒ de yīfu bǐ tā de yīfu guì. 我的衣服比她的衣服贵。	Wǒ de xié méiyǒu tā de xié guì. 我的鞋没有她的鞋贵。	Tā de kùzi hé wǒ de yíyàng. 她的裤子和我的一样。 Wǒ de chènshān hé tā de chènshān yíyàng guì. 我的衬衫和她的衬衫一样贵。

选择 Choose the correct answer.

Choose the correct words in parentheses to complete the conversation. Then practice with your partner.

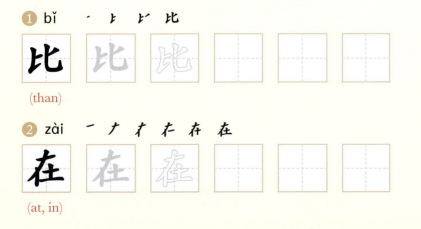

Ānnà de chènshān hěn hǎokàn.
A：安娜的 衬衫 很 好看¹。

Mǎkè de chènshān yě hěn _____ (hǎokàn / měi).
B：马克的 衬衫 也 很 _____ (好看 /美)。

Ānnà hé Mǎkè de chènshān _____ (bǐ / yíyàng) hǎokàn.
A：安娜 和 马克的 衬衫 _____ (比/一样) 好看。

Bǐ'ěr èrshíyī suì. Lǐ Lì ne?
B：比尔 21 岁。李丽呢?

Lǐ Lì _____ (bǐ / méiyǒu) Bǐ'ěr _____ (dà / xiǎo), Lǐ Lì èrshí suì.
A：李丽 _____ (比/ 没有) 比尔 _____ (大/ 小),李丽 20 岁。

😊 休息一下 Break Time

Practice writing the following two characters using the proper stroke order indicated below.

1 bǐ ` ㇏ ㇏ 比

比 比 比

(than)

2 zài 一 ㇒ ㇏ 在 在 在

在 在 在

(at, in)

---

¹ *Hǎokàn* 好看 here means "beautiful". It also means "wonderful" in Chinese. For example:

Zhè bù diànyǐng hěn hǎokàn. 这部电影很好看。
This film is wonderful.

Zhè běn shū hěn hǎokàn.
这本书很好看。
This book is wonderful.

听与说　Listen and Speak

Listen to the recording and read silently. Listen again and repeat the sentences after you hear them, and then practice the conversation in pairs.

At a Bicycle Shop

Wang Damin takes Jenny to a second-hand bicycle shop. He is a hard bargainer and helps Jenny buy a pink bike.

Wáng Dàmín:　Nǐmen yǒu hóngsè de zìxíngchē ma?
王大民：　你们 有 红色 的自行车 吗？

Diànzhǔ:　Wǒmen zhǐ yǒu fěnsè hé hēisè de.
店主：　我们 只 有 粉色和 黑色 的。

Wáng Dàmín:　Nǐ gèng xǐhuan nǎge yánsè?
王大民：　你 更 喜欢哪个颜色？

Zhēnnī:　Wǒ gèng xǐhuan fěnsè. Wǒ xiǎng mǎi
珍妮：　我 更 喜欢粉色。我 想 买

fěnsè de.
粉色的。

Wáng Dàmín:　Lǎobǎn, zhè liàng fěnsè de duōshao qián?
王大民：　老板[1]，这 辆 粉色的 多少 钱？

Diànzhǔ:　Bāshí Měiyuán.
店主：　80 美元。

Wáng Dàmín:　Tài guì le, piányi diǎnr ba.
王大民：　太贵了，便宜点儿吧。

Diànzhǔ:　Qīshí Měiyuán ba, zhè shì zuìdījià le.
店主：　70 美元 吧，这是 最低价了。

Wang Damin:　Do you have red bicycles?
Shop Owner:　We only have pink and black ones.
Wang Damin:　Which one do you like?
Jenny:　I prefer pink. I want to buy a pink one.
Wang Damin:　Sir, how much is this pink bike?
Shop Owner:　80 dollars.
Wang Damin:　That's too expensive. Could you lower the price a little bit?
Shop Owner:　How about 70 dollars? I am afraid this is the best I can do.

---

[1] *Lǎobǎn* 老板 is commonly used in Chinese to refer to supervisors, managers, storekeepers or people of higher rank.

Required Words and Expressions

yǒu 有	to have	
hóngsè 红色	red	
zìxíngchē 自行车	bicycle	
fěnsè 粉色	pink	
hēisè 黑色	black	
gèng 更	more	
yánsè 颜色	color	
xiǎng 想	to want	
lǎobǎn 老板	boss	
liàng 辆	(measure word for vehicles)	
Měiyuán 美元	U.S. dollar	
tài 太	too	
piányi 便宜	cheap	
zuìdījià 最低价	the lowest price	

Word Order: Create sentences by arranging the following words in the appropriate order.

1. ① 很 (hěn)　② 粉色 (fěnsè)　③ 好看 (hǎokàn) _____

2. ① 多少 (duōshao)　② 自行车 (zìxíngchē)　③ 粉色 (fěnsè)　④ 钱 (qián)

3. ① 喜欢 (xǐhuan)　② 种 (zhǒng)　③ 更 (gèng)　④ 你 (nǐ)
   ⑤ 颜色 (yánsè)　⑥ 哪 (nǎ) _____

C 二人练习 **Pair Work**

Enjoy Bargaining: With a partner, practice bargaining.

A：这 辆 自行车 多少 钱？
Zhè liàng zìxíngchē duōshao qián?

B：100 块。
Yìbǎi kuài.

A：太 贵 了。便宜点儿吧。
Tài guì le. Piányi diǎnr ba.

B：80 块 吧。这 是 最低价了。
Bāshí kuài ba. Zhè shì zuìdījià le.

Culture Box

In China, you can bargain in most markets except for those large stores which have set prices on their goods. If you want to buy something in a free market in China, bargaining can make for an interesting experience. Chinese often use the following sentences when they are bargaining in the market:

Kěyǐ piányi diǎnr ma?
可以便宜点儿吗?
Can you lower the price?

Kěyǐ dǎzhé ma?
可以打折吗?
Can you give me a discount?

Tài guì le! Wǒ bù mǎi le.
太贵了! 我不买了。
It's too expensive! I won't buy it.

D 小组活动 **Group Work**

The Best Choice: According to the information in the chart, share your preferences with your team members, then work together to agree on an item, its color and price that you're willing to pay.

A：这 辆 黑色 的 自行车 很 好。我 喜欢 黑色。
Zhè liàng hēisè de zìxíngchē hěn hǎo. Wǒ xǐhuan hēisè.

B：我 也 喜欢 黑色。
Wǒ yě xǐhuan hēisè.

C：那 辆 红色 的 更 好。我 更 喜欢 红色。
Nà liàng hóngsè de gèng hǎo. Wǒ gèng xǐhuan hóngsè.

D：粉色 的 自行车 比 红色 的 更 漂亮。
Fěnsè de zìxíngchē bǐ hóngsè de gèng piàoliang.

……

zìxíngchē 自行车	fěnsè 粉色	piàoliang 漂亮	yě 也
wàitào 外套	hóngsè 红色	kù 酷	gèng 更
wéijīn 围巾	hēisè 黑色	guì 贵	bǐ 比
píxié 皮鞋	lánsè 蓝色	piányi 便宜	méiyǒu 没有

05 颜色 Colors

𝒜 听与说 Listen and Speak

Listen to the recording and read silently. Listen again and repeat the colors after you hear them.

chéngsè 橙色
huángsè 黄色
fěnsè 粉色
báisè 白色
qiǎnlǜsè 浅绿色
hóngsè 红色
hēisè 黑色
huīsè 灰色
lǜsè 绿色
zǐsè 紫色
shēnlánsè 深蓝色
lánsè 蓝色
qiǎnlánsè 浅蓝色
shēnlǜsè 深绿色

ℬ 二人练习 Pair Work

Favorite Colors: Ask your partner's favorite colors.

Nǐ zuì xǐhuan nǎ zhǒng yánsè?
A：你 最 喜欢 哪 种 颜色？

Lánsè. Nǐ zuì xǐhuan nǎ zhǒng yánsè?
B：蓝色。你 最 喜欢 哪 种 颜色？

Báisè, lǜsè, hóngsè wǒ dōu xǐhuan.
A：白色、绿色、红色 我 都 喜欢。

𝒞 班级活动 Class Activity

What does he/she wear? In groups, take turns describing your classmates' clothing.

Tā chuānle yí jiàn lǜsè de chènshān, yì tiáo hēisè de
她 穿了 一件 绿色的 衬衫 、一条 黑色的

kùzi, hěn piàoliang.
裤子，很 漂亮。

Expanded Words and Expressions

qiǎn 浅	light, shallow
shēn 深	dark, deep
báisè 白色	white
huángsè 黄色	yellow
lǜsè 绿色	green
lánsè 蓝色	blue
zuì 最	most
chuān 穿	to wear

06 词汇扩展　Word Power

听与说　Listen and Speak

Where can you buy the things in the left column? Match the things with the places in the right column. Then listen and repeat.

	cídiǎn			yàofáng	
1	词典	dictionary	a.	药房	drugstore
	zhǐténgyào			yóujú	
2	止疼药	pain reliever	b.	邮局	post office
	miànbāo			jiāyóuzhàn	
3	面包	bread	c.	加油站	gas station
	yóupiào			kuàicāndiàn	
4	邮票	stamp	d.	快餐店	fast-food restaurant
	qìyóu			chāoshì	
5	汽油	gasoline	e.	超市	supermarket
	xié			shāngchǎng	
6	鞋	shoe	f.	商场	mall
	hànbǎobāo			shūdiàn	
7	汉堡包	hamburger	g.	书店	bookstore
	èrshǒuchē			jiùhuò shìchǎng	
8	二手车	second-hand car	h.	旧货 市场	flea market

听与说　Listen and Speak

Listen to the recording and read silently. Listen again and repeat the sentences after you hear them, and then practice the conversations in pairs.

1. A: Can I help you?
   B: I am just looking around.
2. A: Madam, do you have size L for this dress?
   B: Yes. Here it is. Does it fit you well?
3. A: May I use a credit card?
   B: Sorry, we only accept cash.

1.
   Nǐ yào mǎi shénme?
   A：你要 买 什么？
   Wǒ suíbiàn kànkan.
   B：我 随便 看看。

2.
   Lǎobǎn, yǒu dàhào de ma?
   A：老板，有 大号 的 吗？
   Yǒu. Nín kàn zhè jiàn héshì ma?
   B：有。您 看 这 件 合适 吗？

3.
   Kěyǐ yòng xìnyòngkǎ ma?
   A：可以 用 信用卡 吗？
   Duìbuqǐ, wǒmen zhǐ shōu xiànjīn.
   B：对不起，我们 只 收 现金。

Expanded Words and Expressions

suíbiàn 随便	as one pleases	
dàhào 大号	large size	
héshì 合适	suitable	
yòng 用	to use	
xìnyòngkǎ 信用卡	credit card	
shōu 收	to receive, to accept	
xiànjīn 现金	cash	

☺ 休息一下　Break Time

Listen to the recording and read silently. Listen again and repeat the sentence after you hear it.

Pay attention to the pronunciation of the three consonants *s*, *sh*, *r* and the tones of *an* while repeating the sentence. Then compete with a partner, trying to say the sentence as quickly and accurately as you can.

Sān shān rào sì shuǐ, sì shuǐ rào sān shān.
三 山 绕 四 水，四 水 绕 三 山。

Three hills surround four rivers, and four rivers surround three hills.

08 文化掠影　Culture Snapshot

☐ In China, **bargaining** is very common, especially in the market. Bargaining is considered a strategy for negotiation, an expression of persuasive power, and a tactical mind game. The joy lies in the sense of accomplishment rather than the deal itself. Since thrift is considered a virtue in the daily life of the Chinese people, those who earn their bread with diligence and wisdom understand the concept that a penny saved is a penny earned. On the other hand, by understanding the psychological mindset of the buyers, the sellers have also built up a strategy of pricing that has taken into account the percentage of possible bargaining. For instance, if a seller needs to make a minimum profit of 2 dollars on a pound of vegetables, the price will likely be set at 3 dollars. In this way, the bargainer will be happy about receiving a lower price, while the seller is still content with the profit gained from the sale.

☐ **Color** is important in Chinese culture, as many colors are considered to be either auspicious (*jílì* 吉利) or inauspicious (*bù jílì* 不吉利). In other words, colors can have positive or negative connotations. For example, in Chinese society, red is generally considered a lucky color – Chinese brides and bridegrooms often wear red during their wedding ceremony, and red envelopes (*hóngbāo* 红包) containing a monetary gift are given during holidays or special occasions. Because red traditionally symbolizes happiness, it is strictly forbidden at funerals. You should also avoid writing your name (or anyone else's) in red ink, as this symbolizes the death of the person whose name is written in red.

1 Expressing Quantity Using Measure Words

In Mandarin Chinese, numbers must occur with a measure word or classifier in order to modify nouns. When the exact quantity of any object is needed, the appropriate classifier must appear after the number and before the noun.

yí gè hànzì
一个汉字
one Chinese character

liǎng gè rén
两 个人
two people

yí liàng zìxíngchē
一 辆 自行车
one bicycle

sān jiàn chènshān
三 件 衬衫
three shirts

yì tiáo kùzi
一条 裤子
one pair of trousers

yì shuāng xié
一 双 鞋
one pair of shoes

sān běn shū
三 本 书
three books

liǎng běn hùzhào
两 本 护照
two passports

Tip

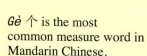

Gè 个 is the most common measure word in Mandarin Chinese.

Tip

Sometimes nouns can be used as measure words. For example:

yì bēi chá
一杯 茶   a cup of tea

liǎng wǎn mǐfàn
两 碗 米饭 two bowls of rice

2 Expressing Comparison Using the Preposition 比

Preposition 比 occurs in constructions that compare two or more things along the same dimension. You can use the following structure when you get the result of comparison.

A+比+B+adjective (the result of comparison)

(1) A: How old are you?
     B: I am 19. How about you?
     A: I am older than you. I am 20.
     C: I am 18. I am younger than you both.

Nǐ duō dà?
(1) A：你 多 大?

Wǒ shíjiǔ suì.   Nǐ ne?
     B：我 19 岁。你呢?

Wǒ bǐ nǐ dà.   Wǒ èrshí suì.
     A：我 比你 大。我 20 岁。

Wǒ shíbā suì,   wǒ bǐ nǐmen xiǎo.
     C：我 18 岁，我 比 你们 小 [1]。

---

[1] *Xiǎo* 小 here means "young".

If the result of a comparison is negative, you can choose one of the following structures.

A+不+比+B+ adjective (the result of comparison)
A+没 (有) +B+adjective (the result of comparison)

Please note the differences between 不比 and 没有.

Tā bù bǐ nǐ gāo.
(2) 他 不 比 你 高。

Tā méiyǒu nǐ gāo.
(3) 他 没有 你 高。

(2) He isn't taller than you. (He is shorter or he is the same height as you.)
(3) He is shorter than you.

To express equality, use the pattern A+和+B+一样（+adjective）.

Nǐ de yīfu hé Màikè de yīfu yí yàng.
(4) A：你 的 衣服 和 迈克 的 衣服 一 样 。

Duì, wǒ hé Màikè zhōumò yìqǐ qù shāngchǎng mǎi de.
B：对，我 和 迈克 周末 一起去 商场 买 的。

(4) A: Your jacket is exactly like Mike's.
B: Yeah. We both got ours at a mall last weekend.

Wǒ hé wǒ gēge yí yàng gāo.
(5) 我 和 我 哥哥 一 样 高。

(5) I'm as tall as my brother.

3 The Different Usages of 了

Compare the following sentences and pay attention to the usages of 了.

Verb+了: The auxiliary 了 indicates the action happened in the past when it appears behind a verb.

Tā zhǐ huāle yìbǎi kuài qián.
(1) 他 只 花 了 100 块 钱。

Lǐ Lì mǎile yì tiáo wéijīn.
(2) 李丽 买了 一 条 围巾。

(1) He only spent 100 yuan.
(2) Li Li bought a scarf.

Sentence+了: The modal particle 了 occurs at the end of a sentence, and adjectives or nouns can also appear before it.

Tài guì le!
(3) 太 贵 了[1]！

Zhè shì zuìdījià le.
(4) 这 是 最低价了。

(3) It's too expensive!
(4) This is the lowest price.

---

[1] "太……了" with an adjective expresses the idea of "very much" or "too much".

10 语法练习 Grammar Practice

1 Make complete sentences following the examples given.

①
<small>yì tiáo</small>   <small>kùzi / wéijīn/ pídài</small>
一 条   裤子/围巾/皮带
<small>jiàn</small>   <small>yīfu / chènshān</small>
件   衣服/ 衬衫
<small>liàng</small>   <small>zìxíngchē</small>
辆   自行车

②
<small>Tā hé wǒ yíyàng gāo.</small>
他 和 我 一样 高。
<small>tā de yīfu</small>   <small>wǒ de</small>   <small>piàoliang</small>
他的衣服   我的   漂亮
<small>zhè shuāng xié</small>   <small>nà shuāng</small>   <small>dà</small>
这 双 鞋   那 双   大

③
<small>Wǒ bǐ tā dà.</small>
我 比 他 大。
<small>tā de péngyou</small>   <small>wǒ de</small>   <small>duō</small>
他的 朋 友   我的   多
<small>mèimei</small>   <small>tā</small>   <small>kě'ài</small>
妹妹   他   可爱

④
<small>Wǒ méiyǒu tā shuài.</small>
我 没有 他 帅。
<small>hēisè</small>   <small>hóngsè</small>   <small>hǎokàn</small>
黑色   红色   好 看
<small>chènshān</small>   <small>wàitào</small>   <small>guì</small>
衬 衫   外套   贵

2 Complete the following sentences with the words given.

<small>liàng</small>	<small>tiáo</small>	<small>bēi</small>	<small>tài</small>	<small>méiyǒu</small>	<small>yíyàng</small>	<small>bǐ</small>	<small>hé</small>
辆	条	杯	太	没有	一样	比	和

①
<small>Nǐ xiǎng hē shénme?</small>   <small>Wǒ xiǎng hē yì</small>   <small>kělè.</small>
A：你 想 喝 什么？   B：我 想 喝 一 _____ 可乐。

②
<small>Zhè</small>   <small>zìxíngchē</small>   <small>guì le.</small>
这 _____ 自行车 _____ 贵 了。

③
<small>Zhè</small>   <small>kùzi</small>   <small>nà</small>   <small>kùzi</small>   <small>, dōu shì èrbǎi kuài qián.</small>
这 _____ 裤子 _____ 那 _____ 裤子 _____ ，都 是 200 块 钱。

④
<small>Hóng de</small>   <small>lǜ de guì, lǜ de</small>   <small>hóng de guì.</small>
红 的 _____ 绿 的贵，绿 的 _____ 红 的贵。

3 Complete the following conversations.

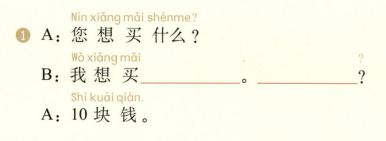

①
<small>Nín xiǎng mǎi shénme?</small>
A：您 想 买 什么？
<small>Wǒ xiǎng mǎi</small>
B：我 想 买 _____。 _____？
<small>Shí kuài qián.</small>
A：10 块 钱。

……

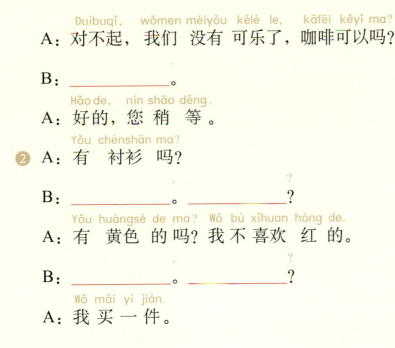

A：Duìbuqǐ, wǒmen méiyǒu kělè le, kāfēi kěyǐ ma?
对不起，我们 没有 可乐了，咖啡可以吗？

B：_____。

A：Hǎo de, nín shāo děng.
好的，您 稍 等。

② A：Yǒu chènshān ma?
有 衬衫 吗？

B：_____。_____？

A：Yǒu huángsè de ma? Wǒ bù xǐhuan hóng de.
有 黄色 的吗？我不喜欢 红的。

B：_____。_____？

A：Wǒ mǎi yí jiàn.
我 买 一件。

Expanded Words and Expressions

shāo děng
稍 等   wait a moment

11 语音提示 Pronunciation Tips

1 Tone Changes of yī 一

Repeat the following phrases after your teacher, paying attention to the pronunciation of 一.

yì jiā shāngchǎng	yì tiáo pídài	yì běn shū
一家 商场	一 条 皮带	一 本 书

yí gè rén	yí jiàn yīfu	yíyàng
一个 人	一 件 衣服	一样

一 + the 1st /2nd /3rd tone ⟶ 一 changes to the 4th tone
一 + the 4th tone ⟶ 一 changes to the 2nd tone

2 The Semi-3rd Tone

Read the following words or phrases, paying attention to the changes of the 3rd tone.

hǎokàn	kǎnjià	fěnsè
好看	砍价	粉色

xǐhuan	yǒu méiyǒu	zěnmeyàng
喜欢	有 没有	怎么样

Tip

Remember that when a 3rd tone syllable is directly followed by a non-3rd tone, it becomes a semi-3rd tone.

Sentence Stress 🎧

Listen and read, then mark the stress of each sentence.

Màikè de yīfu hé nǐ de yīfu yíyàng hǎokàn.
迈克的 衣服 和 你 的 衣服 一样 好看。

Wǒ yě shì zài Xiùshuǐ Jiē mǎi de.
我 也 是 在 秀水 街 买 的。

Wǒ gèng xǐhuan fěnsè.
我 更 喜欢 粉色。

Tài guì le!
太贵了!

Tip

Sentence stress usually appears on the word that conveys the most important information of the sentence. The proper stress can make your speaking more natural and effective.

12 汉字书写 Writing Chinese Characters

1 笔顺 Stroke Order

When writing a Chinese character, it is important to follow the correct stroke order. The general principles are as follows.

Diǎn de shūxiě shùnxù
点 的 书写 顺序 The Stroke Order of Dot

diǎn zài zhèng shàng huò zuǒ shàng, xiān xiě
点 在 正 上 或 左 上, 先 写
when on the top middle or top left, the dot before other strokes

eg. wén 文 (character)

eg. mén 门 (door)

diǎn zài yòu shàng huò zì de lǐbian, hòu xiě
点 在 右 上 或 字 的 里边, 后 写
when on the top right or inside the character, the dot after other strokes

eg. shū 书 (book)

eg. tài 太 (too)

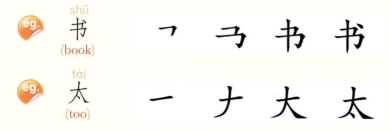

You can write it!

Practice writing the following Chinese characters. Don't forget to follow the correct stroke order!

duō ノ ク タ タ 多 多
多 多
(many, much)

shǎo ｜ ⺌ ⼩ ⺌
少 少
(little, few)

jià ノ イ イ 价 价 价
价 价
(price)

qián ノ ⺊ ⺯ ⺬ 钅 钅 钅 钱 钱 钱
钱 钱
(money)

mǎi ⺮ ⺮ ⺮ 买 买 买
买 买
(to buy)

mài 一 十 士 志 志 卖 卖 卖
卖 卖
(to sell)

hēi ｜ ⼝ ⼞ ⽥ ⽥ 甲 里 里 黑 黑 黑
黑 黑
(black)

sè ノ ク ⼛ 各 各 色
色 色
(color)

duōshao
多 少
(how many/much)

jiàqián
价 钱
(price)

mǎimai
买 卖
(business)

hēisè
黑 色
(black)

---

2 汉字的演变 **Evolution of Chinese Characters**

 雨 → 雨 → 雨

Listening

1 Listen to the following words and mark the missing tones. 🎧

yifu	zixingche	kanjia	fense	pianyi	duoshao
衣服	自行车	砍价	粉色	便宜	多少

2 Listen to the following conversation and complete the sentences with the correct characters in parentheses. 🎧

Nín hǎo, nín xiǎng mǎi shénme?
A：您 好，您 想 买 什么？

Wǒ xiǎng mǎi yí jiàn　　　　(fēngyī / T xù). Yǒu　　　　(hóngsè / huángsè) de ma?
B：我 想 买 一件 ＿＿＿＿ (a. 风衣/ b.T恤)。有 ＿＿＿＿(a. 红色 / b. 黄色) 的 吗？

Méiyǒu, yǒu　　　　(hēisè / lánsè) hé báisè de.
A：没有，有 ＿＿＿＿(a. 黑色/ b.蓝色) 和 白色的。

Hǎo, wǒ mǎi yí jiàn báisè de. Duōshao qián yí jiàn?
B：好，我 买 一件 白色的。 多少 钱 一件？

(Yìbǎi wǔshí / Yìbǎi liùshí) kuài.
A：＿＿＿＿ (a. 150 / b. 160) 块 。

Tàiguì le,　　　　(shǎo / piányi) diǎnr ba.
B：太贵了，＿＿＿＿(a. 少 / b. 便宜) 点儿吧。

Yìbǎi èrshí kuài ba, zuìdījià le.
A： 120 块 吧，最低价了。

3 Listen to the recording and decide whether the following picture is true or false. 🎧

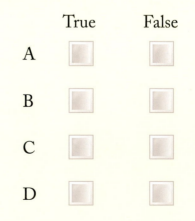

	True	False
A	☐	☐
B	☐	☐
C	☐	☐
D	☐	☐

Speaking

1 With a partner, read the following conversation aloud.

Měiměi: Kěkě, nǐ xiàwǔ zuò shénme?
美美：可可，你下午做什么？

Kěkě: Wǒ xiàwǔ qù Xiùshuǐ Jiē mǎi lǐwù.
可可：我下午去秀水街买礼物。

Měiměi: Wǒ yě qù kànkan.
美美：我也去看看。

Kěkě: Nǐ hěn xǐhuan qù nàr mǎi dōngxi ma?
可可：你很喜欢去那儿买东西[1]吗？

Měiměi: Shìde, nàr de dōngxi hěn piányi.
美美：是的，那儿的东西很便宜。

Diànyuán: Nǐmen xǐhuan shénme yánsè de yīfu?
店员：你们喜欢什么颜色的衣服？

Měiměi: Hóngsè de.
美美：红色的。

Diànyuán: Nǐ kàn zhè jiàn zěnmeyàng?
店员：你看这件怎么样？

Měiměi: Búcuò.
美美：不错。

Kěkě: Duōshao qián?
可可：多少钱？

Diànyuán: Yìbǎi kuài.
店员：100 块。

Měiměi: Tài guì le. Bāshí kuài zěnmeyàng?
美美：太贵了。80 块怎么样？

Diànyuán: Bùxíng.
店员：不行。

Kěkě: Wǒmen zǒu ba. Tài guì, bù mǎi le.
可可：我们走吧。太贵，不买了。

Diànyuán: Hǎo ba, hǎo ba, mài gěi nǐmen.
店员：好吧，好吧，卖给你们。

Expanded Words and Expressions

dōngxi
东西   thing, stuff

mài
卖   to sell

bùcuò
不错   not bad

---

[1] Dōngxi 东西 means "things" while dōngxī 东西 means "east and west".

2 Take turns answering the following questions with a partner.

Jīntiān xiàwǔ Kěkě hé Měiměi zuò shénme le?
1. 今天下午可可和美美做什么了？

Měiměi wèishénme xǐhuan qù Xiùshuǐ Jiē mǎi dōngxi?
2. 美美为什么喜欢去秀水街买东西？

Tāmen xǐhuan shénme yánsè de yīfu?
3. 她们喜欢什么颜色的衣服？

Tāmen mǎi yīfu huāle duōshao qián?
4. 她们买衣服花了多少钱？

1. What did Keke and Meimei do this afternoon?
2. Why does Meimei like shopping in the Silk Street?
3. What colors do they like to wear?
4. How much did they pay for the dress?

3 Now practice the conversation from Activity 1 with your partner, substituting your own information where you can.

Reading

Nǐ xǐhuan guàngjiē ma?
你喜欢 逛街 吗？

Nǚrén bǐ nánrén gèng xǐhuan guàngjiē. Jīntiān, Xiǎoměi hé
女人比男人 更 喜欢 逛街 。今天， 小美 和
jǐ gè péngyou yìqǐ qù guàng shāngchǎng, mǎile jǐ jiàn piàoliang
几个 朋友 一起去 逛 商场 ，买了几件 漂亮
yīfu, yánsè búcuò, jiàqián yě bú guì.
衣服，颜色 不错，价钱 也 不贵。

Qiángqiang bù xǐhuan guàngjiē. Tā xǐhuan wǎngshàng gòuwù.
强强 不喜欢 逛街。他喜欢 网上 购物。
Zài wǎngshang mǎi dōngxi búyòng huā tài duō shíjiān, jiàgé
在 网 上 买东西不用 花 太 多 时间，价格
yě hěn piányi. Qiángqiang zuì xǐhuan de gòuwù wǎngzhàn shì
也 很 便宜。 强强 最喜欢 的 购物 网站 是
"Táobǎo Wǎng".
"淘宝 网"。

Expanded Words and Expressions

guàngjiē
逛街 to go shopping

wǎngzhàn
网站 website

1. What did Xiaomei buy today?
2. Who like shopping more, men or women? Why?

1 Fill in the blanks.

  méiyǒu   xǐhuan guàngjiē.
① _____ 没有 _____ 喜欢 逛街 。

Qiángqiang xǐhuan zài   mǎi dōngxi.
② 强强 喜欢 在 _____ 买 东西。

2 Answer the questions.

Xiǎoměi jīntiān mǎile shénme?
1. 小美 今天 买了 什么 ？

Nǚrén hé nánrén shéi gèng xǐhuan guàngjiē? Wèishénme?
2. 女人 和 男人 谁 更 喜欢 逛街 ？ 为什么 ？

3. "价格" 和 文章 中 哪个 词 的 意思 一样?
   Jiàgé hé wénzhāng zhōng nǎge cí de yìsi yíyàng?

4. "网上 购物" 是 什么 意思?
   "Wǎngshàng gòuwù" shì shénme yìsi?

5. 强强 为什么 喜欢 网上 购物?
   Qiángqiang wèishénme xǐhuan wǎngshàng gòuwù?

3. Can you find a word in the article which has the same meaning of *jiàgé* 价格?

4. What does *wǎngshàng gòuwù* 网上购物 mean?

5. Why does Qiangqiang like *wǎngshàng gòuwù* 网上购物?

Writing

You are going to a party next week and need something to wear. According to the following information, decide what you are going to wear and then make a shopping list.

niúzǎikù
牛仔裤 ￥150

T xùshān
T恤衫 ￥90

píxié
皮鞋 ￥320

máoyī
毛衣 ￥240

wàitào
外套 ￥200

liányīqún
连衣裙 ￥180

Expanded Words and Expressions

máoyī 毛衣	sweater
wàitào 外套	coat
liányīqún 连衣裙	dress

My Shopping List	Budget	Why I Chose It

Word List of Unit 5

Required Words and Expressions
(For Comprehension and Both Oral and Written Communication)

Míngcí 名词 (Nouns)

粉色	fěnsè	pink
黑色	hēisè	black
红色	hóngsè	red
老板	lǎobǎn	boss
美元	Měiyuán	U.S. dollar
钱	qián	money
颜色	yánsè	color
衣服	yīfu	clothes
自行车	zìxíngchē	bicycle

Dòngcí 动词 (Verbs)

花	huā	to spend (money or time)
会	huì	to be able to, can
砍价	kǎnjià	to bargain
买	mǎi	to buy
想	xiǎng	to want
有	yǒu	to have

Xíngróngcí 形容词 (Adjectives)

贵	guì	expensive
便宜	piányi	cheap
一样	yīyàng	the same

Fùcí 副词 (Adverbs)

更	gèng	more
太	tài	too
为什么	wèishénme	why
只	zhǐ	just, only

Jiècí 介词 (Preposition)

比	bǐ	than

Liáncí 连词 (Conjunction)

因为	yīnwèi	because

Liàngcí 量词 (Measure Words)

件	jiàn	(measure word for clothes, things, etc.)
块	kuài	*yuan* (spoken form)
辆	liàng	(measure word for vehicles)
元	yuán	*yuan*

Chángyòng biǎodá 常用表达 (Expression)

最低价	zuìdījià	the lowest price

Expanded Words and Expressions
(For Comprehension and Oral Communication)

Míngcí 名词 (Nouns)

T恤衫	T xùshān	T-shirt
白色	báisè	white
东西	dōngxi	thing, stuff
黄色	huángsè	yellow
裤子	kùzi	trousers
蓝色	lánsè	blue
连衣裙	liányīqún	dress
绿色	lǜsè	green
毛衣	máoyī	sweater
牛仔裤	niúzǎikù	jeans
商场	shāngchǎng	mall
外套	wàitào	coat
网站	wǎngzhàn	website
现金	xiànjīn	cash
鞋	xié	shoes

信用卡	xìnyòngkǎ	credit card

Dòngcí 动词 (Verbs)

穿	chuān	to wear
逛街	guàngjiē	to go shopping
卖	mài	to sell
收	shōu	to receive, to accept
用	yòng	to use

Xíngróngcí 形容词 (Adjectives)

不错	bùcuò	not bad
大号	dàhào	large size
合适	héshì	suitable
浅	qiǎn	light, shallow
深	shēn	dark, deep

随便	suíbiàn	as one pleases

Fùcí 副词 (Adverb)

最	zuì	most

Liàngcí 量词 (Measure Words)

双	shuāng	(measure word for a pair)
条	tiáo	(measure word for something long and narrow)

Chángyòng biǎodá 常用表达 (Expression)

稍等	shāo děng	wait a moment

Suggested Words and Expressions
(For Comprehension Only)

Míngcí 名词 (Nouns)

价格	jiàgé	price
价钱	jiàqián	price

Chángyòng biǎodá 常用表达 (Expression)

网上购物	wǎngshàng gòuwù	online shopping

Unit 6 第六单元
Dì-liù dānyuán

Fine Food

Tiān xià měi shí

天下美食

The ability to order Chinese food in Chinese is considered both a challenge and a luxury in Chinese language learning. Just as in other parts of the world, many Chinese people enjoy cooking and eating traditional dishes; however, the amount of time spent in preparation and the skills required to make authentic Chinese food are simply amazing. Dishes are given special names based not only on their ingredients, but also on their color, smell, and taste. Perhaps one of the most enjoyable cultural experiences is to visit different restaurants in China or in Chinatown and to be able to order dishes in Chinese.

In this unit, you will learn:

FUNCTION

☐ to talk and ask about experiences：你吃过 "火山飞雪" 吗？/我从来没吃过。

☐ to ask about and describe the taste of food：今天我想吃点儿辣的。

☐ to ask about opinions and make choices：你要米饭还是面条？/我要一杯水。

☐ to make suggestions：我们再点两杯饮料吧。

GRAMMAR

☐ to express things you have done using the particle 过

☐ to ask others to make a choice using "是……还是……？"

☐ to use 的 phrases to indicate people or things

CULTURE

☐ famous Chinese dishes

☐ courtesies at dining tables

听与说　Listen and Speak

Listen to the recording and read silently. Listen again and repeat the sentences after you hear them, and then practice the conversation in pairs.

In a Chinese Restaurant

Jenny and Wang Damin talk about Chinese cuisine and culture while they have lunch in a restaurant.

Zhēnnī:
珍妮：　Zhège cài zhēn hǎochī.　Wǒ cónglái méi
这个 菜 真 好吃。我 从来 没
chīguo.　Tā jiào shénme míngzi?
吃过。它 叫 什么 名字？

Wáng Dàmín:
王大民：　Zhège jiào "Huǒshān Fēixuě".　Xīhóngshì shì
这个叫 "火山 飞雪"。西红柿是
"huǒ",　báitáng shì "xuě".
"火"，白糖 是 "雪"。
Zěnmeyàng?　Zhège càimíng[1] yǒuyìsi ba?
怎么样？这个 菜名[1] 有意思吧？

Zhēnnī:
珍妮：　Zhōngguó càimíng zhēn yǒu xuéwen a!
中国 菜名 真 有 学问啊！

Wáng Dàmín:
王大民：　Duì le,　nǐ yào mǐfàn háishi miàntiáo?
对了，你要 米饭 还是 面条？

Zhēnnī:
珍妮：　Dōu kěyǐ.
都可以。

Wáng Dàmín:
王大民：　Wǒmen zài diǎn[2] liǎng bēi yǐnliào ba.
我们 再 点[2] 两 杯 饮料吧。

Zhēnnī:
珍妮：　Wǒ yào yì bēi shuǐ.
我要 一杯 水。

Jenny: This dish is delicious. I've never had it before. What's it called?

Wang: It is called "Flying Snow on the Volcano". The tomato represents the fire and the sugar represents the snow. What do you think? Is the name of the dish interesting?

Jenny: Chinese dishes' names are of so much knowledge.

Wang: By the way, do you want rice or noodles?

Jenny: Either one is fine.

Wang: Let's order two drinks.

Jenny: I'd like a cup of water.

---

[1] *Càimíng* 菜名 means "name of the dish".

[2] *Diǎn* 点 here means order food or drinks. It also means call the roll, or choose songs for someone through radio, television or in KTV. For example, *diǎn cài* 点菜 (order dishes), *diǎn míng* 点名 (call the roll), *diǎn gē* 点歌 (choose songs).

Required Words and Expressions

cài	菜	dish
hǎochī	好吃	delicious
cónglái	从来	always
méi	没	not
guo	过	(time marker to express the past)
tā	它	it
xīhóngshì	西红柿	tomato
báitáng	白糖	sugar
xuéwen	学问	knowledge
yào	要	to want
mǐfàn	米饭	rice
háishi	还是	or
miàntiáo	面条	noodles
zài	再	again
diǎn	点	to order
yǐnliào	饮料	beverage
shuǐ	水	water

B 个人练习 Self-practice

Word Order: Create sentences by arranging the following words in the appropriate order.

1. ①吃 ②我 ③过 ④从来 ⑤没 _____
  chī wǒ guo cónglái méi

2. ①菜 ②这个 ③好吃 ④真 _____
  cài zhège hǎochī zhēn

3. ①你 ②米饭 ③要 ④面条 ⑤还是 _____
  nǐ mǐfàn yào miàntiáo háishi

C 二人练习 Pair Work

What's your favorite food? With a partner, practice asking what his or her favorite food is.

Nǐ yào chī mǐfàn háishi miàntiáo?
A：你 要 吃 米饭 还是 面条 ？

Wǒ yào chī miàntiáo.
B：我 要 吃 面条。

Nǐ yào hē shuǐ háishi hē yǐnliào?
A：你 要 喝 水 还是 喝 饮料？

Wǒ yào hē yǐnliào.
B：我 要 喝 饮料。

D 小组活动 Group Work

Talk about Chinese Food: In groups of three or four, take turns telling your classmates about different Chinese dishes you have tried.

Nǐ chīguo Mápó Dòufu ma?
A：你 吃过 麻婆 豆腐 吗？

Wǒ méi chīguo.
B：我 没 吃过。

Wǒ chīguo.
C：我 吃过。

Wǒ jīngcháng chī.
D：我 经常 吃。

Expanded Words and Expressions

jīngcháng
经常 often

Spotlight

Expanded Words and Expressions

suān 酸	sour
kǔ 苦	bitter
xián 咸	salty

Culture Box

As you learned in *Episode 1*, the names of Chinese dishes are often very descriptive. In some cases they even have historical significance. For example, *Gōngbǎo Jīdīng* 宫保鸡丁 (Kung Pao Chicken) was named after a minister of the Qing Dynasty named Ding Baozhen. His official title or rank was 宫保, meaning palatial guardian.

1. Bitter Melon in Sauce
2. Peking Roast Duck
3. Kung Pao Chicken
4. Boiled Fish with Chili Sauce
5. Noodles Served with Fried Bean Sauce
6. Sweet and Sour Fish
7. Hot and Sour Soup
8. Mapo Tofu

A 听与说 Listen and Speak

Listen to the recording and read silently. Listen again and repeat the names of the dishes after you hear them.

Dishes Popular with International Students in China

Liángbàn Kǔguā
1 凉拌 苦瓜

Běijīng Kǎoyā
2 北京 烤鸭

Gōngbǎo Jīdīng
3 宫保 鸡丁

Shuǐzhǔyú
4 水煮鱼

Zhájiàngmiàn
5 炸 酱 面

Tángcùyú
6 糖醋鱼

Suānlàtāng
7 酸辣汤

Mápó Dòufu
8 麻婆豆腐

B 二人练习 Pair Work

Talking about Chinese Dishes: With a partner, take turns guessing and describing the flavor of the foods in Activity A.

03 句型操练 Sentence Patterns

𝒜 听与说 Listen and Speak

Listen to the recording and read silently. Listen again and repeat the sentences after you hear them.

v.+过

Nǐ chīguo Huǒshān Fēixuě ma?
你 吃过 火山 飞雪 吗?

Wǒ chīguo Huǒshān Fēixuě.
我 吃过 火山 飞雪。

Wǒ méi chīguo Huǒshān Fēixuě.
我 没 吃过 火山 飞雪。

ℬ 选择 Choose the correct answer.

Choose the correct words in parentheses to complete the conversations. Then practice with your partner.

Nǐ kànguo 《Kǒngzǐ》 zhè bù diànyǐng ma?
1. A：你 看过 《孔子》这部 电影 吗?
   Wǒ (méi/bú) kànguo, tīngshuō búcuò.
   B：我 _____（没/不）看过, 听说 不错。

Nǐ (kàn bu kàn / kàn méi kànguo) zhè běn shū?
2. A：你 _____（看不看 / 看 没 看过）这本 书?
   Hǎo a, gěi wǒ kànkan.
   B：好啊, 给 我 看看。

Nǐ tīng (guo /—) Zhōu Jiélún de gē ma?
3. A：你 听 _____（过 /—）周 杰伦[1]的 歌 吗?
   Dāngrán tīngguo, tā de gē hěn hǎotīng.
   B：当然 听过, 他的 歌 很 好听。

---

[1] *Zhōu Jiélún* 周杰伦 is a famous singer from Taiwan, China.

听与说　Listen and Speak 🎧

Listen to the recording and read silently. Listen again and repeat the sentences after you hear them, and then practice the conversation in pairs.

On Campus

Bill is hungry after class, so he asks Li Li where they can go to get something to eat.

比尔：　Wǒ è le,　jīntiān xiǎng chī diǎnr là de.
比尔：　我饿了，今天 想 吃点儿辣的。

李丽：　Wǒmen qù Hǎidǐlāo¹ ba.　Nàr de huǒguō
李丽：　我们去海底捞¹吧。那儿的 火锅

wèidào tèbié hǎo,　fúwù yě hěn zhōudào.
味道特别 好，服务也很 周到。

比尔：　Tīngshuō qù nà jiā fànguǎn chīfàn de rén
比尔：　听说 去那家饭馆²吃饭的人

tèbié duō.
特别多。

李丽：　Shì a.　Wǒmen kěyǐ yìbiān děng zuò,
李丽：　是啊。我们可以一边 等 座，

yìbiān chī miǎnfèi shuǐguǒ.
一边吃 免费 水果。

比尔：　Miǎnfèi de?　Tài hǎo le!　Wǒ xǐhuan.
比尔：　免费 的？太 好了！我喜欢。

李丽：　Wǒmen zǒu bā!
李丽：　我们 走 吧!

Bill: I'm starving. I want to eat something spicy today.
Li Li: Let's go to Haidilao. The hotpot there is especially delicious, and the service is also really good.
Bill: I've heard that too many people go to that restaurant.
Li Li: Yes. We can eat free fruit while waiting for seats.
Bill: Free? That sounds good to me. I like it.
Li Li: Let's go!

---

¹ *Hǎidǐlāo* 海底捞 is the name of a famous hotpot restaurant. Its literal meaning is "to scrape from the seabed".

² In oral Chinese, *fànguǎn* 饭馆 is usually pronounced as *fànguǎnr* 饭馆儿.

Required Words and Expressions

è 饿	hungry	
là 辣	spicy	
nàr 那儿	there	
huǒguō 火锅	hotpot	
wèidào 味道	taste	
tèbié 特别	especially	
fúwù 服务	to serve	
zhōudào 周到	thoughtful	
jiā 家	(measure word for restaurants, stores, schools, etc.)	
fànguǎn 饭馆	restaurant	
fàn 饭	meal	
yībiān ...... 一边...... yībiān ...... 一边......	to do different things at the same time	
děng 等	to wait	
zuò 座	seat	
miǎnfèi 免费	to be free of charge	
shuǐguǒ 水果	fruit	

𝓑 个人练习 Self-practice

Word Order: Create sentences by arranging the following words in the appropriate order.

<table>
<tr><td>jīntiān</td><td>xiǎng</td><td>diǎnr</td><td>là</td><td>de</td></tr>
</table>

1. ①今天　②想　③点儿　④辣　⑤的
   chī
   ⑥吃 ＿＿＿＿＿＿＿＿

<table>
<tr><td>wèidào</td><td>yě</td><td>tèbié</td><td>nàr de</td><td>huǒguō</td></tr>
</table>

2. ①味道　②也　③特别　④那儿的　⑤火锅
   hǎo　　fúwù　　zhōudào　　hěn
   ⑥好　⑦服务　⑧周到　⑨很 ＿＿＿＿＿＿＿

<table>
<tr><td>kěyǐ</td><td>shuǐguǒ</td><td>yìbiān</td><td>yìbiān</td><td>děng zuò</td></tr>
</table>

3. ①可以　②水果　③一边　④一边　⑤等座
   wǒmen　　chī　　miǎnfèi
   ⑥我们　⑦吃　⑧免费 ＿＿＿＿＿＿＿

𝓒 二人练习 Pair Work

Recommend Restaurant for Your Partner: With a partner, practice suggesting a type of food and recommending a suitable restaurant.

Jīntiān wǒ xiǎng chī là de.
A：今天 我 想 吃 辣的。

Wǒmen qù Hǎidǐlāo ba.　Nàr de huǒguō wèidào hǎo,
B：我们 去海底捞吧。那儿的 火锅 味道 好，
fúwù yě hěn zhōudào.
服务也 很 周到 。

𝓓 小组活动 Group Work

Perform and Say: One student should perform two actions simultaneously while the rest of the group describe which two activities he or she is doing.

Tā/ Tā yìbiān chànggē, yìbiān tiàowǔ.
他/她 一边 唱歌，一边 跳舞。

zǒu	pǎo	kàn	tīng	shuō	xiào
走	跑	看	听	说	笑
to walk	to run	to look	to listen	to say	to laugh

05 健康食物 Good Food for Good Health

A 听与说 Listen and Speak

Listen to the recording and read silently. Listen again and repeat the phrases after you hear them.

1
hóngsè shíwù: xīhóngshì, hónglàjiāo, cǎoméi
红色 食物：西红柿、 红辣椒 、 草莓
Red foods: tomatoes, red peppers, strawberries

Nourish the heart and ease tiredness

2
huángsè shíwù: yùmǐ, huángdòu, nánguā
黄色 食物：玉米、 黄豆 、 南瓜
Yellow foods: corn, soybeans, pumpkins

Nourish the spleen and stomach

3
lǜsè shíwù: xīlánhuā, qíncài
绿色食物：西兰花、芹菜
Green foods: broccoli, celery

Nourish the liver and help digestion

4
hēisè shíwù: hēimù'ěr, hēizhīma
黑色食物：黑木耳、黑芝麻
Black foods: black fungi, black sesame

Nourish the kidneys

5
báisè shíwù: dōngguā, báiluóbo, shānyào
白色食物： 冬 瓜、白萝卜、 山药
White foods: white gourds, white radishes, Chinese yams

Nourish the lungs

6
lánzǐsè shíwù: qiézi, zǐ pútáo, lánméi
蓝紫色食物：茄子、紫葡萄、蓝莓
Blue/purple foods: eggplants, purple grapes, blueberries

Nourish the heart and blood vessels

B 二人练习 Pair Work

Favorite Food: With a partner, take turns telling each other about your favorite foods, making sure to describe their colors and tastes.

Nǐ xǐhuan shénme shíwù?
你 喜欢 什么 食物?
Wǒ xǐhuan
我喜欢＿＿＿＿＿＿＿＿＿＿＿＿＿＿＿＿＿

Nǐ bù xǐhuan shénme shíwù?
你 不 喜欢 什么 食物?
Wǒ bù xǐhuan
我 不 喜欢＿＿＿＿＿＿＿＿＿＿＿＿＿＿＿

06 阅读　Reading

吃 饭　At the Restaurant

Fúwùyuán, diǎn cài.
A：服务员，点 菜。

Gěi nín càidān.
B：给 您 菜单。

Yào yí gè Tángcùyú, yí gè Gōngbǎo Jīdīng, liǎng wǎn mǐfàn.
A：要 一个 糖醋鱼，一个 宫保 鸡丁，两 碗 米饭。

Liǎng wèi hē diǎnr shénme?
B：两 位 喝点儿 什么？

Lái diǎnr yǐnliào ba. Liǎng bēi kělè.
A：来 点儿 饮料 吧。 两 杯 可乐。

Fúwùyuán, zhège cài tài xián le.
A：服务员，这个 菜 太 咸 了。

Shì ma? Duìbuqǐ, wǒmen gěi nín huàn yí fèn.
B：是 吗？对不起，我们 给 您 换 一份。

Fúwùyuán, mǎidān! Yígòng duōshao qián?
A：服务员，买单！ 一共 多少 钱？

Nín yígòng xiāofèile yìbǎi kuài.
B：您 一共 消费了 100 块。

Answer the following questions according to the conversation.

Tāmen diǎnle shénme cài?
1. 他们 点了 什么 菜？

Tāmen hēle shénme?
2. 他们 喝了 什么？

Cài de wèidào zěnmeyàng?
3. 菜的 味道 怎么样？

Tāmen yígòng huāle duōshao qián?
4. 他们 一共 花了 多少 钱？

Expanded Words and Expressions	
càidān 菜单	menu
wèi 位	(measure word <formal> used to refer to people)
mǎidān 买单	to pay the bill
yīgòng 一共	altogether
xiāofèi 消费	to consume

1. What dishes do they order?
2. What do they drink?
3. How do the dishes taste?
4. How much does the meal cost?

☺ 休息一下　Break Time

Practice writing the following two characters using the proper stroke order indicated below.

❶ shuǐ 　 亅 ㇁ ㇁ 水

水
(water)

❷ huǒ 　 、 ㇀ 丷 火

火
(fire)

07 餐桌礼仪 Table Manners

Expanded Words and Expressions

dǎnào 打闹	to play in a boisterous way
ràng 让	to let somebody have it
jiā 夹	to clip
qiǎng 抢	to vie for

Why do people play in a boisterous way while dining?

1. When it's time to sit, offering the best seat: "No, you take this seat!"
2. When it's time to eat, forcing food on guests: "Try this, please!"
3. When it's time to pay, vying for the chance to pay: "Today it's my treat!"

Culture Box

In China, one of many ways to show respect and friendship toward guests is to offer them the most distinguished seat at the table. At the end of the meal, both the host and the guest often want to pay for the meal in order to express their goodwill.

Tip

Fènghuáng 凤凰 is a beautiful and mysterious bird in ancient Chinese legend.

听与说 Listen and Speak 🎧

Listen to the recording and read silently. Listen again and repeat the sentences after you hear them, and then practice the sentences in pairs.

Wèishénme rénmen yìbiān chīfàn yìbiān dǎnào ne?
为什么 人们 一边 吃饭 一边 打闹 呢?

Zuòxià de shíhou ràng lái ràng qù:
1. 坐下 的 时候 让 来 让 去:
"Nín zuò, nín zuò!"
"您 坐,您 坐!"

Chī cài de shíhou jiā lái jiā qù:
2. 吃 菜 的 时候 夹 来 夹 去:
"Nín chī zhège!"
"您 吃 这个!"

Mǎidān de shíhou qiǎng lái qiǎng qù:
3. 买单 的 时候 抢 来 抢 去:
"Jīntiān wǒ qǐngkè!"
"今天 我 请客!"

☺ 休息一下 Break Time 🎧

Listen to the recording and read silently. Listen again and repeat the sentence after you hear it.

Pay attention to the pronunciation of the two consonants *h* and *f* while repeating the sentence. Then compete with a partner, trying to say the sentence as quickly and accurately as you can.

fěnhóng fènghuáng, lán fènghuáng.
粉红 凤凰,蓝 凤凰。
pink phoenix, and blue phoenix.

Hóng fènghuáng, huáng fènghuáng,
红 凤凰, 黄 凤凰,
Red phoenix, yellow phoenix,

08 文化掠影　Culture Snapshot

☐ In **Chinese cuisine**, many dishes have symbolic or metaphorical names. Dishes are also known for their color, taste, and smell. For instance, *Mǎyǐ Shàngshù* 蚂蚁上树 (Ants Climbing up Trees) is a popular dish. The ants are represented by ground pork, while rice noodles represent the trees. Other common dishes that are popular in the U.S. include *Mápó Dòufu* 麻婆豆腐 (Mapo Tofu) and *Zuǒ Zōngtáng Jī* 左宗棠鸡 (General Tso's Chicken).

☐ Chinese culture has long been considered **a collective culture**, an idea that is also reflected at the dinner table. While in the U.S. each individual tends to order his or her own dish, in China the host usually orders for the whole table. In Western countries, most dining tables are square or rectangular, allowing each person his or her own space. In Chinese restaurants, tables are usually round, and the guests share all the dishes. If more than ten people are dining together, a Lazy Susan is used in the center of the table to rotate the dishes. The dichotomy of individual vs. collective culture is being challenged as we move toward a more global society; however, these subtle cultural differences can still be easily noted.

☐ With regard to table manners, Chinese people like **a boisterous and enthusiastic atmosphere**. Chinese are used to loud conversation and physical gestures when eating in a restaurant with family or friends, while Westerners tend to prefer quiet places for private conversations. Chinese consider noise from crowds as a sign of enjoyment. Although many restaurants in China do have private dining rooms for those who need them, the majority of ordinary Chinese people feel relaxed in a crowded dining hall, surrounded by people talking, shouting and laughing.

1 **Expressing Things You Have Done Using the Particle 过**

The aspectual particle 过 expresses that an event has been experienced with respect to some time reference.

verb + 过

(1) I have eaten a dish called "Flying Snow on the Volcano" before.

Wǒ chīguo Huǒshān Fēixuě.
(1) 我吃过 火山 飞雪。

没（有）+ verb + 过

(2) A: Have you been to Beijing before?
B: No, I haven't.

Nǐ qùguo Běijīng ma?
(2) A：你去过 北京 吗？
Wǒ méi (yǒu) qùguo.
B：我 没（有）去过。

verb + 没 + verb + 过? = verb + 过 + 吗?

(3) A: Have you ever seen Li Li?
B: Yes, only once.

Nǐ jiàn méi jiànguo Lǐ Lì?
(3) A：你 见 没 见过 李丽？
= Nǐ jiànguo Lǐ Lì ma?
=你 见过 李丽 吗？
Jiànguo yí cì.
B：见过 一次。

2 **Asking Others to Make a Choice Using "是……还是……？"**

As a conjunction, 还是 joins two declarative clauses. When used in a question, it represents an either/or choice to the respondent. This is known as an alternative question. 是 can be omitted as seen in Example 2.

(1) A: Are you American or British?
B: I am British.

Nǐ shì Měiguórén háishi Yīngguórén?
(1) A：你是 美国人 还是 英国人 ？
Wǒ shì Yīngguórén.
B：我 是 英国人 。

(2) A: Do you prefer rice or noodles?
B: I want rice.

Nǐ (shì) chī mǐfàn háishi chī miàntiáo?
(2) A：你（是）吃 米饭 还是 吃 面条 ？
Wǒ chī mǐfàn.
B：我 吃 米饭。

还是 can join two words by itself when the situation is very specific.

(3) A: What would you like to drink? Cola or coffee?
B: Coffee.

Nǐ hē shénme? Kělè háishi kāfēi?
(3) A：你喝 什么？可乐 还是 咖啡？
Kāfēi.
B：咖啡。

You may also end an alternative question with the modal particle *ne* 呢, but please note that you cannot use *ma* 吗 or *ba* 吧 in this context.

Nǐ shì Měiguórén háishi Yīngguórén ne?
① 你 是 美国人 还是 英国人 呢？

Nǐ chī mǐfàn háishi chī miàntiáo ne?
② 你 吃 米饭 还是 吃 面条 呢?
Nǐ hē shénme? Kělè háishi kāfēi ne?
③ 你喝 什么? 可乐还是 咖啡呢?

You can also ask an alternative question by listing a series of key words with a rising tone.

Nǐ qù nǎr? Běijīng? Shànghǎi? Sūzhōu?
(4) A：你去哪儿? 北京? 上海? 苏州?
Běijīng.
B：北京。

(4) A: Where would you like to go? Beijing? Shanghai? Suzhou?
B: Beijing.

3 Using 的 phrases to Indicate People or Things

By adding the particle 的 after a noun, pronoun, verb, adjective or phrase, you can create a noun phrase to indicate people or things. These noun phrases function just like nouns.

chī   chī de
(1) 吃 ⟶ 吃的
Wǒ yào mǎi diǎnr chī de.
我 要 买 点儿 吃的。

là   là de
(2) 辣 ⟶ 辣的
Wǒ xiǎng chī diǎnr là de.
我 想 吃点儿 辣的。

mǎi   wǒ mǎi de
(3) 买 ⟶ 我 买的
Bǐ' ěr mǎi de yīfu bǐ wǒ mǎi de piányi.
比尔 买的 衣服 比我 买 的 便宜。

(1) eat⟶ something to eat
I want to buy something to eat.
(2) spicy⟶ something spicy
I want to eat something spicy.
(3) buy⟶ something I bought
The piece of clothing Bill has bought is cheaper than mine.

Can you find other 的 phrases in this unit?

10 语法练习 Grammar Practice

1 Make complete sentences following the examples given.

Nǐ qùguo Běijīng ma?
❶ A：你 去过 北京 吗?
Qùguo. /Méi qùguo.
B：去过。/没 去过。
chī   Běijīng Kǎoyā
吃   北京 烤鸭
kàn   zhè běn shū
看   这 本 书

Wǒ xiǎng chī diǎnr là de.
❸ 我 想 吃点儿 辣的。
tián de
甜的
xián de
咸的

Nǐ chī miàntiáo háishi mǐfàn?
❷ 你吃 面条 还是 米饭?
hē kělè   kāfēi
喝 可乐   咖啡
qù chāoshì   fànguǎn
去 超市   饭馆

Tā yìbiān hē chá, yìbiān kàn shū.
❹ 他 一边 喝茶，一边 看书。
shàngwǎng   hē kāfēi
上 网   喝咖啡
chànggē   tiàowǔ
唱歌   跳舞

2 Complete the following sentences with the words given.

miǎnfèi	guo	wèidào	háishi	le
免费	过	味道	还是	了

1 A：
Wǒ méi chī ___ Zhōngguócài，hǎochī ma?
我 没 吃 ___ 中国菜 ，好吃 吗?

B：
Wǒ yě méi chī ___，wǒmen qù shìshi ba?
我 也 没 吃 ___，我们 去 试试 吧?

2 A：
Wǒ è ___. Wǎnshang chī shénme?
我 饿 ___。 晚上 吃 什么 ?

B：
Wǒmen chī bǐsà ba.
我们 吃 比萨 吧。

3 A：
Wǒmen qù zhè jiā fànguǎn ba，yǒu ___ de yǐnliào hē.
我们 去 这 家 饭馆 吧，有 ___ 的 饮料 喝。

B：
Hǎo de.
好的。

4 A：
Nǐ xǐhuan chī shénme ___ de huǒguō?
你 喜欢 吃 什么 ___ 的 火锅?

B：
Là de.
辣的。

5 A：
Yáo Míng shì Měiguórén ___ Zhōngguórén?
姚 明 是 美国人 ___ 中国人 ?

B：
Tā shì Zhōngguórén.
他 是 中国人 。

3 Answer the following questions about yourself.

1
Nǐ qùguo nǎxiē guójiā? Nǎge guójiā zuì yǒuyìsi?
你 去过 哪些 国家? 哪个 国家 最 有意思?

_____

2
Nǐ zuòguo fàn ma? Nǐ xǐhuan zuò shénme cài?
你 做过 饭 吗? 你 喜欢 做 什么 菜?

_____

3
Nǐ kànguo Zhōngguó diànyǐng ma? Kànguo nǎ bù Zhōngguó diànyǐng?
你 看过 中国 电影 吗? 看过 哪部 中国 电影 ?

_____

4
Nǐ gěi māma sòngguo lǐwù ma? Nǐ sòngguo shénme lǐwù?
你 给 妈妈 送过 礼物 吗? 你 送 过 什么 礼物?

_____

11 语音提示 Pronunciation Tips

1 -n and -ng

Read the following syllables, paying close attention to the pronunciation of the finals.

tán – táng	fàn – fàng
xiān – xiāng	shān – shāng
mín – míng	zhēn – zhēng
yīn – yīng	fēn – fēng

Tip

When pronouncing the front nasal -n, place the tip of the tongue at the back of the front upper teeth. The back nasal final -ng, however, is pronounced with back of the tongue touching the soft palate, with a stronger nasal sound than -n.

2 R-ending Retroflexion

Listen and read, paying close attention to the pronunciation of -r.

nàr	zhèr	nǎr
那儿	这儿	哪儿
děng zuòr	càimíngr	fànguǎnr
等 座儿	菜名儿	饭馆儿
hē diǎnr	lái diǎnr	chī diǎnr
喝 点儿	来 点儿	吃 点儿

Tip

R-ending retroflexion or *érhuà* 儿化 happens when -er is added to the end of another final. This change is made in writing by adding r to the end of the syllable in Pinyin and by adding 儿 after the final character of the word. If the original final ends in a vowel, just curl your tongue back to make -r after pronouncing the original final. In the pronunciation of words like *míngr* and *diǎnr*, the consonant of the original final is dropped in order to pronounce the final -r.

3 Intonation of the Exclamatory Sentence

Listen and read, paying close attention to the intonation of each sentence.

Tài hǎo le!
太 好 了!

Nǐ jīntiān zhēn piàoliang!
你 今天 真 漂亮!

Zhōngguó càimíng zhēn yǒu xuéwen a!
中国 菜名 真 有 学问 啊!

Tip

Exclamatory sentences are typically full of feeling. The sentence stresses like adverbs of degree should receive more emphasis. Can you find where the stress is placed in the sentences to the left?

12 汉字书写 Writing Chinese Characters

1 笔顺 Stroke Order

When writing a Chinese character, it is important to follow the correct stroke order. The general principles are as follows.

Sānbāowéi jiégòu de zì
三包围 结构的字 Three-Side Enclosure

You have seen characters that are fully enclosed or that are enclosed on two sides. There are also three types of three-side enclosures.

quēkǒu xiàng shàng, xiān lǐ hòu wài
缺口 向 上，先里后外 up gap: from inside outwards

eg. xiōng
凶
(fierce) ノ メ 凶 凶

quēkǒu xiàng xià, xiān wài hòu lǐ
缺口 向 下，先外后里 down gap: from outside inwards

eg. fēng
风
(wind) ノ 几 风 风

quēkǒu xiàng yòu, xiān shàng hòu lǐ zài zuǒxià
缺口 向 右，先 上 后里再左下 right gap: from top inwards before bottom left

eg. qū
区
(district) 一 フ 又 区

You can write it!

Practice writing the following Chinese characters. Don't forget to follow the correct stroke order!

è ノ ㇒ ㇏ ㇏ ㇏ 饣 饣 饿 饿 饿
饿
(hungry)

chī 丨 冂 口 叱 叱 吃
吃
(to eat)

guo 一 寸 寸 寸 讨 过
过
(time marker to express the past)

xué ⺀ ⺊ ⺍ ⺍ ⺍ 学 学 学
学
(to learn)

wèn 丶 门 门 问 问 问
问
(to ask)

zhōu ノ 几 月 月 冎 用 周 周
周
(circle)

dào 一 T I 马 圣 至 到 到	**yī** 一	
到 到	一 一	
(to arrive)	(one)	
biān フ カ 力 边 边	**mǐ** 丶 丶 ソ 半 米 米	
边 边	米 米	
(side)	(rice)	
fàn 丿 丶 乞 忙 饣 饭 饭	**miàn** 一 一 丆 丙 丙 而 而 面 面	
饭 饭	面 面	
(meal)	(powder)	
tiáo 丿 夂 夂 冬 条 条 条	**huǒ** 丶 丷 火 火	
条 条	火 火	
(strip)	(fire)	
guō 丿 卜 上 乍 钅 钅 钉 钉 钌 钌 锅 锅 锅	**yībiān**	
锅 锅	一 边	
(pot, pan)	(to do different things at the same time)	
chīguo	**xuéwen**	
吃 过	学 问	
(have eaten)	(knowledge)	
zhōudào	**mǐfàn**	
周 到	米 饭	
(thoughtful)	(rice)	
miàntiáo	**huǒguō**	
面 条	火 锅	
(noodles)	(hotpot)	

这个菜真好吃！ Zhège cài zhēn hǎochī !

(The dish is so delicious!)

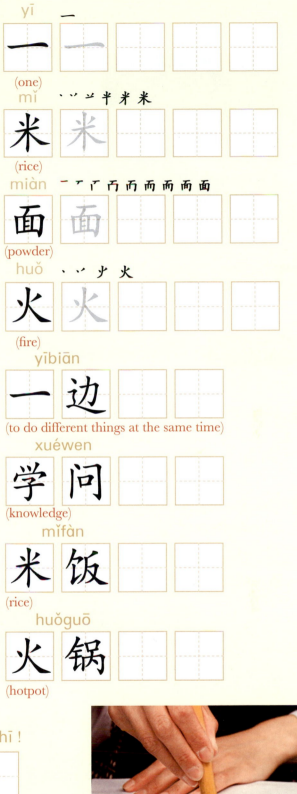

2 汉字的演变 Evolution of Chinese Characters

13 综合练习　Integrative Practice

Listening

1 Listen to the following words and mark the missing tones.

xuewen	mifan	weidao	haochi	Zhongguocai	miantiao	huoguo	paidui	mianfei
学问	米饭	味道	好吃	中国菜	面条	火锅	排队	免费

2 Listen to the following conversations and complete the sentences with the correct characters in parentheses.

❶
Nǐ chī shénme? Miàntiáo háishi mǐfàn?
A：你 吃 什么？ 面条 还是 米饭？

Wǒ zuótiān chīle mǐfàn, jīntiān xiǎng chī _____ (miàntiáo/ mǐfàn).
B：我 昨天 吃了米饭，今天 想 吃 _____（a. 面 条 /b.米饭）。

❷
Nín yào shénme?
A：您 要 什么？

Wǒ yào _____ (yì wǎn miàntiáo/ yì wǎn mǐfàn).
B：我 要 _____（a.一碗 面 条 /b.一碗 米饭）。

❸
Huǒguō yǒu shénme wèidào de?
A：火锅 有 什么 味道 的?

Huǒguō yǒu _____ (là de/ tián de), yě yǒu _____ (suān de/ xián de).
B：火锅 有 _____（a.辣的/b.甜的），也 有 _____（a. 酸 的/b. 咸 的）。

3 Listen to the recording and complete the following table.

Zhōngguócài de tèdiǎn
中国菜 的特点

dōng 东 (east)	nán 南 (south)	xī 西 (west)	běi 北 (north)
là 辣			

Expanded Words and Expressions

tèdiǎn
特点　　characteristic

4 Listen to the recording again and decide whether the following statements are true or false.

　　　　　　　　　　　　　　　　T　　F

Wǒ hěn xǐhuan chī là de.
① 我很 喜欢 吃辣的。　　□　□

Wǒ zuì xǐhuan chī Sìchuān huǒguō.
② 我最 喜欢 吃 四川 火锅。　　□　□

Niúròumiàn hěn là yě hěn xiāng.
③ 牛肉面 很辣也很 香 。　　□　□

Speaking

1 With a partner, read the following conversation aloud.

Xiǎowēi:　Nǐ chīguo Zhōngguócài ma?
小薇 ：你吃过 中国菜 吗?

Ā Lóng:　Chīguo.
阿龙 ：吃过。

Xiǎowēi:　Wèidào zěnmeyàng?
小薇 ：味道 怎么样 ?

Ā Lóng:　Yǒudiǎnr là.
阿龙 ：有点儿辣。

Xiǎowēi:　Zhōngguócài yě yǒu bú là de.　Wǒ hěn xǐhuan chī là
小薇 ： 中国菜 也有 不辣的。我很 喜欢 吃辣
de,　nǐ ne?
的，你呢?

Ā Lóng:　Wǒ ya,　suān,　tián,　kǔ,　là dōu néng chī.
阿龙 ：我呀， 酸 、 甜 、苦、辣都 能 吃。

Xiǎowēi:　Wǎnshang wǒmen qù chī Sìchuān huǒguō,
小薇 ： 晚上 我们 去吃 四川 火锅，
zěnmeyàng?
怎么样 ?

Ā Lóng:　Hǎo a!
阿龙 ：好啊!

1. Has Ah Long eaten Chinese food? How does he think about it?
2. What tastes does Xiaowei like?
3. What tastes does Ah Long like?
4. What are they in the mood to eat for dinner?

2 Take turns answering the following questions with a partner.

Ā Lóng chīguo Zhōngguócài ma? Tā juéde zěnmeyàng?
1. 阿龙 吃过 中国菜 吗?他觉得 怎么样 ?

Xiǎowēi xǐhuan shénme wèidào?
2. 小薇 喜欢 什么 味道?

Ā Lóng xǐhuan shénme wèidào?
3. 阿龙 喜欢 什么 味道?

Tāmen wǎnshang qù chī shénme?
4. 他们 晚上 去吃 什么?

3 Now practice the conversation from Activity 1 with your partner, substituting your own information where you can.

Reading

Welcome to *Xiān* 鲜 restaurant!

Càidān 菜单	Menu
Liángcài 凉菜	**Cold Dishes**
Liángbàn Kǔguā 凉拌 苦瓜	Bitter Melon in Sauce
Xīhóngshì bàn Báitáng 西红柿 拌 白糖	Tomato Mixed with Sugar
Rècài 热菜	**Hot Dishes**
Gōngbǎo Jīdīng 官保 鸡丁	Kung Pao Chicken
Tángcùyú 糖醋鱼	Sweet and Sour Fish
Tāng 汤	**Soup**
Suānlàtāng 酸辣汤	Hot and Sour Soup
Zhǔshí 主食	**Staple Food**
Zhájiàngmiàn 炸酱面	Noodles Served with Fried Bean Sauce
Jiǎozi 饺子	Dumpling
Mǐfàn 米饭	Rice
Yǐnliào 饮料	**Beverages**
Chá 茶	Tea
Kělè 可乐	Cola
Guǒzhī 果汁	Juice
Píjiǔ 啤酒	Beer

Expanded Words and Expressions

liángcài 凉菜	cold dish
rècài 热菜	hot dish
tāng 汤	soup
zhǔshí 主食	staple food
guǒzhī 果汁	juice
píjiǔ 啤酒	beer

Nǐ xiǎng chī diǎnr shénme?
1. 你 想 吃点儿 什么？

Nǐ xǐhuan hē shénme yǐnliào?
2. 你喜欢 喝 什么 饮料？

Nǐ chīguo "jiǎozi" ma?
3. 你吃过"饺子"吗？

Zhè fèn càidān shang shénme cài zuì xīyǐn nǐ?
4. 这 份 菜单 上 什么 菜 最吸引你？

Nǐ zhīdào "xiān" de yìsi ma?
5. 你知道"鲜"的意思吗？

1. What do you want to eat?
2. What kind of beverages do you like?
3. Have you ever eaten *jiǎozi* 饺子?
4. Which dish on the menu appeals to you most?
5. Do you know what *xiān* 鲜 means here?

Writing

Describe your favorite dish in Chinese, including its ingredients and flavors.

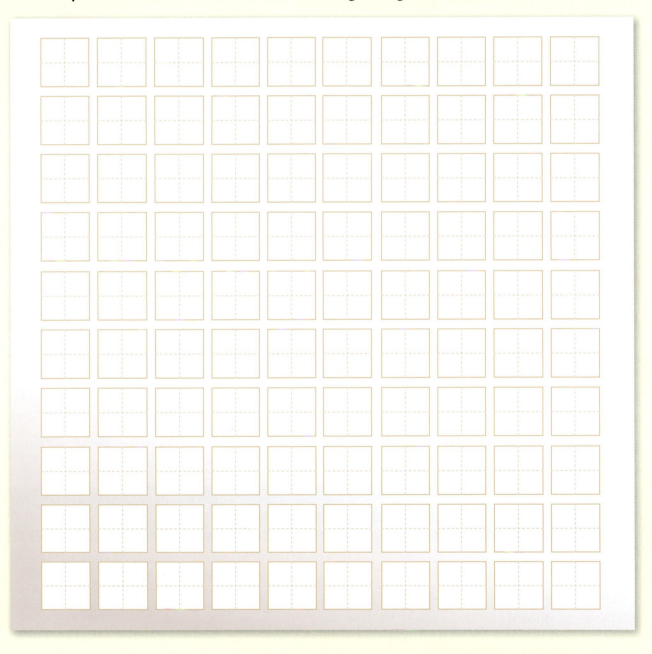

Word List of Unit 6

Required Words and Expressions
(For Comprehension and both Oral and Written Communication)

Míngcí 名词 (Nouns)

白糖	báitáng	sugar
菜	cài	dish
饭	fàn	meal
饭馆	fànguǎn	restaurant
火锅	huǒguō	hotpot
米饭	mǐfàn	rice
面条	miàntiáo	noodles
水	shuǐ	water
水果	shuǐguǒ	fruit
味道	wèidào	taste
西红柿	xīhóngshì	tomato
学问	xuéwen	knowledge
饮料	yǐnliào	beverage
座	zuò	seat

Dòngcí 动词 (Verbs)

等	děng	to wait
点	diǎn	to order
服务	fúwù	to serve
免费	miǎnfèi	to be free of charge
要	yào	to want

Xíngróngcí 形容词 (Adjectives)

饿	è	hungry
好吃	hǎochī	delicious
辣	là	spicy
周到	zhōudào	thoughtful

Dàicí 代词 (Pronouns)

那儿	nàr	there
它	tā	it

Fùcí 副词 (Adverbs)

从来	cónglái	always
没	méi	not
特别	tèbié	especially
再	zài	again

Liáncí 连词 (Conjunction)

还是	háishi	or

Zhùcí 助词 (Auxiliary Word)

过	guo	(time marker to express the past)

Liàngcí 量词 (Measure Word)

家	jiā	(measure word for restaurants, stores, schools, etc.)

Chángyòng biǎodá 常用表达 (Expression)

一边……一边……	yībiān… yībiān…	to do different things at the same time

Expanded Words and Expressions
(For Comprehension and Oral Communication)

Míngcí 名词 (Nouns)

菜单	càidān	menu
果汁	guǒzhī	juice
凉菜	liángcài	cold dish
啤酒	píjiǔ	beer
热菜	rècài	hot dish

汤	tāng	soup
特点	tèdiǎn	characteristic
主食	zhǔshí	staple food

Dòngcí 动词（Verbs）

打闹	dǎnào	to play in a boisterous way
夹	jiā	to clip
买单	mǎidān	to pay the bill
抢	qiǎng	to vie for
让	ràng	to let somebody have it
消费	xiāofèi	to consume

Xíngróngcí 形容词（Adjectives）

苦	kǔ	bitter

酸	suān	sour
咸	xián	salty

Fùcí 副词（Adverbs）

经常	jīngcháng	often
一共	yīgòng	altogether

Liàngcí 量词（Measure Word）

位	wèi	(measure word <formal> used to refer to people)

Chángyòng biǎodá 常用表达（Expression）

试试	shìshi	to have a try

Suggested Words and Expressions
(For Comprehension only)

Míngcí 名词（Nouns）

饺子	jiǎozi	dumpling
炸酱面	Zhájiàngmiàn	Noodles Served with Fried Bean Sauce

Xíngróngcí 形容词（Adjective）

鲜	xiān	fresh, delicious

Chángyòng biǎodá 常用表达（Expressions）

北京烤鸭	Běijīng Kǎoyā	Peking Roast Duck
宫保鸡丁	Gōngbǎo Jīdīng	Kung Pao Chicken
凉拌苦瓜	Liángbàn Kǔguā	Bitter Melon in Sauce
麻婆豆腐	Mápó Dòufu	Mapo Tofu
水煮鱼	Shuǐzhǔyú	Boiled Fish with Chili Sauce
酸辣汤	Suānlàtāng	Hot and Sour Soup
糖醋鱼	Tángcùyú	Sweet and Sour Fish

01 语音营　Pronunciation Kit

A Read the following characters and words, and group them according to the tones.

去　走　找　周　谁　对　忙　回　看　书
件　钱　元　吧　花　块　比　贵　会　更
没　过　它　要　点　饿　想　辣　汤　太

声调 （Tones）	字 （Characters）
ー （一声）	周
／ （二声）	谁
∨ （三声）	走
＼ （四声）	件
· （轻声）	吧

上课　颜色　一起　听说　特别　时候　免费
主演　便宜　衣服　因为　砍价　好看　一样
多少　酒吧　那儿　当然　主意　最近　还是
味道　上网　饮料

声调 （Tones）	词 （Words）
ー ＋ ー/／/∨/＼	听说
／ ＋ ー/／/∨/＼	颜色
∨ ＋ ー/／/∨/＼	主演
＼ ＋ ー/／/∨/＼	上网
ー/／/∨/＼ ＋ ·	时候

Cataract on Mount Lu

Li Bai (Tang Dynasty)

The sunlit Censer Peak exhales a wreath of cloud;
Like an upended stream the cataract sounds loud.
Its torrent dashes down three thousand feet from high;
As if the Silver River fell from azure sky.

(Translated by Xu Yuanchong)

B Listen to the recording, and read the following poem with a partner, paying close attention to the pronunciation of each syllable as well as the flow of each line.

Wàng Lú Shān Pùbù

望 庐 山 瀑布

Lǐ Bái （Táng）

李白 （唐）

Rì zhào xiānglú shēng zǐyān,　　Yáo kàn pùbù guà qiánchuān.

日照 香炉 生 紫烟，遥 看 瀑布 挂 前川 。

Fēiliú zhí xià sānqiān chǐ,　　Yí shì yínhé luò jiǔtiān.

飞流 直下 三千 尺，　疑 是 银河 落 九天。

Group the following words with similar patterns or functions.

麻婆豆腐　西装　书店　邮局　牛仔裤　打电玩　宫保鸡丁

黄　咖啡　可乐　蓝　果汁　唱歌　火锅

连衣裙　糖醋鱼　衬衫　看电影　茶　绿　电影院

银行　黑　图书馆　T恤　红　水　跳舞

What would you like to do in your spare time?

Which clothing is not your style?

What places do you usually go to?

Can you list some Chinese dishes?

What do you like to drink for dinner?

Which colors do you like to wear?

03 见字知意 Understanding the Meanings of the Chinese Characters

What other characters have you learned with the following radicals? List as many as you can.

衤：衬 _____

辶：过 _____

火：烤 _____

纟：红 _____

04 最佳活动与场所 Best Activities and Places

Your teacher will divide the class into two groups. Each person in Group A should make a list of things they want to do, and then write it on a yellow card. Group B should make a list of places they want to go, and then write each place on a red card. Once the cards have been prepared, mix them up and have each student choose one card. Try to find your partner by circulating around the room, conversing with your classmates about where they want to go or what they want to do in Chinese according to the card they get. Use the examples in Activity B as a model.

𝒜 Fun Activities

饭馆	看电影	酒吧	上网
电影院	做饭	咖啡馆	唱歌
学校	跳舞	……	……

ℬ Invitation

Míngtiān xiàwǔ nǐ yǒukòng ma? Wǒmen qù fànguǎn chīfàn zěnmeyàng?
A：明天 下午 你 有 空 吗？我们 去 饭馆 吃饭 怎么样？

Tài hǎo le. Wǒmen shénme shíhou jiàn?
B：太 好 了。我们 什么 时候 见？/

Bù hǎoyìsi, wǒ míngtiān yào qù diànyǐngyuàn kàn diànyǐng.
不好意思，我 明天 要 去 电影院 看 电 影。

……
A：……

Wǒmen zài nǎr jiàn? Nà hòutiān zěnmeyàng?
B：我们 在 哪儿 见？/ 那 后天 怎么样？

……
A：……

05 价廉物美　Buy and Sell

A Pair Work

Role Play: With a partner, take turns acting as a salesperson and a customer selling and buying four of the items listed below. The salesperson should mark the price for each item, then the customer can bargain to get a good deal.

学生A：

自行车	外套	电视	鞋
￥_____	￥_____	￥_____	￥_____

学生B：

相机	地图	手机	字典
￥_____	￥_____	￥_____	￥_____

B Class Activity

Who's the best? After the bargaining is complete, each pair should report to the class the cheapest and most expensive items sold. Then the class should choose the best salesperson and the best bargainer.

06 采访　Interview

你喜欢吃什么，不喜欢吃什么？ What do you like or dislike?

1. 水果　我喜欢吃香蕉，不喜欢吃苹果。

2. 凉菜　_____

3. 热菜　_____

4. 饮料　_____

5. 主食　_____

Tip

xiāngjiāo
香蕉　　banana

píngguǒ
苹果　　apple

07 点菜 Ordering Dishes

A In groups of three, choose your favorite Chinese and Western dishes from the list below, and add others to come up with your own menu.

Recommend

中餐	西餐
两碗米饭	两个汉堡
一份宫保鸡丁	一份牛排
一份水煮鱼	一份沙拉
两杯茶	两杯咖啡

Our Menu

B Role Play

In groups of three, practice the following dialogue, with two members acting as customers and the third acting as a waiter or waitress.

A：您好！吃点儿什么？

B：<u>一份宫保鸡丁。</u>

C：<u>一份水煮鱼。</u>

A：主食吃点儿什么？

B：<u>两碗米饭。</u>

A：喝点儿什么？

C：<u>两杯茶。</u>

A：你们有忌口的吗？

B：不要太辣。

Tip

hànbǎo 汉堡	hamburger
niúpái 牛排	steak
shālā 沙拉	salad
jìkǒu 忌口	to avoid certain food (because of illness or other reasons)

Let's review the storylines together!

Listening

Listen to the recording, and read the text below in Reading silently.

Reading

Pair Work

Check the Pronunciation: With a partner, take turns reading the following text. Student A reads the characters without Pinyin while Student B helps check pronunciation as needed. Then switch roles and read the second section.

What did Li Li and Bill do?

1. 比尔来中国学习汉语。他认识的第一个中国朋友是李丽。在机场，他们第一次见面。李丽觉得比尔的汉语不错。

2. 比尔请李丽去喝茶，李丽送给他一份特别的礼物——一张中国地图。

3. 山田和比尔一样，也是北京大学的留学生。他是日本人，他的汉语很好，大家都叫他"小北京"。

4. 比尔和新朋友山田去听中国文化课。下课后，比尔和山田去图书馆找李丽，他们一起去KTV唱歌。

5. 比尔在秀水街买了一件衣服，花了150块钱。迈克比比尔少花了50块，买到了一样的衣服。山田说因为迈克更会砍价。

6. 李丽和比尔去海底捞吃火锅。那儿的顾客特别多。他们一边吃免费水果，一边等座。

1. Bǐ'ěr lái Zhōngguó xuéxí Hànyǔ. Tā rènshi de dì-yī gè Zhōngguó péngyou shì Lǐ Lì. Zài jīchǎng, tāmen dì-yī cì jiànmiàn. Lǐ Lì juéde Bǐ'ěr de Hànyǔ búcuò.

2. Bǐ'ěr qǐng Lǐ Lì qù hē chá, Lǐ Lì sòng gěi tā yí fèn tèbié de lǐwù —— yì zhāng Zhōngguó dìtú.

3. Shāntián hé Bǐ'ěr yíyàng, yě shì Běijīng Dàxué de liúxuéshēng. Tā shì Rìběnrén, tā de Hànyǔ hěn hǎo, dàjiā dōu jiào tā "xiǎo Běijīng".

4. Bǐ'ěr hé xīn péngyou Shāntián qù tīng Zhōngguó wénhuà kè. Xiàkè hòu, Bǐ'ěr hé Shāntián qù túshūguǎn zhǎo Lǐ Lì, tāmen yìqǐ qù KTV chànggē.

5. Bǐ'ěr zài Xiùshuǐ Jiē mǎile yí jiàn yīfu, huāle 150 kuài qián. Màikè bǐ Bǐ'ěr shǎo huāle 50 kuài, mǎidàole yíyàng de yīfu. Shāntián shuō yīnwèi Màikè gèng huì kǎnjià.

6. Lǐ Lì hé Bǐ'ěr qù Hǎidǐlāo chī huǒguō. Nàr de gùkè tèbié duō. Tāmen yìbiān chī miǎnfèi shuǐguǒ, yìbiān děng zuò.

1. Zhēnnī hé Wáng Dàmín zài Měiguó xué Hànyǔ, tāmen shì tóngxué. Zhēnnī zài tōngxùnlù shang jìxiàle Wáng Dàmín de xìngmíng hé diànhuà hàomǎ. Wáng Dàmín juéde Zhēnnī xiě de hànzì hěn piàoliang.

2. Yí gè Zhōuwǔ de wǎnshang, Zhēnnī qù Wáng Dàmín jiā zuòkè, hé Dàmín de māma yìqǐ liáotiān.

3. Zhēnnī gěi Wáng Dàmín kàn quánjiāfú zhàopiàn, jièshào tā de jiātíng: bàba shì yīshēng, māma shì lǎoshī, gēge Bǐ'ěr zài Zhōngguó liúxué, shì gè "Zhōngguótōng".

4. Wáng Dàmín qǐng Zhēnnī zhōumò yìqǐ qù kàn《Kǒngzǐ》, Zhēnnī hěn kāixīn. Zhè bù diànyǐng shì Zhōu Rùnfā zhǔyǎn de, Zhēnnī shì tā de fěnsī.

5. Zhēnnī yào mǎi zìxíngchē. Wáng Dàmín hé tā qù mǎile yí liàng fěnhóngsè de zìxíngchē, huāle 70 Měiyuán. Shāngdiàn de lǎobǎn shuō zhè shì zuìdījià.

6. Wáng Dàmín hé Zhēnnī zài cāntīng chīfàn. Tāmen diǎnle yí gè hěn yǒuyìsi de cài, càimíng jiào "Huǒshān Fēixuě". "Huǒ" shì xīhóngshì, "xuě" shì báitáng. Zhēnnī juéde Zhōngguó càimíng zhēn yǒu xuéwen.

1. Which character do you like most?
2. Which story do you think is the most interesting to you?
3. Do you know the meanings of "觉得，顾客，作客，介绍，商店"?
4. What do you expect to happen as the story continues?

1. 珍妮和王大民在美国学汉语，他们是同学。珍妮在通讯录上记下了王大民的姓名和电话号码。王大民觉得珍妮写的汉字很漂亮。

2. 一个周五的晚上，珍妮去王大民家作客，和大民的妈妈一起聊天。

3. 珍妮给王大民看全家福照片，介绍她的家庭：爸爸是医生，妈妈是老师，哥哥比尔在中国留学，是个"中国通"。

4. 王大民请珍妮周末一起去看《孔子》，珍妮很开心。这部电影是周润发主演的，珍妮是他的粉丝。

5. 珍妮要买自行车。王大民和她去买了一辆粉红色的自行车，花了70美元。商店的老板说这是最低价。

6. 王大民和珍妮在餐厅吃饭。他们点了一个很有意思的菜，菜名叫"火山飞雪"。"火"是西红柿，"雪"是白糖。珍妮觉得中国菜名真有学问。

Speaking

Team Work

Talking about the Story: Discuss the following questions in groups of four.

Nǐ zuì xǐhuan de rénwù shì shéi?
1. 你 最 喜欢 的 人物 是 谁？

Nǐ juéde shàngmian de nǎge gùshi zuì yǒuyìsi?
2. 你 觉得 上面 的 哪个 故事 最 有意思？

Nǐ zhīdào "juéde, gùkè, zuòkè, jièshào, shāngdiàn" zhè
3. 你 知道 "觉得、顾客、作客、介绍、 商店 "这
jǐ gè cí de yìsi ma?
几个 词 的 意思 吗？

Duìyú yǐhòu de gùshi nǐ yǒu shénme qīdài?
4. 对于 以后 的 故事 你 有 什么 期待？

Writing

Let the story continue in your own way!

Team Work

A. Talk with your team members, and using your imagination, write a story about what will happen next. Try to write your story in Chinese, if possible.

B. Try to give a role to each person of your team, and practice performing the story in your group.

C. Perform the story for your class, and then decide which team came up with the best story. Choose one best actor and one best actress.

Grammar Kits   语法要点

1. Word order in Chinese sentences: 我喜欢汉语。

2. Expressing judgement using the verb 是: 我是李丽。

3. Confirming information using Yes-no questions ending with 吗: 你是比尔吗?

4. Using the adverb 很 in sentences with an adjectival predicate: 你的汉语很好。

5. The proximal demonstrative pronoun 这: 这是一张中国地图。

6. Asking what-questions with the interrogative pronoun 什么: 你叫什么名字?

7. The adverbs of range 也 and 都: 我也喜欢喝咖啡。我们都喜欢喝咖啡。

8. How to tell time: 现在几点? 现在十点十分。

9. Asking which-question with the interrogative pronoun 哪: 你是哪国人?

10. Asking others to confirm information using 吗 or verb+不+verb questions: 我们要去看电影, 你去吗/你去不去?

11. Expressing the time of an event or action using time phrases as adverbial phrases: 珍妮和王大民周六晚上八点在电影院门口见。

12. Giving a suggestion or request using the sentence final modal particle 吧: 我们一起去听中国文化课吧。

13. Forming wh-questions using question words 谁, 什么, 什么时候, 哪儿, 哪个: 谁是成龙的粉丝? 你喜欢吃什么菜? 我们什么时候去中国? 珍妮的哥哥在哪儿留学? 他在哪个学校学习?

14. Expressing quantity using measure words: 我们点了三个菜和两杯饮料。

15. Expressing comparison using the preposition 比: 姚明比我高。

16. The different usages of 了: 比尔花了500元买了一件新衣服, 太贵了!

17. Expressing things you have done using the particle 过: 你吃过饺子吗?

18. Asking others to make a choice using "是……还是……?": 你是去图书馆还是去教室?

19. Using 的 phrases to indicate people or things: 我要买点儿吃的。

You can find more grammar kits with explanations in our website.

Word	Pinyin	Part of Speech	Meaning	Unit	New HSK Level
T恤衫	T xùshān	*n.*	T-shirt	U5	★
A 阿姨	āyí	*n.*	aunt	U2	L3
啊	a	*modal particle*	(a modal particle)	U1	L3
安排	ānpái	*v.*	to make arrangements	U4	L4
B 爸爸	bàba	*n.*	father	U3	L1
吧	ba	*modal particle*	(a suggestive particle)	U2	L2
白领	báilǐng	*n.*	white-collar	U4	★
白色	báisè	*n.*	white	U5	★
白糖	báitáng	*n.*	sugar	U6	★
白天	báitiān	*n.*	daytime	U4	★
拜拜	bàibài (baibai)	*v.*	bye-bye	U3	★
半	bàn	*num.*	half	U3	L3
棒	bàng	*adj.*	wonderful	U1	L5
杯	bēi	*n.*	cup	U4	★
北京	Běijīng	*n.*	Beijing	U3	L1
北京烤鸭	Běijīng Kǎoyā		Peking Roast Duck	U6	★
比	bǐ	*prep.*	than	U5	L2
比萨	bǐsà	*n.*	pizza	U2	★
笔	bǐ	*n.*	pen	U2	★
不	bù	*adv.*	not	U1	L1
不错	bùcuò	*adj.*	not bad	U5	★
不见不散	bùjiàn bùsàn		be there or be square	U4	★
不客气	bù kèqi		you're welcome	U2	L1
不行	bùxíng	*v.*	will not do	U4	★
部	bù	*m.*	(a measure word for sets of books, volumes of works and movies, groups of machines)	U4	★
C 猜	cāi	*v.*	to guess	U2	L4
菜	cài	*n.*	dish	U6	L1
菜单	càidān	*n.*	menu	U6	L3
茶	chá	*n.*	tea	U2	L1

Word	Pinyin	Part of Speech	Meaning	Unit	New HSK Level
差	chà	*v.*	to be less than	U3	L3
唱歌	chànggē	*v.*	to sing	U2	L2
超市	chāoshì	*n.*	supermarket	U4	L3
城市	chéngshì	*n.*	city	U1	L3
吃	chī	*v.*	to eat	U1	L1
吃饭	chīfàn	*v.*	to have a meal	U4	★
出差	chūchāi	*v.*	to go on a business trip	U4	L4
出去	chūqu	*v.*	to go out	U1	★
穿	chuān	*v.*	to wear	U5	L2
从来	cónglái	*adv.*	always	U6	L4
D 打电玩	dǎ diànwán		to play video games	U2	★
打工	dǎgōng	*v.*	to do a part-time job	U4	L5
打闹	dǎnào	*v.*	to play in a boisterous way	U6	★
大号	dàhào	*adj.*	large size	U5	★
大家	dàjiā	*pron.*	everybody	U3	L2
大妈	dàmā	*n.*	(the title of a woman older than your parents)	U3	★
大学	dàxué	*n.*	university	U3	★
大学生	dàxuéshēng	*n.*	undergraduate	U4	★
大爷	dàye	*n.*	(the title of a man older than your parents)	U3	★
蛋糕	dàngāo	*n.*	cake	U4	L3
当然	dāngrán	*adv.*	of course	U4	L3
等	děng	*v.*	to wait	U6	L2
地图	dìtú	*n.*	map	U2	L3
弟弟	dìdi	*n.*	younger brother	U3	L2
点	diǎn	*m.*	o'clock	U3	L1
		v.	to order	U6	L1
电话	diànhuà	*n.*	phone	U1	★
电视节目	diànshì jiémù	*n.*	TV program	U1	★
电影	diànyǐng	*n.*	movie	U4	L1
电影院	diànyǐngyuàn	*n.*	movie theater	U4	★

Word	Pinyin	Part of Speech	Meaning	Unit	New HSK Level
电子邮箱	diànzǐ yóuxiāng	n.	e-mail address	U1	★
调研	diàoyán	v.	to research	U4	★
东西	dōngxi	n.	thing, stuff	U5	L1
动物	dòngwù	n.	animal	U1	L3
都	dōu	adv.	all	U2	L1
对	duì	adj.	correct	U4	L4
对不起	duìbuqǐ	v.	to be sorry	U4	L1
多大	duō dà		how old	U2	★
多少	duōshao	pron.	how many/much	U1	L1
E 饿	è	adj.	hungry	U6	L3
儿子	érzi	n.	son	U3	L1
F 法国	Fǎguó	n.	France	U3	★
饭	fàn	n.	meal	U6	★
饭馆	fànguǎn	n.	restaurant	U6	L1
分	fēn	m.	minute	U3	L3
粉色	fěnsè	n.	pink	U5	L6
服务	fúwù	v.	to serve	U6	★
服务员	fúwùyuán	n.	waiter, waitress	U2	L2
父母	fùmǔ	n.	parents	U4	★
G 干吗	gànmá		why	U4	★
高	gāo	adj.	tall	U1	L2
高兴	gāoxìng	adj.	glad	U1	L1
哥哥	gēge	n.	elder brother	U3	L2
个	gè	m.	(a commonly used measure word)	U3	L1
更	gèng	adv.	more	U5	L3
工程师	gōngchéngshī	n.	engineer	U3	L5
工作	gōngzuò	n./v.	job; to work	U3	L1
公司	gōngsī	n.	company	U3	L2
宫保鸡丁	Gōngbǎo Jīdīng		Kung Pao Chicken	U6	★
购物	gòuwù	v.	to go shopping	U2	L4
逛街	guàngjiē	v.	to go shopping	U5	★
贵	guì	adj.	expensive	U5	L2
国	guó	n.	country	U3	★

Word	Pinyin	Part of Speech	Meaning	Unit	New HSK Level
果汁	guǒzhī	*n.*	juice	U6	L3
过奖	guòjiǎng	*v.*	to overpraise, to flatter	U2	L6
过	guo	*aux.*	(time marker to express the past)	U6	L2
H 还是	háishi	*conj.*	or	U6	L3
韩国	Hánguó	*n.*	South Korea	U3	★
汉语	Hànyǔ	*n.*	Chinese	U1	L1
汉字	hànzì	*n.*	Chinese character	U1	★
好	hǎo	*adj.*	good	U1	L1
好吃	hǎochī	*adj.*	delicious	U6	L2
好的	hǎo de		OK	U2	★
号码	hàomǎ	*n.*	number	U1	L4
喝	hē	*v.*	to drink	U2	L1
合适	héshì	*adj.*	suitable	U5	L4
和	hé	*conj.*	and	U3	L1
黑色	hēisè	*n.*	black	U5	★
很	hěn	*adv.*	very	U1	L1
红色	hóngsè	*n.*	red	U5	★
护士	hùshi	*n.*	nurse	U3	L4
护照	hùzhào	*n.*	passport	U2	L3
花	huā	*n.*	flower	U2	L3
		v.	to spend (money or time)	U5	L4
黄色	huángsè	*n.*	yellow	U5	★
回	huí	*v.*	to return	U4	L1
会	huì	*v.*	to be able to, can	U5	L1
火锅	huǒguō	*n.*	hotpot	U6	★
J 几	jǐ	*num.*	how many	U3	L1
计划	jìhuà	*n./v.*	plan; to plan	U4	L4
记者	jìzhě	*n.*	journalist	U3	L4
加拿大	Jiānádà	*n.*	Canada	U3	★
夹	jiā	*v.*	to clip	U6	★
家	jiā	*n.*	home, family	U3	L1
		m.	(measure word for restaurants, stores, schools, etc.)	U6	L1
家人	jiārén	*n.*	family member	U3	★

Word	Pinyin	Part of Speech	Meaning	Unit	New HSK Level
家庭主妇	jiātíng zhǔfù	n.	housewife	U3	★
价格	jiàgé	n.	price	U5	L4
价钱	jiàqián	n.	price	U5	★
见到	jiàndào	v.	to have seen	U1	★
见面	jiànmiàn	v.	to meet	U4	L3
见外	jiànwài	v.	to regard somebody as an outsider	U2	★
件	jiàn	m.	(measure word for clothes, things, etc.)	U5	L2
健身房	jiànshēnfáng	n.	gymnasium	U4	L5
饺子	jiǎozi	n.	dumpling	U6	L4
叫	jiào	v.	to name; to call	U1	L1
街	jiē	n.	street	U4	★
姐姐	jiějie	n.	elder sister	U3	L2
今年	jīnnián	n.	this year	U2	★
今天	jīntiān	n.	today	U2	L1
经常	jīngcháng	adv.	often	U6	L3
经理	jīnglǐ	n.	manager	U3	L3
酒吧	jiǔbā	n.	bar	U4	L5
K 咖啡	kāfēi	n.	coffee	U2	L2
咖啡馆	kāfēiguǎn	n.	café	U4	★
开会	kāihuì	v.	to have a meeting	U4	★
开始	kāishǐ	v.	to begin, to start	U4	L2
开心	kāixīn	adj.	happy	U2	L5
砍价	kǎnjià	v.	to bargain	U5	★
看	kàn	v.	to look	U2	L1
看起来	kànqǐlai	v.	seem to be	U2	★
看书	kàn shū	v.	to read	U2	★
可爱	kě'ài	adj.	lovely, cute	U1	L3
可乐	kělè	n.	cola	U2	★
可以	kěyǐ	v.	may	U4	L2
刻	kè	m.	quarter (of an hour)	U3	L3
客户	kèhù	n.	client	U4	L6
客气	kèqi	adj.	polite, couteous	U2	★
口	kǒu	m.	(a measure word for family members)	U3	L3

Word	Pinyin	Part of Speech	Meaning	Unit	New HSK Level
苦	kǔ	*adj.*	bitter	U6	L4
裤子	kùzi	*n.*	trousers	U5	L3
酷	kù	*adj.*	cool	U1	★
块	kuài	*m.*	*yuan* (spoken form)	U5	L1
快乐	kuàilè	*adj.*	happy, joyful	U1	L2
L 辣	là	*adj.*	spicy	U6	L4
蓝色	lánsè	*n.*	blue	U5	★
老	lǎo	*adj.*	old; regular	U4	L3
老板	lǎobǎn	*n.*	boss	U5	L5
老师	lǎoshī	*n.*	teacher	U3	L1
了	le	*aux.*	(a modal particle indicating the event already happened)	U1	L1
		modal particle	(a particle)	U2	L1
礼物	lǐwù	*n.*	gift, present	U2	L3
连衣裙	liányīqún	*n.*	dress	U5	★
凉拌苦瓜	Liángbàn Kǔguā		Bitter Melon in Sauce	U6	★
凉菜	liángcài	*n.*	cold dish	U6	★
辆	liàng	*m.*	(measure word for vehicles)	U5	L3
留学生	liúxuéshēng	*n.*	international student	U3	★
律师	lǜshī	*n.*	lawyer	U3	L4
绿色	lǜsè	*n.*	green	U5	★
M 妈妈	māma	*n.*	mother	U2	L1
麻婆豆腐	Mápó Dòufu		Mapo Tofu	U6	★
马马虎虎	mǎmǎ hǔhǔ (mǎmǎ hūhū)	*adj.*	just so-so; careless	U2	★
吗	ma	*modal particle*	(a question particle)	U1	L1
买	mǎi	*v.*	to buy	U5	L1
买单	mǎidān	*v.*	to pay the bill	U6	★
卖	mài	*v.*	to sell	U5	L2
忙	máng	*adj.*	busy	U4	L2
毛衣	máoyī	*n.*	sweater	U5	★
没	méi	*adv.*	not	U6	L1
没问题	méi wèntí		no problem	U4	★
没有	méiyǒu	*adv.*	not have	U1	★
美	měi	*adj.*	beautiful	U1	★

Word	Pinyin	Part of Speech	Meaning	Unit	New HSK Level
美国	Měiguó	*n.*	the United States of America	U3	★
美元	Měiyuán	*n.*	U.S. dollar	U5	★
妹妹	mèimei	*n.*	younger sister	U3	L2
门口	ménkǒu	*n.*	gate, entrance	U4	★
米饭	mǐfàn	*n.*	rice	U6	L1
免费	miǎnfèi	*v.*	to be free of charge	U6	L4
面条	miàntiáo	*n.*	noodles	U6	L3
名字	míngzi	*n.*	name	U1	L1
明天	míngtiān	*n.*	tomorrow	U3	L1
明星	míngxīng	*n.*	star	U1	L5
墨西哥	Mòxīgē	*n.*	Mexico	U3	★
N 哪	nǎ	*pron.*	which	U3	L1
哪儿	nǎr	*pron.*	where	U3	L1
哪里哪里	nǎli nǎli		it's not that nice, I am flattered	U1	★
那	nà	*pron. /conj.*	that; then	U4	L1
那儿	nàr	*pron.*	there	U6	L1
奶奶	nǎinai	*n.*	grandma (on the father's side)	U3	L3
男	nán	*adj.*	male	U3	★
呢	ne	*modal particle*	(a question particle)	U2	L1
你	nǐ	*pron.*	you	U1	L1
你的	nǐ de		your	U1	★
你们	nǐmen	*pron.*	you (plural)	U2	★
年轻	niánqīng	*adj.*	young	U2	L3
您	nín	*pron.*	you (polite form)	U1	L2
牛仔裤	niúzǎikù	*n.*	jeans	U5	L5
女	nǔ	*adj.*	female	U3	★
女儿	nǔ'ér	*n.*	daughter	U3	L1
女朋友	nǔpéngyou	*n.*	girlfriend	U2	★
女士	nǔshì	*n.*	lady	U3	L5
P 拍照	pāizhào	*v.*	to take pictures	U4	★
旁听	pángtīng	*v.*	to audit	U4	★
朋友	péngyou	*n.*	friend	U2	L1
啤酒	píjiǔ	*n.*	beer	U6	L3

Word	Pinyin	Part of Speech	Meaning	Unit	New HSK Level
便宜	piányi	*adj.*	cheap	U5	L2
漂亮	piàoliang	*adj.*	beautiful	U1	L1
Q 妻子	qīzi	*n.*	wife	U3	L2
钱	qián	*n.*	money	U5	L1
钱包	qiánbāo	*n.*	wallet	U2	★
浅	qiǎn	*adj.*	light, shallow	U5	L5
抢	qiǎng	*v.*	to vie for	U6	L5
巧克力	qiǎokèlì	*n.*	chocolate	U2	L4
琴声	qínshēng	*n.*	piano sound	U1	★
请	qǐng	*v.*	please	U2	L1
请客	qǐngkè	*v.*	to treat	U2	L4
请问	qǐngwèn		May I ask...?	U1	★
去	qù	*v.*	to go	U4	L1
全家福	quánjiāfú	*n.*	family photo	U3	★
R 让	ràng	*v.*	to let somebody have it	U6	L2
热菜	rècài	*n.*	hotdish	U6	★
人	rén	*n.*	people	U3	L1
认识	rènshi	*v.*	to know	U2	L1
日本	Rìběn	*n.*	Japan	U3	★
S 商场	shāngchǎng	*n.*	mall	U5	★
商人	shāngrén	*n.*	businessman	U3	★
上海	Shànghǎi	*n.*	Shanghai	U1	★
上课	shàngkè	*v.*	to have a class	U4	★
上网	shàngwǎng	*v.*	to surf the Internet	U4	L3
上午	shàngwǔ	*n.*	morning	U3	L1
稍等	shāo děng		wait a moment	U5	★
谁	shéi	*pron.*	who	U4	L1
深	shēn	*adj.*	dark, deep	U5	L4
什么	shénme	*pron.*	what	U1	L1
生日	shēngrì	*n.*	birthday	U1	L2
时候	shíhou	*n.*	moment, time	U4	L1
市场	shìchǎng	*n.*	market	U4	L4
是	shì	*v.*	to be	U1	L1

Word	Pinyin	Part of Speech	Meaning	Unit	New HSK Level
试试	shìshi		to have a try	U6	★
收	shōu	v.	to receive, to accept	U5	L4
收下	shōuxià	v.	to accept	U2	★
手机	shǒujī	n.	cell phone	U2	L2
书	shū	n.	book	U2	L1
叔叔	shūshu	n.	uncle	U3	L3
帅	shuài	adj.	handsome	U1	L4
双	shuāng	m.	(measure word for a pair)	U5	L3
水	shuǐ	n.	water	U6	L1
水果	shuǐguǒ	n.	fruit	U6	L1
水煮鱼	Shuǐzhǔyú		Boiled Fish with Chili Sauce	U6	★
睡觉	shuìjiào	v.	to sleep	U2	L1
说	shuō	v.	to speak	U3	★
送给	sòng gěi		to send to, to give to	U2	★
宿舍	sùshè	n.	dormitory	U4	L5
酸	suān	adj.	sour	U6	L4
酸辣汤	Suānlàtāng		Hot and Sour Soup	U6	★
随便	suíbiàn	adj.	as one pleases	U5	L4
岁	suì	m.	year (of age)	U2	L1
T 他	tā	pron.	he, him	U1	L1
它	tā	pron.	it	U6	L2
她	tā	pron.	she, her	U1	L1
他们	tāmen	pron.	they, them	U1	★
她们	tāmen	pron.	they, them	U1	★
太	tài	adv.	too	U5	L1
汤	tāng	n.	soup	U6	L4
糖醋鱼	Tángcùyú		Sweet and Sour Fish	U6	★
特别	tèbié	adv.	especially	U6	L3
特点	tèdiǎn	n.	characteristic	U6	L4
甜	tián	adj.	sweet	U1	L3
条	tiáo	m.	(a measure word for something long and narrow)	U5	L3
跳舞	tiàowǔ	v.	to dance	U4	L2
听说	tīngshuō	v.	it's said, people say	U4	★

Word	Pinyin	Part of Speech	Meaning	Unit	New HSK Level
同学	tóngxué	*n.*	classmate	U3	L1
图书馆	túshūguǎn	*n.*	library	U4	L3
W 外套	wàitào	*n.*	coat	U5	★
玩	wán	*v.*	to play	U4	L2
晚上	wǎnshang	*n.*	night	U3	L2
网上购物	wǎngshàng gòuwù		online shopping	U5	★
网站	wǎngzhàn	*n.*	website	U5	L4
为什么	wèishénme	*adv.*	why	U5	L2
位	wèi	*m.*	(measure word <formal> used to refer to people)	U6	L3
味道	wèidào	*n.*	taste	U6	L4
文化	wénhuà	*n.*	culture	U4	L3
我	wǒ	*pron.*	I, me	U1	L1
X 西红柿	xīhóngshì	*n.*	tomato	U6	L4
希望	xīwàng	*n./v.*	hope; to hope	U2	L2
喜欢	xǐhuan	*v.*	to like	U2	L1
下课	xiàkè	*v.*	to dismiss a class	U4	★
下午	xiàwǔ	*n.*	afternoon	U3	L1
先生	xiānsheng	*n.*	sir, mister	U3	L1
鲜	xiān	*adj.*	fresh, delicious	U6	★
咸	xián	*adj.*	salty	U6	L4
现金	xiànjīn	*n.*	cash	U5	L5
现在	xiànzài	*n.*	now	U3	L1
想	xiǎng	*v.*	to want	U5	L1
相机	xiàngjī	*n.*	camera	U2	★
消费	xiāofèi	*v.*	to consume	U6	L5
小	xiǎo	*adj.*	little	U3	L1
笑容	xiàoróng	*n.*	smile	U1	★
鞋	xié	*n.*	shoes	U5	L3
写博客	xiě bókè		to write a blog	U2	★
谢谢	xièxie	*v.*	thank you	U2	L1
心理学家	xīnlǐxuéjiā	*n.*	psychologist	U3	★
心意	xīnyì	*n.*	regard	U2	★
信用卡	xìnyòngkǎ	*n.*	credit card	U5	L4

Word	Pinyin	Part of Speech	Meaning	Unit	New HSK Level
姓	xìng	n./v.	surname; to be surnamed	U1	L2
姓名	xìngmíng	n.	full name	U1	★
熊猫	xióngmāo	n.	panda	U1	L3
学生	xuésheng	n.	student	U3	L1
学问	xuéwen	n.	knowledge	U6	L5
学习	xuéxí	v.	to study	U3	L1
学校	xuéxiào	n.	school	U3	L1
Y 呀	ya	modal particle	(a particle)	U4	L4
颜色	yánsè	n.	color	U5	L2
要	yào	v.	to want	U6	L2
爷爷	yéye	n.	grandpa (on the father's side)	U3	L3
也	yě	adv.	too	U1	L2
衣服	yīfu	n.	clothes	U5	L1
医生	yīshēng	n.	doctor	U3	L1
一边⋯⋯ 一边⋯⋯	yībiān... yībiān...		to do different things at the same time	U6	L3
一点儿	yīdiǎnr		a little, a bit	U2	★
一定	yīdìng	adv.	surely	U4	L3
一共	yīgòng	adv.	altogether	U6	L3
一起	yīqǐ	adv.	together	U4	L2
一些	yīxiē		some	U2	★
一样	yīyàng	adj.	same	U5	L3
以后	yǐhòu	n.	after	U4	L3
意大利	Yìdàlì	n.	Italy	U3	★
因为	yīnwèi	conj.	because	U5	L2
饮料	yǐnliào	n.	beverage	U6	L4
印度	Yìndù	n.	India	U3	★
用	yòng	v.	to use	U5	L3
幽默	yōumò	adj.	humorous	U2	L4
有	yǒu	v.	to have	U5	L1
有空	yǒukòng	v.	to have free time	U4	★
有意思	yǒuyìsi		interesting	U3	★
有约	yǒu yuē		to have a date	U4	★
瑜伽	yújiā	n.	yoga	U4	★

Word	Pinyin	Part of Speech	Meaning	Unit	New HSK Level
元	yuán	*m.*	*yuan*	U5	L2
再	zài	*adv.*	again	U6	L2
再见	zàijiàn	*v.*	goodbye	U3	L1
在	zài	*prep.*	in	U3	L1
早上	zǎoshang	*n.*	(early) morning	U1	L2
怎么样	zěnmeyàng	*pron.*	how, how about	U4	L1
炸酱面	Zhájiàngmiàn	*n.*	Noodles Served with Fried Bean Sauce	U6	★
占座	zhàn zuò		to get a seat	U4	★
找	zhǎo	*v.*	to find	U4	L2
这	zhè	*pron.*	this	U2	L1
真	zhēn	*adv.*	really, truly	U2	L2
知道	zhīdào	*v.*	to know	U4	L2
职员	zhíyuán	*n.*	office clerk	U3	★
只	zhǐ	*adv.*	just, only	U5	L3
中国	Zhōngguó	*n.*	China	U2	L1
中国通	Zhōngguótōng	*n.*	an expert on China	U3	★
中午	zhōngwǔ	*n.*	noon	U3	L1
周到	zhōudào	*adj.*	thoughtful	U6	L5
周六	Zhōuliù	*n.*	Saturday	U4	★
主食	zhǔshí	*n.*	staple food	U6	★
主演	zhǔyǎn	*n.*	starring actor/actress	U4	★
主意	zhǔyi (zhúyi)	*n.*	idea	U4	L4
自行车	zìxíngchē	*n.*	bicycle	U5	L2
自由职业者	zìyóu zhíyè zhě	*n.*	freelancer	U4	★
字典	zìdiǎn	*n.*	dictionary	U2	L3
走	zǒu	*v.*	to walk, to go	U4	L2
最	zuì	*adv.*	most	U5	L2
最低价	zuìdījià		the lowest price	U5	★
最近	zuìjìn	*n.*	recent	U4	L3
最喜爱的	zuì xǐ' ài de		favorite	U1	★
座	zuò	*n.*	seat	U6	L4
做	zuò	*v.*	to do	U3	L1
做饭	zuòfàn		to cook	U2	★

adj.	adjective
adv.	adverb
aux.	auxiliary word
conj.	conjunction
int.	interjection
m.	measure word
n.	noun
num.	number
obj.	object
particle	particle
pron.	pronoun
subj.	subject
v.	verb

Notes